THE SAVI REPORT

Sexual Abuse and Violence in Ireland

Hannah McGee, Rebecca Garavan,
Mairéad de Barra, Joanne Byrne and Ronán Conroy
Royal College of Surgeons in Ireland

The Liffey Press
in association with
Dublin Rape Crisis Centre

Published by
The Liffey Press
307 Clontarf Road
Dublin 3, Ireland

© 2002 Dublin Rape Crisis Centre

A catalogue record of this book is
available from the British Library.

ISBN 1-904148-10-7

Printed in the Republic of Ireland by Colour Books Ltd.

CONTENTS

SECTION I: INTRODUCTION

SECTION II: SAVI SURVEY

SECTION IV: DISCUSSION, CONCLUSIONS AND
RECOMMENDATIONS

SAVI Study Monitoring Group

Sinead Hanley *(Barrister and Consultant), private practice (CHAIR)*

Olive Braiden *(former Director) (1999-2000), Dublin Rape Crisis Centre*

Geraldine Connolly *(Counselling Psychologist), Head of Clinical Services, Dublin Rape Crisis Centre*

Dr Sheila Greene *(Developmental Psychologist), Children's Research Centre, Trinity College Dublin*

James Martin *(Principal Officer), Garda Administration Division, Department of Justice, Equality and Law Reform*

Angela Noonan *(Assistant Principal), Child Care Policy Unit, Department of Health and Children*

Dr Bernadette O'Sullivan *(Clinical Psychologist), Vico and Clanwilliam Institute, Dublin (and Board member, Dublin Rape Crisis Centre)*

Dermot Ryan *(Assistant Principal) (member 1999-2000), Department of Health and Children*

Dr Helen Russell *(Sociologist), Economic and Social Research Institute*

Health Services Research Centre, Department of Psychology, Royal College of Surgeons in Ireland

The Health Services Research Centre (HSRC) was established in 1997 at the Department of Psychology, Royal College of Surgeons in Ireland. Its aim is to promote quality in Irish healthcare through research. Its work facilitates co-operation among re-searchers, health professionals, policy makers and health service users. Recently completed projects include assessments of the health status and healthcare access of homeless men and women; of those infected by hepatitis C through State-provided blood products; and of older people in Ireland. Ongoing work includes evaluation of barriers to organ donation; patient satisfaction with hospital out-patient services; Traveller health service experiences; and patient access to cardiac services. Its work is funded by Government agencies and voluntary bodies. [www.rcsi.ie]

The Views expressed in this report are those of the authors and do not necessarily reflect the views or policies of the sponsors.

FOREWORD

Micheál Martin, TD
Minister for Health and Children

As Minister for Health and Children, I was happy to provide funding towards this research project carried out by the Health Services Research Centre, Department of Psychology, Royal College of Surgeons in Ireland on behalf of the Dublin Rape Crisis Centre and I now welcome its publication.

Both men and women were interviewed as part of this survey and the report describes, *inter alia*, their personal experiences of, and attitudes towards, all forms of sexual violence both as adults and as children. We are continually learning how best to treat victims of sexual violence, both at a personal and professional level. As we are all too aware, the impact of rape and sexual assault can have a traumatic effect on victims and services must be in a position to respond appropriately. I hope that the findings of this report will contribute to the further development of appropriate responses by all those concerned with the provision of services to victims of sexual violence, whether they are male or female, adult or child. In recent years there has been a growing recognition of the complementary roles of the statutory and the voluntary agencies in providing services for victims of rape and sexual assault and I would like to commend the work of the Dublin Rape Crisis Centre which has been to the forefront in this area.

I welcome the publication of this report and I look forward with interest to studying its findings and recommendations.

FOREWORD

John O'Donoghue, TD
Minister for Justice, Equality and Law Reform

I am pleased that my Department was able to support the undertaking of this research into the prevalence of sexual violence in Ireland. It will add to the growing body of research on this important subject. Last year, for example, I published the study "Attrition in Sexual Assault Offence Cases in Ireland".

As Minister for Justice, Equality and Law Reform, I recognise that any act of violence can have a devastating effect on the victim. When this violence is an act of rape or sexual assault, the effect must be even more traumatic. Rape and sexual assault are heinous crimes and, as a society, we must take a stand to tackle them. That is why the penalties for sexual offences are severe, and rightly so. These are forms of offending on which interventions, other than purely law-and-order-type interventions, also have a vital role to play. The role of educators, in particular, is obviously crucial. In that context, research projects give us important information to help all involved respond better to the special needs of victims.

It is an old saying, but prevention is always better than cure, and we must try to prevent crimes of rape and sexual assault. I hope that the research undertaken will help us to achieve this and more.

FOREWORD

Breda Allen
Dublin Rape Crisis Centre

This is a groundbreaking study, the importance of which cannot be overestimated. Up to now the only figures available were based on the number of people seeking counselling or reporting to the Gardaí. We were aware that this only represented "the tip of the iceberg". We knew that those people who sought help were a minority of those sexually victimised and there was no way to establish the number of people who do not seek help.

The lack of information available meant that the Dublin Rape Crisis Centre could not:

- Carry out a comprehensive public awareness campaign because there was no information about the "silent majority"

- Prepare comprehensive plans for the development of services

- Target appropriate groups who are most in need of information about services and who need most encouragement in order to access available services.

I believe that this very wide-ranging report will help us, and other Rape Crisis Centres around the country, to develop relevant services and provide effective help to as many people as possible. For many years we in the Dublin Rape Crisis Centre have known that there was an ever-increasing demand for our services, yet we were unable to estimate with any degree of accuracy whether the problem of sexual violence was increasing or decreasing.

While this study is of major importance, it is only through the regular repetition of this type of research study that we can be informed, and provide information about, increases or decreases in sexual crimes in Ireland. The Dublin Rape Crisis Centre recommends that this be a first baseline study that will be repeated at regular intervals in the future.

I wish to publicly recognise the contribution of The Atlantic Philanthropies to this study. When the Dublin Rape Crisis Centre first outlined the idea for such a study in 1999, they responded generously to the project in terms of financial aid, advice and support in making this idea a reality.

A special debt of gratitude is due to the excellent team who carried out this research and are the authors of the Report. They are: Professor Hannah McGee, Director of the Health Services Research Centre at the Royal College of Surgeons in Ireland, and her colleagues Rebecca Garavan, Mairéad de Barra, Joanne Byrne and Ronán Conroy. The entire team worked hard over three years to bring this important work to fruition.

Above all, the Dublin Rape Crisis Centre wishes to sincerely thank each of the 3,120 participants in this study who disclosed their experiences and attitudes in a lengthy interview. We recognise their generosity in agreeing to participate in what was a challenging and at times difficult interview, and that by so doing they chose to make their experiences available for the greater good of all victims of sexual violence.

We also wish to thank and acknowledge the Department of Health and Children, including the Health Promotion Unit in that Department, and the Department of Justice, Equality and Law Reform for their financial contributions to the project.

Breda Allen, Chairperson
Dublin Rape Crisis Centre
March 2002

PREFACE

The Sexual Abuse and Violence in Ireland (SAVI) Study was conducted at the Health Services Research Centre, Department of Psychology at the Royal College of Surgeons in Ireland (RCSI). We were very pleased to have the opportunity to address such a challenging and important issue in contemporary Ireland. Many people made this project possible. We firstly applaud the initiative of the Dublin Rape Crisis Centre in proposing the project, in funding a feasibility study to consider how such a project could be completed in a safe and valid manner and in eliciting contributions from key Government Departments — the Department of Health and Children and the Department of Justice, Equality and Law Reform — towards the cost of undertaking the main study. From the outset, a Study Monitoring Group provided excellent support and guidance to us on the project. Members of that Group are listed on page xi. A particular thanks to Sinéad Hanley, Chair of the Group, for making this such a constructive forum for all involved. Thanks also to staff at the Dublin Rape Crisis Centre for liaison throughout the project, in particular to Geraldine Connolly, Director of Clinical Services and Maria Byrne, Administrator.

Study planning involved meetings and discussions in Ireland, the UK and the US. Particular thanks to the following for professional input into study design issues in sexual violence: Dr Nancy Thoennes and Dr Pat Tjaden, Centre for Policy Research, Denver; Dr Mary Koss, University of Arizona; Dr Dean Kilpatrick, University of South Carolina; Dr Judith Siegel and Dr Neil Malamuth, University of California at Los Angeles; Professor Sylvia Walby,

University of Leeds; Dr Liz Kelly and Dr Linda Regan, University of North London; and Professor Michael King, Royal Free Hospital, London. In Ireland, James Williams of the Survey Unit, Economic and Social Research Institute, Dublin and Dr Michael Breen of the Department of Media and Communications Studies, University of Limerick provided invaluable advice on the telephone survey methodology in the Irish setting. Many others provided information or advice including Pauline Beegan, Dublin; Dr Shane Alright, Trinity College Dublin; Dr Elizabeth Dunne, University College Cork, Dr Máire Leane, University College Cork and Dr Patrick Walsh, Granada Institute Dublin.

It was not possible to conduct the study without a variety of safety mechanisms. Thank you to all of the rape crisis centres nationally and to the Granada Institute for agreeing to provide prompt services to those who decided they needed professional help for the problems they described to us in the study. Fiona Neary, National Coordinator of the Network of Rape Crisis Centres of Ireland was particularly helpful in facilitating this. Many professionals and organisations were interviewed for the study — those in the prison services, services for learning disability, psychiatric services, Pavee Point (a Travelling Community organisation) and Ruhama (a support organisation for women in prostitution) along with other individuals from academic, research and service-provision communities, who shared their knowledge with us. We would like to express our special appreciation and thanks to a small number of carefully selected people who had personally experienced sexual violence and who generously provided their perspectives on drafts of the SAVI questionnaire to ensure that the finalised measure was phrased in an acceptable and sensitive manner.

Within the College (RCSI), many people across departments helped us to make the study possible. Within the Department of Psychology, everyone has lived with and helped out with the project for nearly three years. Particular thanks to Mrs Linda Hunt for sterling administrative support and to Professor Ciaran O'Boyle, Dr Anne Hickey, Ms Helen Goode and Ms Eva Doherty for professional advice. The project was finally possible because we were able to bring together a truly great team of telephone interviewers. Fifteen people trained and worked together over five months covering morning to night and Monday to Saturday in their survey calls. Their names are: Joanne Byrne, Clara Connolly, Catriona Ellis, Frances Foley, Loraine Hayes, James Kelly, Caroline Kennedy, Colette Leigh, Colma McCarthy, Afshana Naeem, Siobain O'Donnell, Emma Riggs, Leah Schneider, Astrid Walsh and Regina Walsh. Their commitment to the quality of their work and to the well-being of interviewees was impressive and their support for each other through challenging interviews equally so. They all stayed for the whole period of the project calls — a testimony to their commitment and team approach. Thanks to each of them for making the study a reality.

We opted to call the study "SAVI", a play on the word "savvy" meaning "to have understanding of". It seemed a good aspiration to have for a project aiming to provide an evidence base for such a sensitive and under-explored issue in Ireland. The reader is the judge of how successful we have been in that aspiration. We hope that the report as compiled goes some way to repaying the faith and efforts of so many people who helped in the overall study. We also hope that the report will facilitate a constructive focus on the topic of sexual violence in contemporary Ireland.

The project has been very stimulating but also very demanding. Thanks to our immediate families and friends who have had to put up with our demands and preoccupations with the project. We each have our personal dedications for the project — our families and friends and those we personally know who have been affected by sexual violence. Our collective dedication as a research team goes to those who entrusted the stories of their lives to us.

Thank you, one and all.

Hannah McGee
Rebecca Garavan
Mairéad de Barra
Joanne Byrne
Ronán Conroy
Royal College of Surgeons in Ireland

Dedication

Over 3,000 people took part in the SAVI Study. Many recounted difficult and painful personal experiences of sexual violence. All took the time to discuss with us very personal and sensitive aspects of their lives. The study's unique contribution is this substantial input from so many members of the Irish public. We thank them for their time and trust and dedicate this book to them.

List of Tables and Figures

List of Tables

List of Figures

EXECUTIVE SUMMARY

BACKGROUND

The prevalence of sexual violence in Ireland is unknown. Incomplete evidence from crime statistics, previous research reports and service uptake figures is insufficient to understand the nature and extent of the problem and to plan and evaluate services and preventive interventions.

The main aim of the SAVI study was to estimate the prevalence of various forms of sexual violence among Irish women and men across the lifespan from childhood through adulthood.

Additional aims of the study were to describe who had been abused, the perpetrators of abuse, the context in which abuse occurred and some psychological consequences of abuse; to describe the pattern of disclosure of such abuse to others, including professionals; to document public beliefs about and perceived prevalence of sexual violence; to assess public willingness to disclose abuse to others in the event of a future experience; to document particular challenges experienced in addressing sexual violence by marginalised groups; and to make recommendations for future developments in the areas of public awareness, prevention, service delivery and policy development.

METHOD

A survey assessing the prevalence of sexual violence was conducted by anonymous telephone interviews with randomly selected participants from the general population in Ireland. They were interviewed at home telephone numbers in the period March to June 2001.

Many ethical and safety considerations were built into the study design to ensure that a high quality and sensitive approach was used. Interviewers were highly qualified and underwent additional training and regular supervision in the conduct of the interviews. A wide range of safety mechanisms were put in place to reassure participants about study authenticity and to provide them with access to professional services if required.

RESULTS

Study Population

Over 3,000 randomly selected Irish adults took part in the study (n = 3,118). This represented a 71 per cent participation rate of those invited. For a telephone survey, and on such a sensitive topic, this very high participation rate means that the findings can be taken as broadly representative of the general population in Ireland. The information available can therefore provide important and previously unavailable information on the extent and nature of sexual violence in Irish society.

Prevalence of Sexual Violence

Child Sexual Abuse (defined as sexual abuse of children and adolescents under age 17 years)

- **Girls**: One in five women (20.4 per cent) reported experiencing contact sexual abuse in childhood with a further one in ten (10.0 per cent) reporting non-contact sexual abuse. In over a quarter of cases of contact abuse (i.e. 5.6 per cent of all girls), the abuse involved penetrative sex — either vaginal, anal or oral sex.

- **Boys**: One in six men (16.2 per cent) reported experiencing contact sexual abuse in childhood with a further one in fourteen (7.4 per cent) reporting non-contact sexual abuse. In one of every six cases of contact abuse (i.e. 2.7 per cent of all boys), the abuse involved penetrative sex — either anal or oral sex.

Adult Sexual Assault (defined as sexual violence against women or men aged 17 years and above)

- **Women**: One in five women (20.4 per cent) reported experiencing contact sexual assault as adults with a further one in twenty (5.1 per cent) reporting unwanted non-contact sexual experiences. Over a quarter of cases of contact abuse in adulthood (i.e. 6.1 per cent of all women) involved penetrative sex.

- **Men**: One in ten men (9.7 per cent) reported experiencing contact sexual assault as adults with a further 2.7 per cent reporting unwanted non-contact sexual experiences. One in ten cases of contact abuse in adulthood (i.e. 0.9 per cent of all men) involved penetrative sex.

Lifetime Experience of Sexual Abuse and Assault

- **Women**: More than four in ten (42 per cent) of women reported some form of sexual abuse or assault in their lifetime. The most serious form of abuse, penetrative abuse, was experienced by 10 per cent of women. Attempted penetration or contact abuse was experienced by 21 per cent, with a further 10 per cent experiencing non-contact abuse.

- **Men**: Over a quarter of men (28 per cent) reported some form of sexual abuse or assault in their lifetime. Penetrative abuse was experienced by 3 per cent of men. Attempted penetration or contact abuse was experienced by 18 per cent, with a further 7 per cent experiencing non-contact abuse.

Characteristics of Sexual Abuse and Violence in Childhood and Adulthood

- Overall, almost one-third of women and a quarter of men reported some level of sexual abuse in childhood. Attempted or actual penetrative sex was experienced by 7.6 per cent of girls and 4.2 per cent of boys. Equivalent rape or attempted rape figures in adulthood were 7.4 per cent for women and 1.5 per cent for men. Hence, girls and women were more likely to be subjected to serious sexual crimes than boys and men. Levels of serious sexual crimes committed against women remained similar from childhood through adulthood. Risks for men were lower as children than they were for women and decreased three-fold from childhood to adult life.

- Of those disclosing abuse, over one-quarter (27.7 per cent) of women and one-fifth (19.5 per cent) of men were abused by different perpetrators as both children and adults (i.e. "revictimised"). For women, experiencing penetrative sexual abuse in childhood was associated with a sixteen-fold increase in risk of adult penetrative sexual abuse, and with a five-fold increase in risk of adult contact sexual violence. For men, experiencing penetrative sexual abuse in childhood was associated with a sixteen-fold increase in the risk of adult penetrative sexual violence, and an approximately twelve-fold increase in the risk of adult contact sexual violence. It is not possible to say that childhood abuse "causes" adult revictimisation. Childhood sexual abuse is, however, an important marker of increased risk of adult sexual violence.

- Most sexual abuse in childhood and adolescence occurred in the pre-pubescent period, with two-thirds (67 per cent) of abused girls and 62 per cent of abused boys having experienced abuse by twelve years of age.

- In four of ten cases (40 per cent), the experience of child sexual abuse was an ongoing, rather than a single, abuse event. For many of those who experienced ongoing abuse (58 per cent of girls and 42 per cent of boys), the duration of abuse was longer than one year.

- A third (36 per cent) of those who had experienced sexual abuse as a child now believe that their abuser was also abusing other children at the time.

Characteristics of Perpetrators and Context of Sexual Violence

- Most perpetrators of child sexual abuse (89 per cent) were men acting alone. Seven per cent of children were abused by one female perpetrator. In 4 per cent of cases more than one abuser was involved in the same incident(s).

Perpetrators of Child Sexual Abuse

- **Girls**: A quarter (24 per cent) of perpetrators against girls were family members, half (52 per cent) were non-family but known to the abused girl and a quarter (24 per cent) were strangers.

- **Boys**: Fewer family members were involved in child sexual abuse of boys. One in seven perpetrators (14 per cent) was a family member with two-thirds (66 per cent) non-family but known to the abused boy. One in five (20 per cent) were strangers.

- In sum, in four-fifths of cases of child sexual abuse, the perpetrator was known to the abused person.

- The perpetrator was another child or adolescent (17 years old or younger) in one out of every four cases.

Perpetrators of Sexual Violence against Adults

- Almost one-quarter (23.6 per cent) of perpetrators of sexual violence against women as adults were intimate partners or ex-partners. This was the case for very few (1.4 per cent) abused men. Instead, most perpetrators of abuse against men were friends or acquaintances (42 per cent). The risk of sexual assault by a stranger was higher for adults (representing 30 per cent of assaults on women and 38 per cent of assaults on men) than for children.

- Alcohol was involved in almost half of the cases of sexual assault that occurred as an adult. Of those who reported that alcohol was involved, both parties were drinking in 57 per cent of cases concerning sexual assault of women, and in 63 per cent of cases concerning sexual assault of men. Where only one party was drinking, the perpetrator was the one drinking in the majority of cases (84 per cent of female and 70 per cent of male assault cases).

Psychological Consequences of Sexual Violence

- Approximately one in three (30 per cent) women and one in four (18 per cent) men reported that their experiences of sexual violence (either in childhood, adulthood or both) had had a moderate or extreme effect on their lives overall.

- A quarter (25 per cent) of women and one in six (16 per cent) men reported having experienced symptoms consistent with a diagnosis of post-traumatic stress disorder (PTSD) at some time in their lives following, and as a consequence of, their experience of sexual violence.

- Those who had experienced sexual violence were significantly more likely to have used medication for anxiety or depression or to have been a psychiatric hospital inpatient than those without such experiences. For instance, those who had experienced attempted or actual penetrative sexual abuse were eight times more likely to have been an inpatient in a psychiatric hospital than those who had not been abused.

Disclosure of Experiences of Sexual Violence

- Almost half (47 per cent) of those who disclosed experiences of sexual violence in this study reported that they had never previously disclosed that abuse to others. Thus in a study of over 3,100 adults, almost 600 people disclosed instances of abuse for the first time to another person.

- Older people were generally less likely than other age groups to have disclosed to others in the past with one exception: most (60 per cent) young men who had experienced child sexual abuse had told no-one prior to the study.

- Most people who disclosed sexual violence did so to friends (71 per cent) or family members (43 per cent). Family members were more likely to be told in the case of child sexual abuse.

- The most common reason people gave for not telling about their abuse as children was because of feeling ashamed or blaming themselves. A quarter of both men and women who had experienced child sexual abuse reported these as the reasons for not telling. These reasons were uncommon for those who had experienced sexual violence as adults. A fifth of adults had not disclosed sexual assault because they thought that what had happened to them was too trivial to tell others.

- Disclosure of sexual violence to professionals was strikingly low. Regarding experiences of adult sexual assault, only one man (of 98 abused, i.e. 1 per cent) and 7.8 per cent of women (19 of 244) had reported their experiences to the Gardaí (i.e. 6 per cent overall of those abused). Patterns were similar regarding experiences of child sexual abuse. Ten men (of 178) and 28 women (of 290) reported their experiences to the Gardaí (i.e. 8 per cent overall of those abused). Disclosure to medical professionals was 6 per cent for adult abuse and 4 per cent for child abuse while disclosure to counsellors/therapists was 12 per cent with 14 per cent of women and 8 per cent of men disclosing to counsellors/therapists.

- Regarding client evaluation of services received from professionals, overall satisfaction with services received was greatest for counsellors and therapists at 81 per cent. About half (56 per cent) of those who reported to the Gardaí were satisfied overall with the service they received with little differences for child or adult abuse. Those who received help from medical professionals were mixed in their ratings, with those who received services for adult sexual assault being almost twice as satisfied with the services they received than those with experiences of child sexual abuse (60 per cent versus 33 per cent).

- Lack of information from the Gardaí and medical personnel was the main source of dissatisfaction with services. Specifically, Gardaí were seen to provide inadequate explanations of procedures being undertaken, and medical personnel were seen as needing to provide more information regarding other available services and options. With regard to counselling services, time waiting to get an appointment was the major source of dissatisfaction.

- Legal redress for sexual crimes, as reported in this study, was the exception rather than the rule. Of 38 individuals who reported child sexual abuse to the Gardaí, six cases (16 per cent) resulted in court proceedings with four guilty verdicts. Of 20 people reporting adult sexual assault, two court cases (10 per cent) were taken with one resulting in a guilty verdict.

Public Perceptions of Sexual Violence

The perceptions of all the participants were taken to represent the "public" perception of sexual violence in Irish society today.

Perceptions of Prevalence of Sexual Violence

- Estimates of the prevalence of adult sexual assault and most types of child sexual abuse by the participants indicated that about half of those interviewed were quite inaccurate about the frequency of such events, either because they over-estimated or underestimated them. Underestimation was more common, with a third underestimating the prevalence of rape among adult women and men, and child abuse by non-family members. However, participant estimates regarding the prevalence of incest were substantially higher than those reported in the present study.

- Participants significantly overestimated the number of cases reported to the Gardaí (estimated 34 per cent women and 16 per cent men; actual percentages 10 per cent women and 6 per cent men) while correctly signalling the gender difference of men being less likely to report than women. Estimates of the likelihood of getting a conviction in court cases were similar to actual reports although actual reports relate to such small numbers that conclusions need to be drawn with caution.

Perceptions of Probability of Disclosure

- When asked to judge whether they would tell others if they themselves were sexually abused, over a quarter of study participants said that they would be unlikely to tell family members. More (41 per cent) felt they probably would not tell friends. Regarding professionals, over a quarter (27 per cent) felt they would be unlikely to tell the Gardaí and almost a quarter were uncertain or thought they would not go to a counsellor. However, most (85 per cent) felt they would disclose to a doctor, some with the added qualification that they would only if medically necessary. Men were more likely to think they would not disclose to all groups except doctors.

Perceptions of Service Access

- Over a quarter of the group (27.6 per cent) reported that they would not know where to go to get professional help for sexual violence if they needed it. Men were significantly less likely than women to be able to identify where they could go for help and young adults of both sexes (those aged 18–24) were less likely than others to know where to seek help. Half of young men (i.e. under age 30) reported that they would not know where to find professional support or services.

Public Beliefs about Sexual Violence

Beliefs about sexual violence were assessed with attitude statements about common rape beliefs.

- Some reported attitudes reflected more accurate views and views which are more supportive to those who are affected by sexual violence. For instance, almost all (92 per cent) agreed that "a date rape can be just as traumatic as rape by a stranger"; 85 per cent agreed that "a raped woman is usually an innocent victim" and 91 per cent disagreed that "child sexual abuse is usually committed by strangers". On the other hand, four in ten (40 per cent) of study participants felt that "accusations of rape are often false".

- Men were significantly more accepting of attitudes reflecting rationalisations or victim-blaming concerning sexual violence than women, particularly with regard to motivation for rape and sexual violence committed against men. Specifically, 47 per cent of men (versus 34 per cent of women) agreed that "the reason most rapists commit rape is overwhelming sexual desire" and 41 per cent of men (versus 27 per cent of women) agreed that "men who sexually assault other men must be gay (homosexual)".

- Attitudes towards media coverage of sexual violence were predominantly positive with three-quarters (76 per cent) believing coverage was beneficial.

Sexual Harassment

- Some form of sexual harassment was experienced at least once during the last 12 months by 16.2 per cent of women and 12.6 per cent of men. Being stalked in a way that was frightening to them was reported by 1 per cent of the participants.

Marginalised Groups

- A large national telephone survey is a useful means of estimating levels of sexual violence for the general population. However, it cannot adequately reflect the experiences of marginalised groups in Ireland. This study selected a range of exemplar groups to illustrate the additional challenges that disclosure and management of sexual violence poses for marginalised groups. The groups selected were homeless women and their children, Traveller women, prisoners, women in prostitution, people with learning disabilities, and those with psychiatric problems.

RECOMMENDATIONS

- *Recommendation 1*: That a comprehensive public awareness campaign on sexual violence be developed, delivered and evaluated in Ireland.

- *Recommendation 2*: That a range of information materials on services for sexual violence be developed and made available in appropriate settings and formats to assist those in need of such services.

- *Recommendation 3*: That barriers to the disclosure of sexual violence be addressed at the level of the general public, professionals and systems.

- *Recommendation 4*: That all those responsible for public awareness, educational, health-related or law enforcement service delivery on the issue of sexual violence incorporate information on vulnerability for specific groups in their activities. These groups include those abused as children, adult women and adult men; perpetrators of abuse; and marginalised groups.

- *Recommendation 5*: That the need for service developments be anticipated and planned on the basis of a comprehensive needs evaluation of evidence for medical, counselling and law enforcement services. This should take into account potential increases in service demand as a consequence of public awareness campaigns. Co-ordination of service development and public awareness strategies is essential. A service needs assessment should be conducted for those who have experienced or otherwise been affected by sexual violence, to include all statutory and voluntary agencies and to address both medical and counselling services.

- *Recommendation 6*: That a range of educational materials on sexual violence in Irish society be developed for relevant professionals; this to complement a national public awareness campaign. In addition, that regular assessment of the user perspective be incorporated into service evaluation and planning for improvement.

- **Recommendation 7**: That a systematic programme of Irish research is needed to inform, support and evaluate developments in addressing sexual violence in the coming years. This should include a regular national survey assessing public attitudes and experiences and critically evaluating changes in both over time.

- **Recommendation 8**: That a Consultative Committee on Sexual Violence be established with the responsibility and authority to ensure that recommendations arising from the SAVI Study and similar reports are acted on by relevant agencies within an appropriate timeframe. This Committee should represent the broad constituency of interests which can contribute to effective management of the societal challenge of sexual violence.

Section I

INTRODUCTION

Chapter 1

GENERAL INTRODUCTION

BACKGROUND TO THE STUDY

Over recent years, there has been a rapidly developing awareness of the profound impact of sexual violence and its consequences, not only on individuals and their families but also on society as a whole. The seriousness of sexual violence is both a cause and a consequence of the particular secrecy with which it has typically been surrounded. Service-based evidence on sexual violence provides incomplete evidence from which to understand its prevalence, to develop insights into the causes and consequences of such violence, to monitor trends and to plan and evaluate the impact of interventions. Acknowledging the need for a wider information base, national studies on the prevalence of sexual violence have recently been completed in countries such as the US, Canada, New Zealand, Finland and Sweden.

In Ireland, national data on child sexual abuse was first collected in 1993 by the Irish Society for the Prevention of Cruelty to Children. Embedded in a larger interview study of adults concerning physical punishment of children, they collected brief self-completed information on personal experiences of childhood sexual abuse (ISPCC, 1993). While this study provided some information on child abuse, the prevalence of sexual assault and violence among adults in Ireland is unknown, as is the attitude of the general public to abuse. Furthermore, the experiences of seeking professional services, including legal services and redress for those who have been abused, have not been evaluated in a comprehensive manner. Neither has there been an evaluation of perceived and actual barriers to care for those who have been abused. In the context of increasing attention to the problem of sexual violence in Ireland, the need for both local (i.e. Irish) and representative information on its prevalence and nature is clear. Such evidence is required to inform service delivery and policy making and to plan, conduct and evaluate interventions to tackle this serious crime. A keen awareness of the need for representative Irish evidence by the Dublin Rape Crisis Centre (DRCC), the largest frontline service provider to those who have experienced sexual violence in Ireland, was the origin and driving force behind this research project. In 1999, the DRCC acquired funding through a private donation for a feasibility study on this complex topic. On successful completion of this study, the present research study was commissioned. Core funding for the main study was also secured by a private donation to the DRCC, and contributions were provided to the DRCC by the Department of Health and Children and the Department of Justice, Equality and Law Reform in order to establish a partnership which could maximise the potential for positive action in relation to the recommendations.

A national prevalence study of sexual abuse and violence was seen as a major contribution to developing an evidence base on sexual violence in Ireland. From the outset, it was envisaged that the survey should encompass abuse across the lifespan, include both women and men, and specifically examine professional service provision for those who experienced such abuse. A random sample of the Irish population was considered the optimal means to acquire this information. However, the conduct of a randomised national study on sexual violence provided significant challenges. Since there was no information to determine if there was a feasible and valid research approach to such a national study in Ireland, a feasibility study was deemed necessary before embarking on a major national survey.

Following extensive consultation in early 2000 with international research teams and with key Irish informants (legal, police, medical, counselling and market research), a telephone survey methodology was examined for its feasibility. The resulting study of 73 participants proved successful according to two major criteria: response rates to the invitation to participate were acceptable, and evidence that participants were willing to disclose episodes of abuse was generated. (The feasibility study is described in greater detail later in this section.)

The conduct of the feasibility study led to the development of the main study proposal and provided valuable information to generate the sample size estimations needed for the main study. While a national prevalence survey was seen as a vital part of developing evidence-based strategies to tackle sexual violence, it was also acknowledged from the outset that a number of marginalised groups in Irish society would not be included, or challenges specific to their exposure to sexual violence addressed, in a general population prevalence survey. The overall study aimed to highlight some of the particular challenges for selected minority groups as a way of acknowledging the very complex challenge of ensuring all citizens can be protected from sexual violence. The overall project — a national prevalence study coupled with more specific examination of the challenges concerning sexual violence for marginalised groups — was entitled the SAVI (Sexual Abuse and Violence in Ireland) Study.

The complexity of the terminology used to describe sexual violence reflects the complexity of the issue itself. There is no offence called "child sexual abuse" in Irish law (see Appendix V: Glossary, for further discussion). The legal terms "sexual assault", "aggravated sexual assault", "rape" and "rape under Section 4" refer to sexual crimes committed regardless of the age of the victim (for further explanation see Bacik, Maunsell and Gogan, 1998). In the SAVI study, three terms are used: sexual violence, sexual assault and sexual abuse.

- The term *sexual violence* is used as an inclusive term to describe all sexual offences, be they committed against adults or children.

- The term sexual assault is used to describe sexual offences involving *physical contact committed against adults* (i.e. aged 17 years or older). It combines the legal categories of sexual assault and rape.

- The term *sexual abuse* is used to describe sexual offences committed *against a person aged under 17 years* (the legal age for consent to sexual relations in Ireland).

Penetrative abuse describes all penetrative acts (penile, digital or with an object) of the mouth, vagina or anus. Other contact abuse refers to sexual abuse involving physical contact without penetration, and generally corresponds to sexual assault or aggravated sexual assault in Irish law (see Appendix V: Glossary for further clarification). Non-contact abuse is used in connection with child sexual abuse to refer to indecent exposure and exposure to pornography. In the case of adults, it refers to unwanted sexually offensive experiences that could not be otherwise classified.

AIMS OF THE PRESENT STUDY

The SAVI study had seven broad aims:

1. To provide reliable estimates of the prevalence of various forms of sexual violence against men and women across the lifespan from childhood through adulthood

2. To describe those who have been abused, the perpetrators of abuse, the context in which abuse occurs, and some of the psychological consequences of abuse

3. To describe the patterns of disclosure of abuse to others, both personal and professional contacts, and to outline decisions made regarding disclosure including barriers to telling others

4. To document and compare public perceptions of the prevalence of various forms of sexual violence with the documented prevalence in this study

5. To evaluate the public perceptions regarding issues related to sexual violence. This ranged from evaluations of beliefs about sexual violence to estimating their own willingness to disclose abuse to others in the event of a future experience of sexual violence

6. To document the particular challenges experienced in addressing sexual violence by marginalised groups in Ireland; this to be achieved by describing an exemplar set of such groups. The groups included were homeless women and their children, Travellers, prisoners, women in prostitution, people with a learning disability, and people in psychiatric services

7. To consolidate information from the general public and those who have experienced abuse in order to make recommendations in the areas of public awareness prevention, service delivery and policy development.

The remainder of Section I outlines international literature on the prevalence of sexual violence and on public perceptions of such violence. Experiences of those abused in terms of disclosure and use of health or related services, and in terms of legal redress for the violence committed against them, is considered. Available Irish evidence is summarised alongside international research.

PREVALENCE OF SEXUAL VIOLENCE: INTERNATIONAL RESEARCH

The prevalence of sexual violence is a particularly challenging figure to determine given that sexual violence is acknowledged to be under-reported by an unknown quantity. Prevalence estimates are known to be influenced by features of the crime and its meaning, such as fear surrounding the consequences of reporting. It is also influenced by design features of the prevalence studies themselves (as discussed in greater detail elsewhere). Not only is under-reporting a hindrance in estimating the true prevalence of sexual violence, but it has consequences that have made under-reporting an ethical concern (World Health Organisation, 1999).

Research which severely under-reports abuse is less likely to accurately identify the associations between risk factors and outcomes. In terms of policy and prevention stemming from such research, valuable programmes and interventions may be moved further down a long list of priorities if the problem is considered to be much smaller than it actually is (Ellsberg, Heise, Pena, Agurto and Winkvist, 2001). These concerns have resulted in various studies to specifically examine the amount of under-reporting. For example, the US National Crime Victimisation (NCV) Survey is a crime telephone poll conducted annually to detect levels of reported and unreported crimes. The National Crime Victim's Centre estimates that the reported levels of rape in the NCV Survey are 6 to 15 times lower than the true levels (Finkelhor, Wolak and Berliner, 2001). In the 1980s in Finland, rapes were reported at the rate of 345 per year, while police estimated that the actual number was more in the region of 6,000-10,000 per year (European Commission, 1997).

Nevertheless, most international studies attempt to account for under-reporting. From these figures, the best estimates indicate that 14–25 per cent of adult women have been raped during their lifetime. At the other end of the continuum, sexual harassment at work will be experienced by 50 per cent of women during their lives (Goodman, Koss and Russo, 1993). Rates of sexual victimisation for men are harder to estimate with reported lifetime levels ranging from 3–31 per cent (Crowder, 1995). In both sexes, most sexual violence occurs before age 18 years of age. Examples of the prevalence levels of sexual violence obtained from a range of international studies using differing methodologies are outlined in Appendix I.

PREVALENCE OF SEXUAL VIOLENCE: IRISH RESEARCH

In Ireland, sexual abuse is now acknowledged as a significant problem. A recent study of patterns of crime in Ireland since 1950 concluded that there was a substantial increase in the number of sexual offences reported in the past 20 years (Young, Read, Barker-Collo and Harrison, 2001). The authors proposed that this was more likely to be due to an increase in the reporting of abuse than to an actual increase in the prevalence of abuse. The number of convictions for sexual crimes was approximately 200 per year in the 1950s and by 1997 had reached approximately 1,000 per year. As of January 2002, the number of men in Irish prisons who have been convicted of sex offences constitute a significant minority: 11.6 per cent (n=350) of the total prison population (Department of Justice, Equality and Law Reform, personal communication).

While recorded crime numbers have increased, there remains the concern that there is significant underreporting of abuse and in particular a shortfall in seeking legal redress. Dublin Rape Crisis Centre figures from 1998–2000 showed that only a quarter of counselling clients for child sexual abuse had reported the abuse to the Gardaí (19 per cent in 1998/9 and 23 per cent in 1999/2000), while a third of those seeking counselling for adult sexual assault had reported to the police (36 per cent in 1998/9 and 33 per cent in 1999/2000) (DRCC, 2000; DRCC, 2001). While there has been some progress concerning the process of reporting sexual abuse to the Gardaí and on through to criminal proceedings, there is an acknowledgement that many barriers still exist in obtaining a court hearing. A recent qualitative study in Cork focused on the experiences of women who had reported abuse to the Cork and Kerry Rape Crisis Centres (Leane, Ryan, Fennell and Egan, 2001). Interviewing eight women and a range of service providers, they identified multiple attrition points from reporting through to court proceedings where cases were removed from consideration by the justice system. The recommendations arising from their study ranged from trial preparation programmes and information packs for those abused, to better education of the public in exposing myths concerning rape or sexual abuse.

Uptake of counselling services which deal with sexual abuse continues to rise. For instance, the Dublin Rape Crisis Centre had 7,500 crisis telephone calls in the period July 1998 to June 1999. These numbers increased to 9,588 in the year 2001 (provisional

2001 data) — this represents a 28 per cent increase. Numbers of first-time callers for recent rape experiences increased from 968 (2000) to 1273 (2001) — a 32 per cent increase. (Earlier analysis by this latter categorisation was not available.) Similarly, CARI (Children at Risk in Ireland — an organisation with a focus on child sexual abuse) reported 239 crisis calls in 1999 with 2,328 in the year 2000. The Irish Society for the Prevention of Cruelty to Children provides summary information on the topic of its calls to Childline telephone services in 2000. Of over 112,000 calls, 2,329 (i.e. 5.2 per cent of all calls where the caller and counsellor had "full communication") involved discussions concerning sexual abuse. Other services, including voluntary services such as Barnardos and the National Network of Rape Crisis Centres, alongside health board services, provide professional support to those experiencing abuse. An overview of their service delivery and changes over time is beyond the scope of this report.

While the previously cited figures provide general trends in Ireland for those who choose to disclose abuse to professional agencies and service providers, numbers based on criminal proceedings and service uptake provide limited insight into the total number of individuals who have been sexually abused in the general population. National studies of the general population may provide more accurate estimates of the levels of violence by including cases which go unreported to authorities and professional bodies. While many countries have regular national crime surveys to identify the nature and level of reported and unreported crime, Ireland does not have a dedicated crime survey strategy to date. However, two national surveys of the prevalence of crime have been conducted. In 1982/83, the Economic and Social Research Institute (ESRI) examined crime in a sample of 8,902 individuals as part of its monthly Consumer Survey (Breen and Rottman, 1985). More recently, in 1998, the Central Statistics Office, as part of its Quarterly Household Survey, researched crime in 39,000 households (Central Statistics Office, 2001). Neither survey, however, addressed the issues of sexual or other interpersonal violence. Using a different focus, the ESRI also conducted a detailed face-to-face interview study on the circumstances of crime with almost 1,000 people who had reported a crime to the Gardaí (Watson, 2000). Topics such as murder and sexual assault were excluded from the study, however, because of their serious and sensitive nature. Another ESRI survey, on the health of women, did ask some questions about violence in general (Wiley and Merriman, 1996). They interviewed 2,988 Irish women aged 18–60 years in 1993 (76 per cent participation rate). When asked if they had ever been beaten, raped, attacked or seriously threatened, 9.9 per cent said "yes". This happened in their own homes in 46 per cent of cases and the attacker was known in 70 per cent of cases (M. Wiley, personal communication). No further breakdown of the type of violence was possible in this large survey.

The only large-scale survey which specifically addressed sexual violence was conducted in 1993 by Irish Marketing Surveys, on behalf of the ISPCC. They undertook a home-based interview study of 1,001 adults selected to be representative of those aged 18–54 nationally. The main focus of the study was personal experiences of, and attitudes towards, disciplining children. At the end of the interview, participants were asked to independently complete a brief pencil-and-paper questionnaire on their experiences of child sexual abuse and to return them to the interviewers in sealed envelopes. This procedure aimed to maximise confidentiality and minimise distress or embarrassment to the participants. Results of this survey indicated that 15 per cent of women and 9 per cent of men reported contact sexual abuse in childhood. Contact abuse occurred more than once in 61 per cent of cases. They estimated, based on these figures, that one in seven Irish women and one in ten men had experienced contact sexual abuse during childhood. In 1993, that constituted approximately 288,000 adults. (Further discussion of the results of the ISPCC study are found in the Results Section alongside the results of this study for comparison purposes.) Finally, a small survey of third-level students (n = 247) was recently conducted by anonymous questionnaire in Dublin (Lalor, 1999). Unwanted sexual experiences for girls before age 16 were noted by 32 per cent of respondents. Numbers of male respondents precluded detailed analysis. The author commentated on "a culture of sexual aggression towards teenage girls" based on his findings from this study.

PREVALENCE AND EXPERIENCE OF SEXUAL VIOLENCE: MARGINALISED GROUPS

General population studies often exclude marginalised groups either intentionally or unintentionally because the methods of access to the population, e.g. telephone contact only or interviews in a dominant language, do not facilitate communication with such groups. Groups can be marginalised from the overall society in a number of ways. There may be language or cultural differences or location-related barriers such as residence in collective or institutional settings, e.g. prisons or armed forces accommodation. The communication problems may extend beyond language to include cognitive or emotional challenges to interaction with others, e.g. those with a learning disability or mental health problems. Groups may also be marginalised because of social judgements about their place in society, e.g. those of a different racial group or those whose identity or lifestyle is not approved of by others in the larger society, e.g. those who are homosexual in orientation or those who work in prostitution. Not all marginalised groups will be expected to be at increased risk of sexual violence. Some, by their in-group's beliefs and their pattern of social interaction with the wider society, may even be at reduced risk. However, the concern with exposure to sexual violence in marginalised groups is both at the level of prevalence and at the level of barriers to disclosing and seeking help following the abuse. An extensive research literature exists on these issues. It will be presented in Section III of the report with reference to the particular marginalised groups addressed in the overall SAVI study. These groups are homeless women, Travellers, prisoners, prostitutes, persons with a learning disability and persons with mental health problems.

ATTITUDES TO SEXUAL VIOLENCE:
INTERNATIONAL RESEARCH

While many studies have attempted to estimate the true prevalence of sexual violence, others have focused on public perceptions of sexual violence and on their general levels of awareness of the issues involved. Because this information has been used primarily in developing prevention and educational strategies, most have focused on the context of child sexual abuse. Finkelhor (1984) surveyed US parents about their perceptions of child sexual abuse. Their prevalence estimates were quite low in comparison to epidemiological data. One-third also felt that strangers were the most likely offenders, followed by parents and step-parents. They perceived abusers as being middle-aged (not younger or older ages) and male, and in general, they did not see younger children (i.e., aged less than five years) as being at risk. Waterman and Foss-Goodman (1984) examined public perceptions of responsibility for offences. When asked about the role of the abused child in abuse, older and male children were seen to be more to blame or to have more responsibility for the abuse.

Although more recent estimates by the public of the prevalence of sexual abuse are not available, the heightened media attention given to the issue internationally has led to what has been called a "moral panic" about the (violent) nature of the world we now live in (Goddard and Saunders, 2001). Kemp (1998) has described contemporary society as being preoccupied with child sexual abuse. In considering the role of the media, Kitzinger (1996) has examined the construction of UK media reports. Intrafamilial stories of child sexual abuse are under-emphasised while those of a more sensationalist nature, e.g. those involving paedophile rings, are highlighted. A similar Australian analysis showed that stories focused on unusual and extra-familial cases (Wilcyzynski and Sinclair, 1999). This fosters the notion of "stranger danger" rather than considering the lack of safety afforded by the home environment for many (children and adults) who are at risk of sexual violence. A comprehensive Swiss study of child sexual abuse also addressed the imbalance between public perceptions and findings based on epidemiological evidence (Ernst et al., 1993). They highlighted the media image of child sexual abuse being very prevalent and being mainly perpetrated against girls (with estimates ranging from 20–50 per cent). Father–daughter incest was portrayed as the most common form of abuse and it was seen as often happening in seemingly intact closely-knit families. Consequences were typically seen as being severe with permanent impairment of the mental health of the abused children. Their research showed that actual prevalence data varied widely, that father–daughter abuse was relatively rare and that it was very difficult to draw conclusions on the family context or long-term consequences of abuse from the available research. While some analyses point to distortions in the media depiction of child sexual abuse, some of these distortions can be seen as attempts to adjust previous perceptions, e.g. from having the public think only of "stranger danger" to realising that many abusers are family members or trusted others. The positive role of the media in promoting public awareness of the issue has been highlighted:

> . . . it is only by highlighting (child sexual abuse) that we can undo the consequences of its invisibility. Public awareness is essential. To the extent that public awareness exists we treat the problem and find resources to deal with it. (Finkelhor, 1992)

A different line of public perception research has focused on what are termed "rape myths". These are identified as personally held beliefs that may promote or condone sexual abuse and also hinder the disclosure and recovery process for those who have been abused. Most research reports on rape myths only address women as the targets of abuse (Burt, 1980). Several rape myth scales have been developed, such as the "Rape Supportive Attitude Scale" (Lottes, 1988) or the "Attitudes toward Rape Victims Scale" (Ward, 1988). These scales have been used in a variety of settings with various groups, including student populations (as part of initiatives to address sexual abuse on university campuses (e.g. Williams, Forster and Petrak et al., 1999), with professional groups (to identify attitudes deemed as unhelpful in groups such as social workers, psychologists, physicians and police officers (e.g. Ward, 1988) and among convicted sex offenders (to identify negative attitudes to address in rehabilitation) (e.g. Marolla and Scully, 1986).

More recent work, from the perspective of acknowledging and managing one's own propensity to abuse others, has investigated the contexts in which men report that they have been sexually coercive or forceful in nature (or have been close to participating in such behaviour) (Malamuth et al., 1991). This work views the beliefs or attitudes which these men hold as precursors to their sexually inappropriate behaviours. It takes a preventive approach and seeks to move some responsibility for preventing abuse to potential abusers. Overall, however, little research on perceptions and attitudes has been conducted with general populations despite the vital importance of this information in planning any public awareness campaigns to address the myths and realities of sexual violence.

ATTITUDES TO SEXUAL VIOLENCE: IRISH RESEARCH

No attitudinal information on sexual violence is available, to our knowledge, in the national Irish setting. One item on the ISPCC (1993) survey showed that the public believed that children should be advised about the danger of sexual abuse (98 per cent of participants felt parents should address the issue and 96 per cent felt schools should also do so). While little is known about Irish attitudes to sexual violence, it is clear that the last decade has raised awareness of sexual violence like no other previous period. High profile sexual abuse cases included the 1992 "X" case (the case of a young girl pregnant by a friend's father who became the focus of a debate on the right to travel abroad for abortion); the 1993 Kilkenny incest case (a father–daughter abuse case); the 1995 McColgan case (a case of family abuse by the father) and the Father Brendan Smyth case (the case of a lifetime legacy of abuse by a priest who was a paedophile). These cases raised questions regarding the public's awareness of child sexual abuse, the management of child abuse by responsible professionals, and the policy and law enforcement context in which sexual abuse is considered.

Alongside this high profile media coverage, there have been legislative and policy developments. Two reports, *Children First — National Guidelines for the Protection and Welfare of Children* (1999) and the *Report of the Task Force on Violence against Women* (1997), were among the most significant developments. Against this background and in the context of calls for public awareness campaigns to highlight the nature and severity of sexual violence (e.g. as a recommendation of the Government's *Report of the Task Force on Violence against Women* (1997) and again of the *First Report of the National Steering Committee on Violence against Women* (1999), some understanding of current Irish attitudes is essential to establish a baseline from which relevant and targeted strategies can be developed.

CHALLENGES IN ESTIMATING THE PREVALENCE OF SEXUAL ABUSE

There are numerous difficulties in conducting prevalence research on sexual abuse and violence. As mentioned previously, the problem of underreporting was one of the primary concerns of this study. Thus, the international literature was reviewed in order to select a method and develop strategies which would minimise under-reporting among participants. In comparing various methodologies across studies in order to determine which strategies work "best", it became clear that many studies cannot be compared directly with one another because they vary in methodology on a number of fronts. In fact, it is almost safe to say that no two studies used exactly the same methodology. Further, each difference, no matter how subtle, may in fact have contributed significantly to the reported response rate and the willingness of the study participants to disclose sensitive information. Walby and Myhill (2001) outlined many of these same considerations for those working in the area of domestic violence and violence against women in general. Their recommendations stem from previous research on methodological issues and lead them to what they call "state of the art" research in this sensitive area. The methodological variations and strategies that seem to be the most influential from the literature are summarised below, but are discussed in more depth in the context of the SAVI Survey in the next chapter:

- The overall method used to collect the data (e.g., postal survey, telephone interview, face-to-face interview, or a combination of methods in a two-stage design)

- Sampling methods (e.g., true random sample of population vs. convenience samples, over-sampling of key groups, differing age cut-off points for inclusion in the sample or designation as child or adult, participation by women and men versus women only)

- Methods used to enhance participation *before* the study commenced (e.g., an introductory letter, media support via TV, radio, newspapers, flyers/posters, etc.)

- Methods used to encourage participation and decrease the refusal rate *during* the data collection period (e.g., multiple opportunities to participate, reminder cards, free-call numbers provided, additional copies of survey sent, reimbursement for participation)

- Methods used to enhance disclosure (e.g., introductory "warm-up" statements to increase rapport, handing participant a card with very sensitive items on it to fill out, using sealed envelopes for certain sections, matching interviewer with participant in terms of gender, race and primary language, introductory statements to establish a non-judgemental atmosphere and increase "normative" context, strategies for ensuring no one else is present and will overhear the interview)

- The context or focus of overall study (e.g., sexual violence as a focus of a study versus sexual violence asked in the context of other experiences/behaviours; studies in which participants were led to believe that the focus of the study was something else as a decoy, such as "views on crime" and "personal safety")

- Construction of questionnaire, including flow, order, and the use of "gating" questions (i.e., participants led through a continuum of less threatening questions asked at the beginning and leading to more sensitive questions at the end; participants only asked certain questions if they have responded affirmatively to previous questions)

- Construction of individual items, including how key terms are defined, such as rape and sexual assault (i.e., participants provided with definitions versus participants being left to determine definitions for themselves).

Although some of the above strategies can be considered more "successful" or even more ethical than others, the success of other strategies may have depended on the cultural context in which they were used. For example, although a telephone interview methodology yielded a high response rate in one country, it may be less successful in a country where a significant subset of the population does not have access to a telephone or is unfamiliar with telephone-type surveys. Wording of key questions may also be culturally specific, especially when questions of a sensitive nature are addressed. Sexually explicit language in one country may be acceptable, while in another country it may actually discourage participation. Ultimately, the methodology selected should reflect an intimate understanding of the cultural context in which the research takes place.

Chapter 2

METHODOLOGICAL CONSIDERATIONS
OF THE SAVI SURVEY

Some of the primary methodological decisions made in the context of this study are described in more detail below.

OVERALL METHOD OF DATA COLLECTION

In theory, a number of research methods are possible for the purposes of a large population survey of sexual violence. However, a growing literature in this area has identified many of the practical advantages and disadvantages of various methods. The first major option is the postal questionnaire. The major advantages of postal questionnaires are their relative ease of administration, and low cost. However, several disadvantages are also associated with postal methods. First, typical response rates of about 30 per cent to unsolicited questionnaires sent to the general public mean that any results obtained are not likely to be representative of the overall population. The postal method has been used in sexual violence research with, for instance, response rates of 40–45 per cent in samples of employed US women (Koss, 1993). This study used a two-stage approach in which a simple question format in a postal survey was used to identify individuals reporting abuse, and who were then invited to take part in a more detailed interview study. However, where the survey is the sole source of information, a more lengthy and complex series of questions will often be needed. Yet if the question format becomes too complex (where some questions are only relevant if earlier questions are answered in the affirmative, e.g. experience with professionals is only relevant if abuse has been disclosed to them), the possibility that participants will make mistakes and inadvertently skip relevant questions is substantial. Since questionnaires must be posted to named individuals at home addresses, assurances about confidentiality, anonymity and random selection to participate may not be sufficient to reassure those invited to participate. Altogether, these considerations make postal surveys an unattractive survey option.

Face-to-face interviews offer many advantages over postal methods, including the opportunity to collect in-depth information and to clarify details concerning abuse. Researchers also believe that the rapport that can be established between an interviewer and a participant during the course of the interview may increase the likelihood that the participant will disclose an experience of abuse if they have experienced one. Because the interviewer is present, they may also be better able to monitor any participant distress and refer them to services if necessary. This is in sharp contrast to the postal methodology in which the researcher will have no information on how the participant reacted to the survey, or whether or not they may need to be referred on to additional support services.

There are also, however, significant drawbacks to face-to-face interviews. Firstly, interview surveys are very time- and resource-consuming. Initial contact must be made with participants and then arrangements for the interview must be agreed. Cancellations and missed interviews mean additional rescheduling is necessary. Travel time and costs must also be added in whether or not the interviewer travels to the participant's home or the participant travels to the researcher. More importantly, in-person interviews with the general public are relatively visible and there are concerns that interviews with (or even invitations for an interview to) those living in the same settings as their abusers could endanger the safety and well-being of those interviewed. Since general population interviews typically take place in the participant's home, there is the additional concern for the safety and welfare of researchers, especially when conducting research on such sensitive issues. Not only is there the possibility that they could find themselves in an unsafe setting or situation (perhaps in a relatively isolated setting), but there is also the more probable dilemma that the researcher will not have a colleague available if they themselves need emotional support following a particularly difficult interview. In light of these concerns, some researchers have recommended that researchers travel in teams to manage both safety and well-being (Kinard, 1996). Of course, interviews requiring two researchers cost much more than those requiring one in terms of both time and money. Therefore, the combination of high "costs" or high risks associated with face-to-face interviewing also make it a relatively unattractive option.

The third major research option is telephone interviewing. The telephone methodology is seen to provide many of the benefits of the face-to-face interviews (e.g., the ability to establish rapport and monitor for distress), yet fewer of the "costs" associated with it. Both participant and interviewer well-being and safety can be more easily managed, as neither party need travel or put themselves in an unfamiliar (and possibly un-supportive) context. In addition, the telephone interview is seen as more "anonymous" than a face-to-face interview; thus the participant may be more assured about confidentiality and thus more likely to report difficult experiences.

Although not a widely used option in Ireland, the use of telephones to conduct surveys is increasing. The ESRI conducts monthly surveys of 1,400 randomly selected households as part of a European Union-wide research system assessing social, health and economic indicators. Some market research companies in Ireland also use telephone survey strategies. In the area of the prevalence of sexual violence, the telephone survey methodology has evolved as the method of choice internationally over the past decade.

A landmark study on physical and sexual violence against women using the telephone methodology was conducted by Statistics Canada in 1993 (Johnson and Sacco, 1995). This national survey of over 12,300 women aged 18+ years has become the blueprint for subsequent national studies elsewhere because of its attention to detail in the planning, execution and question formatting of the study. Telephone coverage for Canada was 99 per cent and they achieved a 63.7 per cent response rate from 19,000 eligible households contacted. Most non-response occurred as "household" refusals, i.e. by the person who answered the phone and before an eligible participant had been invited to participate. When participants were contacted personally, response rates were 91 per cent.

A similar telephone study of 8,000 women and 8,000 men has been conducted in the US (Tjaden and Boyle, 1998). They achieved response rates of 72.1 per cent for women and 68.9 per cent for men. The US study opted to have male interviewers telephone half of the male participants. They checked same-sex and cross-sex interviews and found that women achieved slightly higher study participation rates with male participants than did men (70.0 per cent and 62.3 per cent respectively). However, men reported more incidents of sexual abuse in the previous year to other men than they did to women. Lifetime reports of the prevalence of abuse did not differ (Tjaden et al., 2000). In a similar vein, Australia, New Zealand and Finland have since conducted telephone studies. France completed a national telephone study in 2001. In the UK, an ongoing project extends some of the questions in the annual General Crime Survey to cover aspects of sexual violence in greater detail. While this is not the same as the other studies with a dedicated focus on sexual violence, evidence shows that the higher the number of screening and behaviourally specific questions asked on the topic, the greater the level of disclosure of abuse (Goldman, 2000). Telephone surveys have been estimated to be intermediate between postal and face-to-face interviews in their capacity to facilitate individuals to report abuse (with the lowest rates coming from postal surveys) (Goldman, 2000). In summary, although telephone surveys are relatively new to the Irish population, the relative benefits of such a methodology were thought to outweigh any limitations, and so it was proposed as the methodology to be tested in the feasibility study.

CONTEXT AND FOCUS OF THE PRESENT STUDY

While some research continues to be carried out in which questions about sexual violence are asked in the context of other experiences or behaviours (such as crime, or personal safety), most researchers now agree that multi-purpose or "generic" studies are more likely to arrive at lower estimates of abuse than single-purpose, "dedicated" studies of violence (Ellsberg et al., 2001; World Health Organisation, 1999). Walby and Myhill point out that generic surveys can be restrictive in a number of ways. First, less time and fewer questions can be devoted to a topic like sexual violence within a survey covering all forms of violence. This also leaves little time to establish the rapport needed to discuss sensitive issues. Lastly, setting sensitive questions within a context like crime "might affect the extent to which people are prepared to report incidents which might not be regarded as criminal" (Walby and Myhill, 2001). Further, it is now deemed unethical to use another topic as a decoy, i.e. leading participants to believe that the focus of the study was something else in order to gain their participation.

Given the above considerations, the focus of the SAVI Survey was confined to sexual violence. While it is acknowledged that sexual violence is only one form of abuse (and often co-occurs with other forms of abuse, including neglect and emotional and physical abuse), limiting the focus to sexual violence allowed a more detailed examination of this issue in a depth sufficient to provide a thorough profile of its prevalence, context and consequences.

Further, the psychological consequences of abuse, although briefly examined, were not a primary focus of the study. Most researchers concur that unwanted sexual experiences can have significant negative consequences for an individual's psychological well-being. Research has linked sexual abuse to a variety of psychiatric diagnoses and psychological difficulties, including (but not limited to) major depression, anxiety disorders, dissociative disorders, eating disorders, suicidality, substance abuse, interpersonal and relationship difficulties, sexual dysfunction, loss of self-esteem and behavioural problems. While acknowledging the wide range and extent of the consequences of sexual abuse, a full exploration of these effects was beyond the aim and scope of this study, and would most likely be better achieved through a different methodology (e.g., qualitative, in-depth, face-to-face interviews) and with a more targeted sample. In addition, the extent of the consequences of sexual violence have been thoroughly documented in various populations internationally, with little variation across western cultures, that the need to document the Irish experience is less of a priority than other research needs. Finkelhor (1998) cautions against excessive attention to the already well-documented psychological consequences of abuse at the expense of considering aspects of health and law enforcement services which influence outcomes following sexual violence. Thus only a minimal number of questions regarding psychological consequences were examined in the SAVI study. These included a brief screening measure of post-traumatic stress disorder (PTSD). This was considered to be a useful marker of the levels of distress likely to be seen in such a population.

SAMPLE CONSIDERATIONS

Prevalence rates cannot always be directly compared across studies because even those described as "population" studies may exclude sub-groups of the general population, such as men, those under age 18 years of age or older people. In addition, homeless people, those in group accommodation (e.g., students or trainees), and those in institutional settings (e.g., the armed forces, prisons, psychiatric hospitals or religious communities) are often not included. In this way surveys may not represent the entire population. Of particular concern is emerging evidence that some of the groups excluded are likely to be more vulnerable to abuse or are likely to encounter more or different barriers to disclosing abuse or seeking professional services.

Sample considerations for the SAVI Survey led to a number of specific decisions. Firstly, the study would interview only those who are considered to be adults (aged 18 years or older) by Irish law. However, because experiences of sexual abuse across the life-span were sought, experiences of childhood sexual abuse were obtained through retrospective accounts by the adult participants. Secondly, because men are often excluded from such research, and because of an emerging awareness of the prevalence of sexual abuse of men and their unique barriers to disclosure and access to services, equal numbers of male participants were sought. Thirdly, no upper age limit was set for participation (many previous studies have set age cut-offs for participation, some as low as 55 years). Thus, the experiences of older people would also be obtained. Fourth, as the focus was on the prevalence of abuse for those currently living in Ireland, no attempt was made to document whether the participants contacted were Irish citizens, or whether the abuse actually took place in Ireland. It was felt that the implications for services (with perhaps the exception of police or Gardaí), would be the same since the individuals are currently resident here.

CONSTRUCTION OF THE KEY QUESTIONS AND DEFINITIONS

Another challenge in conducting and comparing studies on the prevalence of sexual violence lies in the large variety of definitions used. For instance, the prevalence of "child sexual abuse" can vary considerably depending on the definition of "child" used. Some researchers have counted only experiences up to age 12. Others use under 18 as the time when a person is considered a "minor" in law, and yet others use under age 16 or 17. What is considered "abuse" varies as well. For example, some studies do not count sexual contacts (wanted or unwanted) if they occur between minors. Others exclude only consenting acts between those within 3 or 5 years of each other where the perpetrator is also a child or teenager (since such acts are regarded differently and as less serious in many legal situations). Finally, studies combine various types of acts differently and often in ways that do not clarify specific inclusion or exclusion criteria, for example, whether counts of "rape" include or exclude acts of forced penetration with objects or fingers. Researchers now suggest that the optimal way to collect accurate information is to provide behaviourally specific definitions rather than summary terms which have varied meanings across the general public (e.g. "put his penis in your vagina against your will" is preferable to "raped you") (Walby and Myhill, 2001; Kilpatrick et al., 2000; Koss, 1993; Wyatt and Doyle Peters, 1986; Russell, 1983). The researcher can then provide the specific prevalence estimates of these experiences as well as combining these very specific categories into larger ones such as "contact" or "non-contact abuse". In this way comparison by others is possible using published or newly developed categories. While many recent international population studies have adopted this strategy, the public acceptability of using very explicit terms to make such specific definitions was largely unknown in the Irish context. The ISPCC (1993) data on child sexual abuse suggested that explicit definitions were not deterrents to response adequacy. The acceptability of such explicit questions became one of the main questions for the feasibility study.

METHODS USED TO ENCOURAGE PARTICIPATION PRIOR TO THE SAVI SURVEY

Previous researchers have used a variety of methods to encourage participation even before their study commences. These include an introductory letter before a telephone call to set up an interview, or media support via TV, radio, or newspapers. No such methods were used in this study. The reasons for this are twofold. Firstly, it was felt that any media attention given to the study might encourage some who were more criminally minded to take advantage of the situation and masquerade as a member of the research team. Thus they could conduct calls of a sexually explicit nature without arousing immediate suspicion by stating that they were part of the team conducting this research. Secondly, attempts to contact people prior to the interview would undermine the reassurances of confidentiality, as names and/or addresses would be needed to do so. Because of the absence of advance publicity, the telephone calls made to the general public were consequently "cold calls", i.e., the participant would have no advance notice to expect a call or to know the topic of the study.

METHODS USED TO ENCOURAGE AGREEMENT TO PARTICIPATE IN THE SAVI SURVEY

Response rates are critical to a study's validity. A low response rate severely limits a researcher's ability to generalise study results to a larger population. In order to increase the likelihood that participants will agree to participate, previous researchers have used various strategies depending on their overall methodology. For example, those conducting postal surveys have sent reminder cards for postal surveys and subsequent additional copies of the survey in case the original was discarded or misplaced. Other researchers have provided multiple opportunities to participate in their study or set up a free-phone number. Others have offered financial reimbursement to entice participation.

Several common strategies recommended for increasing the likelihood that potential participants would be willing to take part and feel comfortable about their participation were considered in the SAVI Survey. Firstly, those who are contacted need to be assured that the study is legitimate, that it is conducted by a reputable agency for legitimate reasons and that these reasons are salient for and endorsed by the potential participant. They also need to feel confident that guarantees such as confidentiality are genuine. Thus, scripts were carefully developed for the interviewers to help explain the purpose of the study, its importance, and how their telephone number was obtained. Several levels of explanation were developed so that the validity of the study could be authenticated for participants. A free-phone number was put in place for the duration of the study. Participants were offered the number so they could ring to authenticate the study before participation or if they had any further questions or concerns (after participation in the study). Alternatively, they could call the main switchboard of the Royal College of Surgeons in Ireland, or their local Garda station. Where potential participants were anxious or unconvinced, the interviewer could offer to fax a letter confirming the study to the person's local Garda station. Secondly, interviewers offered to call back those participants who indicated that the interviewer had reached them at an inconvenient or inappropriate time. Thirdly, participants who initially refused were followed-up with a "conversion call" to allow a second chance at participation. (These calls are a standard part of telephone survey work and are explained in more detail in the section on study procedures.) Finally, men who initially refused an interview offered by a female interviewer were asked if they would prefer to speak to a male interviewer.

METHODS USED TO ENHANCE DISCLOSURE

Related to the above challenge is the task of creating a "safe environment" in which the person taking part feels comfortable enough to disclose any relevant personal experiences. Again, previous research in this area provided the basis for the strategies adopted by the SAVI study. For example, the initial questions in the interview were on non-threatening topics, and these led gradually to more sensitive topics, starting with sexual harassment. Several questions were asked in a graded manner from least to most serious regarding various forms of sexual abuse, thus allowing multiple opportunities for disclosure. As previously stated, the words "rape", "abuse" and "assault" have very different meanings or connotations for people and therefore the researchers provided the behaviourally specific definitions of such abuse. Participants simply had to reply "yes" or "no" to the various experiences presented, thus reducing the possibility of embarrassment or shame in trying to describe their experiences. This method ensures clarity while supporting individuals to communicate difficult information in a relatively non-threatening manner. Perhaps most importantly, feeling able to discuss private views and experiences is dependent on the trust engendered by the researcher. This is established through a combination of the professionalism demonstrated in the study's presentation and the interest and concern expressed by the interviewer for the particular views and experiences of the person taking part. Thus selection and training of interviewers was given the highest priority (as discussed in detail later).

METHODS USED TO ENSURE VALIDITY AND QUALITY OF THE DATA

Various methods have been suggested by previous researchers in this area to counter threats to the validity of their studies. As previously discussed, the precise wording of questions (especially those regarding abuse experiences) has been analysed both within and across research studies, and has resulted in advances in survey construction from a statistical perspective. The fact that sexual experiences are described in specific behavioural terms is an example of these types of safeguards to validity. The international literature was reviewed, and where possible, questions previously used in other studies of sexual violence were used in the SAVI study.

In addition, the survey interview was piloted with a small number of volunteers (five) who had experienced sexual abuse themselves. These few women had all been through Rape Crisis Centre counselling, and were approached by their counsellors about taking part. Counsellors only approached women whom they felt were comfortable discussing their experiences. The purpose of these pilot interviews was to make sure that the survey questions were clear, relevant, comprehensive and sensitive to their experiences.

Another way to ensure validity is to maintain the anonymity of the participants. How confidentiality and anonymity were explained and assured for the participants was previously described in the section on ensuring participation. Other measures taken to maintain confidentiality of the data included assigning each participant a unique study number. Thus, no identifying information, including their telephone number, was recorded on their interview schedule. The telephone numbers were stored securely in a separate location from the completed interviews, as is standard international practice. Maintaining the raw data ensures that studies can be authenticated if queried while protecting the anonymity of the participants.

In order to ensure the quality of the data collected and to verify that the calls were conducted in an ethical and professional manner, calls were monitored in three ways. First, one study co-ordinator was situated in the same room as the interviewers and was thus able to monitor and observe the interviewers throughout the study. This also allowed for immediate and accessible feedback if any concerns were raised by the interviewers themselves. Second, tape recordings of the interviewer's side of randomly selected telephone conversations were recorded and reviewed by the survey co-ordinators. The aim of this was to provide feedback on call strategies and to ensure that interviewer contact with the public was professional and encouraging of participation. Participants' responses to the interviewers and the survey were not taped since permission was not sought as it was felt that asking consent for this would be a further barrier to study participation. Third, for a random selection of approximately six per cent of cases, co-ordinators conducted the follow-up calls to verify the original call and to ask the participant for their evaluation of the quality of the initial call. As an additional method of quality control, weekly feedback sessions provided interviewers with the opportunity to discuss problems in relation to the interview, the data collection procedures or the feedback given to them by the participants.

SAFETY AND ETHICAL CONSIDERATIONS
IN THE SAVI SURVEY

Because of the very nature of sexual violence, the study of such a sensitive and difficult topic is fraught with ethical and safety concerns. A major concern was the risk of opening up painful histories of sexual violence and abuse in situations where this was unsolicited by the person who had suffered the abuse. The researchers were cognisant of the fact that this was a very different situation to one in which a person might choose to disclose such histories themselves.

Thus, it was acknowledged from the onset that these concerns would be made paramount in the planning, execution and reporting of the SAVI Survey. As commissioners of the study, the DRCC set up a Study Monitoring Group immediately following the commissioning of this project. Its purpose was, among other things, to critically evaluate and monitor the conduct of this study. The Monitoring Group was composed of experts in a range of different disciplines (see page xi for details of group membership). In addition, as research undertaken by the Health Services Research Centre at the Royal College of Surgeons in Ireland, ethical approval was sought and granted by the College's Research Ethics Committee. It was at their instigation that a unique policy was adopted of making follow-up calls to all participants in order to assess their level of distress following the interview.

In addition to conducting a considerable literature review, the preparation for the study included consultation with experienced researchers, those who have experienced abuse firsthand, service providers and policy makers in Ireland and abroad. This preparation enabled the research team to take into account ethical and safety concerns from a wide range of vantage points.

A recent and well-recognised framework which addresses safety and ethical issues was developed by the World Health Organisation for research on domestic violence against women (World Health Organisation, 1999). They have outlined several recommendations which specifically concern the safety of participants and researchers, staff selection and support, the management of participant distress, and the support of participants following participation. (Other issues addressed in the document and which are discussed elsewhere in this study are confidentiality, the methodological adequacy of a study and the responsible

use of results. For a complete listing of the WHO recommendations, see Appendix II.) These recommendations were considered
throughout the process of planning and conducting the SAVI
Survey and are described in more detail below.

SAFETY OF PARTICIPANTS

Confidentiality has already been highlighted as important for ensuring participation and the validity of the findings, but can also
be viewed as an important ethical and safety issue. As previously
mentioned, telephone number selection was random; hence the
identity of the participant would be unknown to the interviewer.
Interviewers were also instructed that if they realised they were
interviewing someone known to them, they needed to alert the
participant and discontinue the interview. (This happened once in
the duration of the study, and the situation was recognised before
the interview was started.) No identifying information was included on a participant's completed interview. Sensitive research
data was made inaccessible to all but the research team.

   While confidentiality is fairly easily protected within the research environment, maintaining a participant's confidentiality in
their home environment can be much more difficult. It was felt
that all participants had a right to keep confidential their participation. Thus, it was decided that the purpose of the survey was to
be described to only one person in each household. A person
could not "pass" the phone to other members in the household, if
upon hearing the topic of the survey, they themselves did not
want to participate. In that way, one household member would
not know that another either did not want to participate in the
survey or had, in fact, participated in the survey. In the situation
where an interviewer needed to re-contact a participant and another household member inquired about the nature of the call,
they were told that the person had agreed to participate in a "general health survey".

   A more serious concern is the possibility of retaliatory violence
if a person's participation in the study became known to a

perpetrator. Therefore, prior to beginning any interview, participants were reminded that the topic of the survey was quite sensitive and asked if they were in a situation to take the call without being overheard by others in the household. As a further safeguard, the use of a "code phrase" was explained to the participant before the start of the interview. This phrase (i.e., "I'm too busy right now") was to be used in the event that the participant wanted to alert the interviewer that they were no longer in a private situation, and they needed to stop the interview. For example, if someone unexpectedly came into the room while they were taking part, the participant could use this phrase (thus, not indicating to a third party that they were taking part in a survey). This last strategy was specifically designed to protect those participants who might currently be in a situation of ongoing abuse in which the abuser is living in the same household.

MANAGEMENT OF PARTICIPANT DISTRESS

Several strategies were established to prevent, monitor and manage potential participant distress in the short and long term. First, interviewers were trained to monitor the level of a participant's distress throughout the interview. A range of strategies were built into the interview process, such as asking participants if they were feeling all right, if they would rather discontinue or reschedule the interview, etc. This was done in a standardised manner at certain points in the interview (e.g., at the end of the section regarding sexual experiences if a serious disclosure was made), and at the interviewer's discretion at any other point in the interview if the participant signalled distress in any way.

Since the study had the potential to raise serious concerns for individuals, it was felt appropriate to ask those who disclosed serious abuse (even if they did not appear distressed), if they wished to avail of counselling services. Where participants said "yes", they were to be asked for their general geographic location (county of residence or elsewhere if preferred) and they were given the name of a contact person in the nearest sexual abuse service. This list was generated through the DRCC and the National Network of Rape Crisis Centres and the advice of the Study Monitoring Group. It included contacts to health board and voluntary agencies. Times of office hours, out-of-hours strategies and whether men were seen as clients were clarified in compiling this list. All centres were informed of the existence and nature of the study. All centres agreed that they would provide a priority appointment to any person contacting them saying that they were part of the "Abuse Research Study". The name of the person who knew of, and would facilitate, this arrangement in the particular centre was obtained so it could be provided to participants. This option was to be used in cases of serious distress requiring prompt action if this was what the participant wanted. In this and other unpredictable and serious circumstances, other members of the research team (and Monitoring Group if relevant) were to be consulted regarding the management of the situation. In each case, a detailed record of the management of the case was to be recorded.

If major distress was evident at the time of the interview (or at the time of the follow-up call), the researcher's aim was to support the person temporarily, while encouraging them to gain support from other sources. (One of the main concerns addressed in training was that the interviewers may inappropriately try to take on a counselling role within this research setting. While many interviewers had counselling backgrounds, their role was clarified as that of researcher. The research setting was not seen to be equipped to provide the ongoing support that someone in a distressed situation may need.) One section of the interview was developed (Section S) as a protocol to aid interviewers who encountered a very distressed participant in their role as a researcher. Section S provided suggestions for the interviewer to make to the participant (such as utilising strategies and support systems that they have previously used) while maintaining an empathic stance.

As a way to monitor levels of distress following the interview for all participants, follow-up calls were offered to all those who participated. (For a more detailed description of these calls, see the Procedures section in Chapter 3). At the follow-up call, participants were asked if they were upset following participation in the study. Thus, it allowed a second opportunity for the interviewer to assess participant distress and offer support services if necessary. This strategy appears to be unique to the SAVI Survey as there is no mention of it in other international studies. It was first recommended by the Research Ethics Committee to be included in the feasibility study to ensure the well-being of those participating in such a sensitive study.

As an additional strategy, the Survey free-phone number was offered to all participants should they wish to contact the research team following the interview. This was to allow for some people not evidently distressed at the time of the interview to ask for advice or help at a later point and to facilitate those who did not disclose events during the interview but later wished to record them on further reflection.

INTERVIEWER SELECTION, TRAINING AND SUPPORT

Fifteen interviewers were hired to conduct the interviews. All had previous experience in counselling or crisis telephone help line work (with some having worked for a rape crisis centre), or in social science research, or both. All interviewers had their references checked in order to ensure their suitability for the sensitive nature of the project. In addition, all interviewers had to obtain a letter indicating Garda clearance (i.e., that there was no information on file to indicate a criminal offence likely to interfere with the safety of study participants) before commencing the work.

Regardless of their level of experience, all interviewers were required to attend training specific to the current study. The training was conducted by the three original members of the research team (those who conducted the feasibility study) and an experienced trainer from the Dublin Rape Crisis Centre. Training took place over 12 working days. Topics covered both the interpersonal and research aspects of the position and included: sensitivity training concerning the issues of sexual abuse and violence;

listening skills; the importance of confidentiality; how to administer the survey systematically; how to ensure the quality of the data collected; and how to respond to a participant in distress. Additionally, interviewers were trained on how to monitor and manage their own well-being throughout the study. A combination of methods was used to facilitate training, including lectures, small group work, role plays and videos. Near the end of the training period, interviewers conducted mock telephone interviews with the trainers and were given individualised feedback on their performance. (See Appendix III for a detailed description of each session.)

A number of strategies were established to protect the safety and well-being of the interviewers during this emotionally demanding project. First, as previously described in the section on methodological consideration, the selection of a telephone survey methodology was made partly on the basis of concerns regarding the safety and well-being of the interviewers. (Conducting face-to-face interviews in participants' homes could expose the researcher to potentially dangerous situations if a perpetrator was present.)

In order to manage any distress arising from the interviews and prevent emotional exhaustion, researchers were only allowed to work a maximum of four hours per day in making telephone calls. All telephone calls were to be made from the work setting even if they were working outside peak hours to preserve the privacy of the interviewer's home telephone number. Calls were always made in the dedicated telephone survey rooms where there was more than one researcher at a time. One of three study co-ordinators was always available during the day and in the first few weeks of the study during the evening and on Saturdays. When the study was established, out-of-hours contact was via mobile phone to a designated co-ordinator. This constant access to fellow interviewers and co-ordinators allowed immediate support and management of difficult problems if necessary. Weekly supervision meetings were held to allow time for the interviewers to discuss their reactions to the content and process of the research in addition to more routine concerns. Arrangements were made for confidential, external and free access to counselling if needed by the interviewers because of issues raised by the survey work.

The methodological and ethical considerations outlined above led initially to the development of a feasibility study which examined the effectiveness of these strategies in a more thorough manner in the Irish context. The main aims and results of that feasibility study are described next.

FEASIBILITY STUDY

Aims and Objectives of the Feasibility Study

The primary purpose of the feasibility study was to assess the suitability of the telephone methodology. More specifically, the aims of the feasibility study were to determine:

- If the planned approach would yield an acceptable response rate

- If disclosure levels indicated participants felt willing and able to disclose sensitive issues

- The sample size needed in the main study to achieve a sub-sample of those who have experienced abuse of sufficient size to allow analysis of service use

- That the protocol would not cause undue distress to participants

- What changes would further improve the protocol.

Methodology of the Feasibility Study

The survey developed for the feasibility study was piloted with five volunteers who had experienced sexual abuse and violence firsthand. Following modifications stemming from those pilot interviews, the telephone numbers were generated (as described in the main study). For the feasibility study, three experienced staff were to conduct interviews: two had psychology research and/or clinical experience and one had previous experience as a volunteer rape crisis centre telephone counsellor. The feasibility study was conducted during the summer of 2000. (The survey format, content and procedures they used were nearly identical to those used in the main study, so for brevity, will not be described here.)

Results of the Feasibility Study

A total of 73 participants agreed to participate in the feasibility study within the time period allocated. The total unique telephone numbers attempted to achieve these interviews was 274. Of those 34 per cent were "illegitimate" (i.e. fax, business or public phones). On average, 3.6 calls were required for each legitimate number to reach a final outcome (e.g., completed interview or re-fusal). In 47 per cent of cases, interviews were agreed but for a later time or date. The average time taken to complete an entire transaction with a participant, including the initial contact and agreement, through to the follow-up call was 110 minutes per participant. This included repeat calls to contact the person, re-contact at later scheduled times, interrupted and then continued interviews, etc. The interviews themselves averaged 35 minutes.

The ratio of those who agreed to participate to those who re-fused yielded a 61 per cent response rate. This response rate was deemed acceptable and the interviewers felt that it could be improved on in the larger study with the benefit of experience coming from the feasibility study.

Among those who declined, or were quite hesitant, in partici-pating, some common themes were suspicion about the random nature of the call, or the sensitive nature of the questions. Some participants with "ex-directory" numbers were concerned about access to their number. A set response to these types of reactions was composed to aid interviewers in their efforts to assure the caller that the number was randomly generated. Planned assur-ances of confidentiality, such as use of a free-phone or College telephone call back or offers to contact local Gardaí proved satis-factory for many. One caller refused to participate on the grounds that the study could put an abused person in danger by arousing the suspicion of the perpetrator. This potentially serious concern was thoroughly discussed by the research team and subsequently by the Monitoring Group and outside consultants with expertise in working with sexual offenders. The final decision was that the study would continue to acknowledge the small risk of this outcome while balancing this against the fact that perpetrators will be prompted to action by many more widely available triggers in the environment. Further, concerns about possible actions taken by abusers would prevent the collection of information to understand and address the very same problem.

In terms of willingness of the public to disclose such intimate and difficult experiences over the phone, the feasibility study indicated that they were indeed willing. Not only did participants disclose a range of abuse, from more minor to more serious penetrative abuse, but many disclosed this abuse to the interviewers for the first time. In addition, although the feasibility sample was quite small, and thus the margin of error would be considerable, the rates of abuse disclosed were not unlike those found by other similar international studies of sexual abuse. The data regarding the specific reports of sexual violence were used to calculate the sample size needed to achieve reliable national estimates in the larger study. A sample size which would yield at least 100 men and 100 women reporting serious abuse was calculated.

Finally, the follow-up calls indicated that the interviews were conducted in a manner which did not stimulate distress. There were no reports of participants experiencing significant distress after the initial interview. In fact, follow-up calls were found to be useful and extremely positive experiences. Some participants took the opportunity to recheck who was conducting or funding the study and for what purpose the results would be used. Many expressed positive views on the importance of the study and its timeliness. Given the serious and sensitive nature of the study, it was decided to retain the follow-up interview in the main study to facilitate queries and comments from those who had participated, but also as a positive experience for research interviewers to balance their challenging work.

In conclusion, the telephone survey method was found to be feasible in a small sample of Irish adults. Thus, it was recommended by the research team and accepted by the Study Monitoring Group and sponsors that the telephone survey method be extended to a national study.

Section II

THE SAVI SURVEY

Chapter 3

THE SURVEY

The overall aim of the main study was to provide a broad profile of the level and nature of sexual violence in Ireland. This was to include information about abusers and about disclosure of abuse to others including medical, counselling and legal professionals. Information was to be obtained to inform public awareness strategies, to develop services which facilitate those abused to seek professional help and legal redress, and to identify a focus for prevention strategies. Project leadership and involvement of the Dublin Rape Crisis Centre, in conjunction with the Department of Health and Children and the Department of Justice, Equality and Law Reform meant that key service providers and planners were associated with the conduct and outcome of this study. The broad aims of the study were developed in 1999 with a detailed feasibility project planned for the year 2000. Key issues of safety, acceptability, feasibility and willingness to report abuse needed to be addressed in the feasibility study to determine if the original aims could be evaluated in a larger sample.

SAMPLE SIZE CONSIDERATIONS

A target sample size of approximately 3,000 members of the general public aged 18 years or older was estimated to be necessary on the basis of the feasibility study, to achieve the aims of the main study.

In order to ensure that the sample would be representative of the general population in Ireland, quota estimates by gender and age (young, middle, older age) were drawn up. This allowed a guide to the numbers of men and women in each age group that would need to be targeted in order to match national census data. Without quota management, previous research indicates that older women not in paid employment are over-represented in survey samples.

TELEPHONE SURVEY METHODOLOGY

Telephone calls were conducted using a system called random digit dialing (RDD). This allows the widest coverage of telephone numbers by enabling contact with ex-directory numbers and with new numbers not currently listed in telephone directories. Only landline telephone numbers were used. Recent UK evaluations suggested this to be an appropriate strategy since the vast majority of households with mobile coverage have this in addition to landline telephones. Thus using both sets of numbers would give many households a double or greater chance of being included in sampling. Landline telephone coverage in private households in Ireland is not as high as other countries where telephone surveys are used. For instance, the US coverage is over 95 per cent of the non-institutionalised population while the UK is 96 per cent. In Ireland it is 86 per cent with an estimated 20 per cent increase in uptake from those without phones in every three-month period. While Irish coverage is lower than elsewhere, other means of contacting the widest range of the adult public are even less developed than elsewhere. There is, for instance, no unique postal address system in Ireland.

Lists of telephone numbers were generated as follows using the RANSAM system of the ESRI. The area code is randomly selected from among possible Irish codes and possible "stems" are then identified. The "hundreds bank" method was used where a local telephone number is generated and the last two digits are used to create a full set of 100 numbers ranging from "XXXXX00" to "XXXXX99". A total of 200 sample points (i.e. unique numbers) were generated across the country and the 100 numbers generated with each of these produced clusters of numbers to telephone.

A strict telephone calling and outcome coding system was developed to standardise the methods. Each number dialled was allowed to ring 10 times before cutting off. If there was no reply, numbers were recalled later in the same day or in a different time-block (morning, afternoon or evening) on the next day. Engaged numbers were re-called after 10 minutes. All numbers were called a maximum of 10 times. After 6 unsuccessful calls, the call sheet was passed to a supervisor for review to formally consider the most likely strategy to achieve an answer. Where there were answer machines, messages were not left because they may have caused concern (and may have revealed the study topic to more than one person). Numbers with no replies after 10 attempts were checked with Directory Enquiries to clarify if they were disconnected, not yet given out or public telephones. Where a reply was received to a call, the researcher first clarified whether she was in contact with a private household (only private households were included to maximise privacy for participants). All outcome codes were recorded (see Appendix IVb).

A methodology unique to telephone surveys is the "conversion call" for those people who have declined participation in an unsolicited ("cold call") contact by a researcher. The rationale is to provide an otherwise unavailable opportunity for the potential participant to reconsider participation. The aim is to do this in a way that is facilitating rather than coercing. Conversion calls were to be made by a different interviewer one to two days after the first call. The reasons for re-contact ("it provides us and you with the possibility to reconsider your decision to participate") and an assurance that this was the only re-contact were provided.

SURVEY CONTENT AND MEASURES USED

The interview was divided into 13 sections organised by content and participant-specific factors. Some sections were completed by all participants, while other sections were completed only if relevant to the participant (e.g., experiences with services providers). Figure 3.1 provides a complete listing of all the sections and which were completed by whom. Sections were colour-coded to facilitate interviewers' administration of appropriate sections. Each of the thirteen sections are summarised below.

Figure 3.1: SAVI Telephone Survey Topic Sections

Section	Topic	Who Completed Section
Section 1	Introduction and participant agreement	All participants
Section A	Demographics	All participants
Section B	Public perceptions: violence, education and interventions	All participants
Section C	Rape attitudes	All participants
Section D	Experiences of sexual harassment	All participants
Section E	Experiences of sexual abuse	All participants
Section F	Details of experiences of sexual abuse	Only those who reported abuse
Section G	Personal experiences of, and barriers to, disclosure	Only those who reported abuse
Section H	After-effects of sexual violence	Only those who reported abuse
Section I	Experiences with counselling or therapy services	Only those who reported abuse
Section J	Public beliefs regarding disclosure	All participants
Section K	Conclusions	All participants
Section S	Participant distress	Used *only* if a participant became distressed

Section 1 — Introduction and Participant Agreement

This section facilitated the standardisation of the survey introduction. It ensured that key statements, such as who was conducting the study, its purpose, and its confidential and voluntary nature were given to all participants by the interviewers. Upon agreement to participate, the participant's availability and privacy were checked and the participant's age (over 18 years) was confirmed.

Section A – Demographics

Brief demographic information, such as participant gender, age and marital status, was obtained at the start of the interview.

Section B — Public Perceptions of Violence, Education and Interventions

These introductory sections asked about participant perceptions of crime in Irish society generally; and elicited estimates of the prevalence of various sexual crimes. It also covered participant experiences of, and views on, the education of children concerning sexual abuse.

Section C — Rape Attitudes

Attitudes to sexual issues were evaluated in this section. A series of statements identified as "rape myths" in four previous studies were utilised (for example, "when a woman says 'no' to sexual advances, she really means 'yes'") (Burt, 1980; Ward, 1988; Ong and Ward, 1999 and Williams et al., 1999). Some of these items were modified for use in the Irish population. Participants were asked their level of agreement or disagreement with each statement. However, almost all statements used in previous research reflected views about the abuse of women. Thus some additional statements reflecting attitudes to the abuse of children and men were developed for the present study, for instance, "Child abuse is mostly committed by strangers" and "Men who sexually assault other men must be gay (homosexual)".

Section D — Experiences of Sexual Harassment

Personal experiences with sexually offensive situations or sexual harassment were queried in this section (the phrase "sexual harassment" was not used when asking these questions). Note that the term sexual harassment used in this study is seen as part of the continuum of sexual violence and is broadly defined; other researchers have used a narrower, more legal definition which looks at these experiences only in the context of a work or educational setting. (See the Glossary, Appendix V, for a more detailed description of this term.) Nine of these items were taken from the Sexual Experiences Questionnaire (SEQ-DoD) (Fitzgerald, et al., 1999). Participants were asked if they experienced any of these situations in the last 12 months; thus the questions aimed to assess the incidence of sexual harassment in Ireland rather than the prevalence. Two additional items were developed for this section and were queried for prevalence (lifetime experience). One item regarded experiences with obscene phone calls, while the other examined situations experienced by the person where he or she was the focus of unwanted sexual jokes or activities. The inclusion of items regarding sexual harassment at this point in the survey served as a "lead-in" to the more explicit and difficult questions regarding sexual violence.

Section E — Experiences of Sexual Violence

This section focused on lifetime experiences of sexual violence. The introduction to this section was somewhat lengthier in that it gave participants advance notice of the explicit nature of the questions that were to follow and sought their acknowledgement that they were willing to continue with the survey. The items were behaviourally specific and made explicit the sexual experiences in question. Participants had only to respond with a "yes" or "no" to each item. Both male and female versions of this section were developed so that the wording would be consistent with their gender. Participants were first asked about their experiences as an adult (age 17 and over) and then as a child. Questions asked about the adult experiences emphasised the non-consensual nature of the experiences, while the questions on childhood experiences did not use the same wording since the concept of "consent" is meaningless in the context of child abuse. (However, in order to discriminate abuse from normal or appropriate sexual experimentation and development among peers, the instructions to the participants were changed to make this distinction clear.) The section on childhood experiences also included specific questions about exposure to, or involvement in, childhood pornography. Prompts to the interviewers to monitor for signs of distress from participants were included in this section.

Section F — Details of Experiences of Sexual Abuse

When affirmative answers were given to abuse questions in Section E, this section was deemed relevant. It queried the context of the abuse experienced, including such details as the duration of the abuse, the characteristics of the perpetrator, and the situation in which the abuse occurred. Two versions of this section were developed (versions for childhood and adult experiences) to reflect the different nature of these experiences. If participants reported more than one experience (with a different perpetrator) during either childhood or adulthood, this section (and the next, Section G) was repeated for each incident (up to three incidents — first, last and most distressing). The number of incidents for which data was collected also depended on the level of distress and willingness of the participant to disclose their experiences.

Section G — Personal Experiences of, and Barriers to, Disclosure

This section focused on the context of disclosure. It also examined disclosure to medical and Garda personnel, the reasons why they did or did not disclose and their level of satisfaction with the services these professionals provided, if applicable.

Section H — After-effects of Sexual Violence

This section provided a brief overview of the effects that the experience had on the participant. A brief screening measure of PTSD used in previous research (PTSD Checklist-civilian version (PCL-C) (Andrykowski, 1998)) was provided to give estimates of the levels of PTSD experienced by the participants as a result of their abuse. Participants were also asked in an open-ended question what additional effects the abuse had on their lives, if any.

Section I — Experiences with Counselling or Therapy Services

This section details participant utilisation of psychological services and their levels of satisfaction with those services.

Section J — Public Beliefs Regarding Disclosure

This section asked participants what they might do in a future situation of sexual abuse. More specifically, they were asked how likely they would be to tell someone else (e.g., family, friends, a doctor, a counsellor, Gardaí) about that experience, and where they would go to seek help. The aim was to identify perceived barriers to disclosure and to be able to compare them with barriers as experienced by those who had been abused. Participants were also asked their views of the media coverage of sexual abuse.

Section K — Conclusions

This section collected brief mental health information using the (5-item) standardised measure, the Mental Health Inventory 5 (MHI-5) (Ware et al., 1992). This is a brief general population measure of psychological well-being. Information on previous psychiatric medication or service use or experience of being "in care" was also collected. Here comparisons between those who experienced abuse and those who did not can be made in terms of major markers of mental health experiences. Concluding questions returned to practical questions concerning demographics and permission to re-contact the person in one to two days for a follow-up call.

Section S — Participant Distress

A separate section was developed to serve as a protocol for the interviewer if the participant became distressed or expressed any suicidal ideation during the course of the interview. In either case, this section was immediately referred to and the interview was suspended while the severity of the situation was assessed. This section was developed in consultation with psychiatric colleagues and is consistent with standard clinical practice.

As previously described, interview section arrangement was carefully planned and piloted to ensure that the more serious and sensitive questions were gradually led up to in the survey and that there was a period of more ordinary and unthreatening questions at the end to finish the interview on emotionally neutral topics.

The format of this survey was to collect a large amount of quantitative data — a relatively small amount of information from a large number of people. The report thus included very few case examples or verbatim accounts of aspects of the experience of sexual violence. This is done very eloquently elsewhere, from novels describing a child's perspective on incest (e.g. Moggach, 1998) to factual accounts of the harrowing experiences of abuse and efforts to seek help. There are numerous Irish examples of these (e.g. Doyle, 1988; McKay, 1998).

SURVEY PROCEDURES

Interviewers conducted the surveys between the hours of 9:30 am and 9:00 pm on Mondays to Fridays, and from 10:00 am to 2:00 pm on Saturdays. The evening and weekend shifts were required (based on feasibility study criteria) to facilitate contact with participants who were working full-time. A detailed record of the outcome of each call attempted to each unique telephone number was kept to facilitate organisation, and to calculate response rates and effort required.

Interviewers targeted the first person who answered the phone unless a quota needed to be met (see above). As described earlier, the survey was described to only one person (the target) in each household. Interviewers began each telephone call with a standardised introduction which described the topic and purpose of the survey, the agency which was conducting the survey, an assurance of confidentiality, and the participant's right to refuse or discontinue the survey at any point. Telephone calls were only conducted with landlines at private residences. Where interviewers first spoke with someone who was clearly under the age of 18, they asked to speak to an adult in the household. As an additional safeguard, all those agreeing to participate were asked before the interview started if they were over 18 years old.

Since the calls conducted were "cold" or "out of the blue", participants were asked if they were currently available to participate in the survey or would prefer to be re-contacted at a more suitable time, including at a private line or location. In addition, they were reminded that the topic of the survey was quite sensitive and were asked if they were in a situation to take the call without being overheard. This was done to ensure the safety of the participant, the confidentiality of the call, and the quality of the data by allowing the participant to speak more freely. As a further safeguard, the use of a "code phrase", as discussed earlier, was explained to the participant before the start of the interview. For example, if someone unexpectedly came into the room during the interview while they were taking part, and the participant did not want this person to know that they were taking part in a survey, this phrase would signal a pause. This strategy was specifically designed to protect those participants who may currently be in a situation of ongoing abuse in which the abuser is living in the same household.

Follow-up Procedure

All participants who participated in the survey were asked if they could be re-contacted for a "follow-up" interview one to two days after the initial interview. The calls served multiple purposes: to assess the degree of distress that participants may have felt following the interview; to allow the interviewer another chance to refer participants to appropriate services if necessary; to allow the participant a chance to change their responses; to allow the researcher a chance to clarify any information given in the initial interview that was unclear; and to provide the research team with additional feedback about the survey itself. Follow-up phone calls were semi-structured and were typically quite brief, lasting three to ten minutes.

Data Collection

Data collection began mid-March 2001 and was completed by mid-June 2001. All telephone calls were made by the research team, consisting of 14 women with relevant research and/or counselling experience. One male interviewer conducted a limited number of interviews at the beginning of the data collection period (since previous US experience indicated approximately equivalent response rates for men and women interviewing men (Tjaden and Boyle, 1998)). He discontinued that role since he was about half as successful as women in eliciting participation in the survey.[1] The average duration of an interview was approximately 25 minutes. Only 10 per cent of the interviews took more than 40 minutes to complete.

---

[1] This was the case whether men or women were approached or whether a participant previously contacted by a female researcher who indicated no preference for male or female interviewers was re-contacted. The interviewer in question was an experienced mental health professional, and was selected on the basis of fairness in job interviews and in the absence of any evidence to contraindicate male researcher involvement. Based on our observations of his work, his low response rate was not attributable to his manner or ability in conducting the interviews.

Chapter 4

RESULTS OF THE SAVI SURVEY

An outline of the results of the SAVI Survey is presented in the following order:

o   Response rate to the survey

o   Sample

o   The demographic profile of participants and how representative they are of the general public in Ireland

o   Prevalence figures for child and adult sexual violence

o   Revictimisation

o   The context of abuse, perpetrators and location of abuse

o   Psychological consequences of abuse

o   A description of whether and to whom abuse was disclosed

o   Disclosure to and satisfaction with professional services (Gardaí, medical, counselling)

o   Public views on the barriers to, and likelihood of, disclosure of abuse should they themselves be subjected to sexual abuse or violence

o   The public perceptions of the level of sexual violence in society

o   Public attitudes to sexual violence, including "rape myths", the education of children about the risk of abuse, and media portrayals of abuse o　Prevalence of sexual harassment

o　The effects of participating in the SAVI survey.

RESPONSE RATE

Over 12,000 unique telephone numbers were contacted in the course of the study. Call outcomes were categorised and the response rate calculated using international standards. Figure 4.1 below outlines the broad categories of call outcomes and the number of each type that were obtained (see Appendix IVa and IVb for a detailed outline of call categories).

Figure 4.1: Profile of Unique Telephone Numbers Called and Interviews Conducted for the SAVI Survey

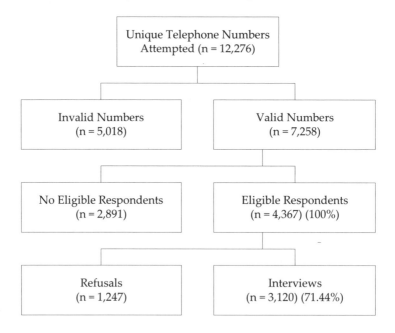

The overall response rate for the study was 71.44 per cent. This is a very high response rate for a public survey in Ireland. For instance, the Economic and Social Research Institute report telephone survey response rates on a range of general topics to be in the region of 62–64 per cent (J. Williams, personal communication). Postal surveys of the general public are similar, for instance, even with follow-up reminders and house calls, as in the case of the SLÁN health survey of the general population; a response rate of 62 per cent was obtained (Friel et al., 1999). The response rate obtained in this study is even more significant considering the sensitive and potentially threatening nature of the topic. It does, however, match closely the rates achieved with similar method- ologies for studies of sexual violence in other countries. For in- stance, in the US, a national survey including 8,005 men and 8,000 women achieved 68.9 per cent and 72.1 per cent response rates respectively (Tjaden and Boyle, 1998). In Canada, a national study of 12,300 women was achieved with a response rate of 63.7 per cent. The majority of refusals in the study were household refus- als. Where the eligible participant was contacted directly when called, response rates were 91 per cent (Johnson and Sacco, 1995). Overall, the high response rate suggests that the results can be considered representative of the general population.

The high response rate was achieved, in part, because of the multiple strategies used to facilitate participation. Among these strategies was the call-back or conversion procedure (see the pro- cedure section in Chapter 3 for a detailed description of these calls). The interviewers achieved a conversion rate of 7 per cent. Thus, almost 1 out 14 of people who initially refused to take part in the study, later agreed to take part after an interviewer re- contacted them.

SAMPLE

A total of 3,120 people were interviewed in the SAVI study. Be- cause the right of the participant to discontinue the survey at any point was highly respected, the interviewers did not push partici- pants to complete the survey. Surveys were analysed for their completeness, and most (95.5 per cent) were considered to be complete. Only 15 participants discontinued the survey before getting to the section on child and adult experiences of sexual abuse (Section E). The survey sample comprised 51 per cent women and 49 per cent men. The age of the participants ranged from 18 years to 90 years.

DEMOGRAPHIC CHARACTERISTICS

The sample was drawn as a national, random-digit dialing sample of telephone households in Ireland. The representativeness of the SAVI sample in terms of the national demographic profile was examined using the most recent census information (Table 4.1). This was the 2001 Quarterly National Household Survey. The gender balance of the SAVI sample was virtually identical to that of the adult general population. Regarding age, the populations were broadly similar. There was, however, a smaller proportion of younger people (i.e. less than age 30), particularly women, in SAVI than in the general population (12.5 versus 23.5 per cent). Proportions of men were more similar (18.9 versus 24.9 per cent). Regarding marital status, proportions of men in the SAVI sample mirrored general population patterns while a smaller proportion of SAVI women were single (19.9 versus 31.5 per cent) compared with the general population. Overall, the proportion of young and single women in SAVI was less than the general population while the male sample was relatively representative of the Irish adult population.

In order to check if these differences in proportion in the SAVI sample would affect the generalisability of the results, prevalence rates of sexual violence were calculated using the original figures and using figures weighted to readjust for the lower numbers of young and single women. This is reported later.

Further demographic characteristics of the SAVI group, such as education, work status and social classification, are outlined in Table 4.2. Published census data is not available with regard to these demographic variables to make comparisons with the general population. Over 60 per cent of the group had Leaving Certificate education or higher with over half of the group in paid or self-employed roles. Almost one in five men (18 per cent) and one in ten women (11 per cent) worked as professionals.

Table 4.1: Demographic Comparison of Age, Marital Status, and Location of Residence of the SAVI Sample and the Population in Ireland

	Men (%)		Women (%)	
Demographic Characteristics[a]	*SAVI*	*General Population*[a]	*SAVI*	*General Population*
Gender	48.6	49.0	51.4	51.0
Age				
20-24[a]	11.3	12.8	6.1	12.1
25-29	7.6	12.1	6.4	11.4
30-39	22.2	20.6	24.4	20.0
40-49	25.2	19.0	23.3	18.4
50-59	14.3	15.7	20.2	14.9
60-69	11.2	10.4	10.1	10.3
70-79	6.8	6.7	7.2	8.2
80+	1.3	2.7	2.3	4.7
Marital Status				
Single	35.3	39.0	19.9	31.5
Married/cohabiting/ divorced/separated	58.6	57.9	68.8	57.5
Widowed	4.1	3.1	9.7	11.0
Residential Location[b]	**SAVI**		**General Population**	
Urban	47% (men and women)		58% (men and women)	
Rural	53% (men and women)		42% (men and women)	

[a] SAVI data was compiled to match available census (QNHS) data. QNHS data in 2001 breakdowns by age, gender and marital status were for private households only. This analysis includes those aged 20+ only since QNHS data for ages 18 and 19 were reported in a larger 15–19-year-old categorisation group.

[b] Residential location data is from the 1996 census as QNHS 2001 does not provide an update by location.

Table 4.2: Demographic Comparison of Education, Work Status and Social Classification of the SAVI Sample

Demographic Characteristics	Men (%)	Women (%)
Education		
Primary school only	15.5	14.9
Up to Group, Junior Certificate	19.9	18.2
Completed Leaving Certificate	30.9	36.0
Completed third level	33.7	31.0
Work Status		
In paid employment	48.0	41.7
Self-employed (farm/business)	25.7	8.0
Home duties	0.9	33.7
Retired	13.1	8.7
Student	7.3	5.2
Other	5.1	2.7
Social Classification		
Professional	17.7	10.7
Intermediate	22.6	30.3
Routine non-manual	21.6	29.0
Skilled manual	20.0	6.9
Semi-skilled manual	12.1	19.1
Unskilled manual	1.1	0.9
Unclassified	4.9	3.1

The Profile of Those Who Did Not Participate in SAVI

A total of 1,247 individuals contacted did not agree to take part in the study. Interviewers recorded whether the person who refused to participate was the first person who answered the phone or the "targeted" individual. In 54 per cent of refusals, the refusal was by the person answering the phone in the household rather than the person who was the target. For example, if a quota was being filled (e.g. asking to speak to women under age 50), another household member would not facilitate the contact. Sometimes a person who was initially contacted, and who had asked the interviewer to call back at a more suitable time was not re-contactable because another member of the household refused to put the interviewer back in touch with the initial person. When possible, limited demographic information was collected for those who refused. As expected, however, many of those who refused to participate also refused to give any personal details. A higher proportion of those who refused were women (59 per cent). This was also the case where refusal was at the level of household rather than the target person (65 per cent of household refusers were women). The approximate age (recorded as less than or greater than age 50) of those who refused was ascertained for 79 per cent of this group. The data indicated that a higher proportion of those refusing to participate were younger people (56 per cent). Again, if possible, all of those who refused were asked why. The most common reasons cited for non-participation (cited by at least 10 people) were "not interested" (41 per cent), "not enough time" (13 per cent), "doesn't pertain to me" and "I'm too old" (1 per cent).

Because the introductory information was provided in a standard sequence, interviewers also took note of how much of the study had been explained to the person before they refused. Of those who refused, 19 per cent did so before they had been told how their telephone number was selected, while 22 per cent refused before they knew the purpose of the study. Given this data, one may conclude that for at least one out of five refusals, their reason for refusal was not the sensitive nature of the topic. A total of 33 per cent refused before they were told how their confidentiality could be assured, 39 per cent before they heard how the results would be used and 65 per cent before they were told how they could check the authenticity of the study if they so wished. This was the case despite the fact that the length of time taken to deliver the introduction of the study to a caller (which contains all of this information) is approximately 30 seconds.

PREVALENCE OF SEXUAL VIOLENCE

Estimating the prevalence of both child and adult sexual abuse and violence in Ireland was one of the main aims of this study. As previously described, a list of behaviourally specific and explicit questions concerning sexual experiences were asked of participants to which they could simply respond "yes" or "no". The category "unsure" was also added, at the suggestion of those who work in this area, to allow for participants who would not be certain as to what happened to them (e.g., as a young child). For the purpose of the prevalence tables, and any analyses using this data, the category "unsure" was re-categorised as a "no". Thus, the estimates provided take quite a conservative approach. Most of the data in this section was analysed by the gender of the participant, as males and females often have significantly different experiences.

Prevalence of Childhood Sexual Abuse

While the adult section makes clear in the introduction that the sexual experiences asked about were non-consensual in nature, the questions regarding childhood experiences did not use the words "against your will" as most experts agree that the concept of "consent" does not apply in the context of childhood. While this point is readily acknowledged, some who are abused may not see themselves as participating against their will or being coerced (e.g., as in early sexual experimentation between older adolescents). Questions were therefore structured so as to make clear to those interviewed that sexual activity which was consensual in adolescence was not to be included. Participants were told the following: "Now, I want to ask you to think back to when you were younger, *before your 17th birthday*. The following questions are also about sexual experiences. Just to be clear, we're not talking about sexual experiences that were 'consensual' or that you agreed to, for example, with a boyfriend or girlfriend who was a similar age to you at the time."

The percentage of participants who indicated "yes" to each item asked about sexual abuse in childhood is reported in Table 4.3.

Table 4.3: Prevalence of Unwanted Sexual Experiences in Childhood (i.e. prior to age 17)

Sexual Experience	Men % (n)	Women % (n)
1. During your childhood or adolescence did anyone ever show you or persuade you to look at pornographic material (for example, magazines, videos, internet, etc.) in a way that made you feel uncomfortable?	6.7 (100)	2.7 (43)
2. Did anyone ever make you or persuade you to take off your clothes, or have you pose alone or with others in a sexually suggestive way or in ways that made you feel confused or uncomfortable in order to photograph or video you?	1.0 (15)	1.3 (20)
3. As a child or adolescent, did anyone expose their sexual organs to you?	12.5 (188)	20.6 (326)
4. During this time did anyone masturbate in front of you?	6.2 (93)	5.3 (84)
5. Did anyone touch your body, including your breasts or genitals, in a sexual way? [a]	11.2 (169)	14.9 (263)
6. During your childhood or adolescence, did anyone try to have you arouse them, or touch their body in a sexual way?	9.7 (146)	9.0 (143)
7. Did anyone rub their genitals against your body in a sexual way?	6.6 (99)	10.1 (160)
8. Did anyone attempt to have sexual intercourse with you?	3.0 (45)	4.6 (72)
9. Did anyone succeed in having sexual intercourse with you?	1.1 (16)	1.7 (26)
10. Did anyone, male or female, make you or persuade you to have oral sex?	1.1 (16)	0.9 (14)
11. Did a man make you or persuade you to have anal sex?	0.9 (14)	0.3 (5)
12. Did anyone put their fingers or objects in your vagina or anus (back passage)? [a]	0.6 (9)	4.4 (69)

[a] When a man was being interviewed, a "male" version of the survey was used; wording was identical to the female version shown above, except for the exclusion of words such as "your breasts" or "your vagina".

Analysis at the level of single items revealed that the most commonly reported experience by both men and women was indecent exposure (item 3) (12.5 per cent of men and 20.6 per cent of women). Of a more serious nature is the second most common experience, that of someone touching their breasts or genitals in a sexual way, with 11.2 per cent of men and 14.9 per cent of women reporting this experience. The most serious forms of abuse (items 9–12), at least in the legal sense, were endorsed by small but significant numbers of men and women. While the percentages of men and women did not vary greatly on a few items (e.g., the number persuaded to have oral sex), significant differences between men and women were found on most items. Overall, women reported greater levels of abuse than men on seven of the twelve items. These individual items regarding sexual experiences in childhood are categorised and discussed further in the section on Lifetime Prevalence.

Prevalence of Unwanted Sexual Experiences as an Adult

Participants were also asked about "unwanted and unwelcome" sexual experiences that occurred in adulthood (age 17 or older). The introduction to this section explained that what the interviewer meant by the terms "unwanted and unwelcome" was "that another person used force or threatened you in some way or took advantage of a situation in which you could not defend yourself, for example when you had had a lot to drink or were asleep". Unwanted sexual experiences as an adult are summarised in Table 4.4. These percentages reflect the total number of people who said yes to each item. Thus, if a participant who was raped was also made touch the perpetrator in a sexual way, both items are counted separately.

Analysis of the experiences reported to have occurred in adulthood suggests that aside from the non-specific item about an attempt of sexual contact (item 1), the most commonly reported experience for both men and women is where someone touched their breasts or genitals against their will (7.1 per cent and 15.8 per cent, respectively). The next most commonly reported experiences involved someone of the opposite sex forcing the participant to touch them (item 4 for men and item 3 for women). For almost all the items, women were more likely to report having experienced this form of abuse. Differences between men and women in the number reporting experiences were seen, with more women being abused on almost all the items. This pattern was much more evident for the experiences reported in adulthood than those in childhood.

Table 4.4: Prevalence of Unwanted Sexual Experiences as an Adult (17 or older)

Sexual Experience	Men	Women
	% (n)	% (n)
1. Have you had an experience that did not involve actual sexual contact between you and another person, but did involve an attempt by someone to force you to have any kind of unwanted sexual contact?	7.9 (119)	18.6 (294)
2. Has anyone, male or female, touched your breasts or genitals against your will?[a]	7.1 (107)	15.8 (250)
3. Has a man made you touch his genitals against your will (aged 17 or older)?	1.1 (17)	6.2 (98)
4. Has a woman made you touch her breasts or her genitals against your will?	4.2 (63)	0.4 (6)
5. Has a man forced you to have sexual intercourse against your will? (By this, so as to be clear, we mean that he put his penis in your vagina)?[b]	n/a	4.3 (68)
6. Has anyone, male or female, made you have oral sex against your will? (By oral sex we mean that a man put his penis in your mouth or that a person, male or female, performed oral sex on you)	0.3 (5)	1.3 (21)
7. Has a man made you have anal sex against your will? (By this we mean that he put his penis in your anus)	0.0 (0)	1.2 (19)

Sexual Experience	Men	Women
	% (n)	% (n)
8. Has anyone put their fingers or objects in your vagina or anus against your will? [a]	0.5 (8)	2.5 (39)
9. Has anyone, male or female, attempted to make you have vaginal, oral or anal sex against your will, but penetration did not occur? [a]	0.9 (13)	3.3 (52)
10. Did you have any other sexual experience against your will that I haven't already mentioned?	2.2 (32)	0.0 (0)

[a] When a man was being interviewed, a "male" version of the survey was used; wording was identical except for the exclusion of words such as "your breasts" or "your vagina".

[b] Men were not asked this question in the survey.

In order to simplify and condense the single experiences listed above, each item was categorised according to both previous research and local professional advice based on categories of criminal behaviour in Ireland.[1] The category "no abuse reported" meant that no items were endorsed by the participant. "Abuse not otherwise specified" was a category specific only to adults, and includes those who described what they considered to be an unwanted sexual experience in an open-ended question (item 10) at the end of the experiences in adulthood section. Thus, the experience they described did not include any of the items specifically queried about and was typically a unique experience. The category "child pornography" includes anyone who endorsed items 1 or 2 from the childhood experiences section, while "indecent exposure" includes those endorsing items 3 or 4 from this same section. These categories are not included in the section on adulthood experiences. "Contact abuse (no penetration)" includes those who had experienced some sexual contact with the perpetrator and includes items 5–7 in the childhood section and items 2–4 in the

---

[1] To redefine the questions from Table 4.4 (child abuse) and Table 4.5 (adult abuse) in terms of Irish legal practice, see Appendix VI.

adulthood section. The category "attempted penetration" includes those who endorsed item 8 in the childhood section and item 9 in the adulthood section. Lastly, the category "penetration/oral sex" combines the most serious forms of abuse and assault, frequently referred to as rape, and includes those who experienced any of items 9–12 in the childhood section or items 5–8 in the adulthood section.

The percentages of men and women who experienced these combined categories of sexual experiences are provided in Table 4.5. Note that in this table, each participant is only counted once. If the participant had previously indicated "yes" to several items either in childhood or adulthood, the most serious of those items was used to categorise that person's experiences. For the purpose of these analyses, the "most serious" category was deemed penetration/oral sex, followed by attempted penetration, contact abuse, indecent exposure, child pornography, abuse not otherwise specified, and lastly, no abuse reported. Thus if someone reported experiencing an item that fell under the category "indecent exposure", but also experienced something considered "contact abuse," that person's experiences are recorded under "contact abuse".

In summary, almost a quarter of the men (24 per cent) and almost one third (30 per cent) of the women reported some level of abuse in childhood. Contact abuse was the most common form of abuse in both childhood and adulthood. Attempted or actual rape was experienced by 4.2 per cent of boys and 7.6 per cent of girls. Equivalent rape and attempted rape figures in adulthood were 1.5 per cent for men and 7.4 per cent for women. Hence the level of serious sexual crimes committed against women remains similar from childhood through adulthood, while risks in childhood for boys are lower than for girls and decrease three-fold from childhood to adult life.

Table 4.5: Types of Unwanted Sexual Experiences by Age at Abuse (child <17 years, or adult) Categorised by Most Serious Level of Abuse Experienced

Most Serious Level of Sexual Abuse/Assault Experienced	Childhood		Adulthood	
	Men *% (n)*	*Women* *% (n)*	*Men* *% (n)*	*Women* *% (n)*
No abuse reported	76.5 (1,151)	69.6 (1,102)	87.6 (1,317)	74.5 (1,180)
Abuse — not otherwise specified[a]	n/a	n/a	2.7 (41)	5.11 (81)
(Child pornography)	2.7 (40)	0.8 (12)	n/a	n/a
(Indecent exposure)	4.7 (70)	9.2 (146)	n/a	n/a
Contact abuse (no penetration)	12.0 (181)	12.8 (203)	8.2 (124)	13 (206)
Attempted penetration	1.5 (22)	2.0 (32)	0.6 (9)	1.3 (20)
Penetration/Oral sex	2.7 (40)	5.6 (89)	0.9 (13)	6.1 (97)
Total	100 (1,504)	100 (1,584)	100 (1,504)	100 (1,584)

[a] This category was created to account for any unwanted sexual experiences in adulthood which participants reported in an open-ended question and did not definitively fit into any of the other categories (Question 1, Table 4.5).

In broad terms, the experience of abuse which started in either childhood or as an adult or both is considered in Table 4.6.

The majority of the sexual abuse and violence that was reported occurred in childhood. For women, 51.3 per cent experienced abuse in childhood only versus 21.0 per cent who experienced abuse only in adulthood. Likewise, for men, 66.1 per cent experienced abuse only in childhood versus 14.4 per cent in adulthood. A significant minority reported abuse both in childhood and in adulthood. Thus, these participants who experienced sexual abuse in childhood were re-victimised in adulthood. The issue of re-victimisation is analysed in more detail later in this section.

Table 4.6: Profile of Age Category (adult vs child) When Abuse Started[a]

When Abuse Started	Men % (n)	Women % (n)
As a child only	66.1 (284)	51.3 (340)
As an adult only	14.4 (62)	21.0 (139)
As both child and adult	19.5 (84)	27.7 (184)
Total	100 (430)	100 (663)

[a] This table counts only experiences of abuse by a new perpetrator or group of perpetrators. Thus abuse which starts in childhood and continues into adulthood is only counted in childhood for this table. Abuse as both a child and adult means that two distinct groups of perpetrators were involved in two separate sets of abuse experiences.

Lifetime Prevalence of Sexual Violence

In order to examine the levels of abuse across the lifetime, participants were re-categorised using the most serious form of abuse they experienced (i.e., regardless of whether it happened in childhood or adulthood) (Table 4.7).

Table 4.7: Types of Unwanted Sexual Experiences Experienced Over a Lifetime Categorised by Most Serious Level of Abuse Experienced

Lifetime Abuse Category	Men % (n)	Women % (n)
No abuse reported	71.4 (1,074)	57.9 (917)
Non-Contact Abuse[a]	7.0 (106)	9.8 (155)
Contact Abuse (no penetration)	16.4 (247)	19.2 (304)
Attempted Penetration	2.0 (30)	2.8 (45)
Penetration/ Oral sex	3.2 (48)	10.2 (162)
Total	100 (1,505)	100 (1,583)

[a] This category is a combination of the child categories of "child pornography" and "indecent exposure" and the adult category of "abuse — not otherwise specified".

Over 40 per cent of women and 28 per cent of men reported some form of sexual abuse or assault that occurred in their lifetime (see also Figures 4.2 and 4.3). Non-penetrative contact abuse was the most common type of abuse reported for both men and women (16 per cent and 19 per cent, respectively). The most serious form of abuse, penetration or forced oral sex, which is considered rape, was experienced by approximately one out of ten women, as compared to approximately one out of 30 men at some point in their lives.

Figure 4.2: Lifetime Prevalence of Sexual Violence for Men

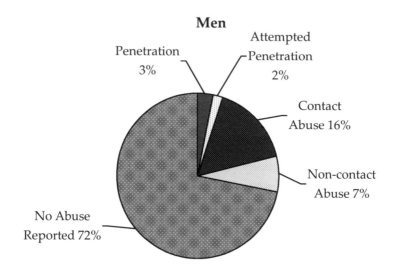

Figure 4.3: Lifetime Prevalence of Sexual Violence for Women

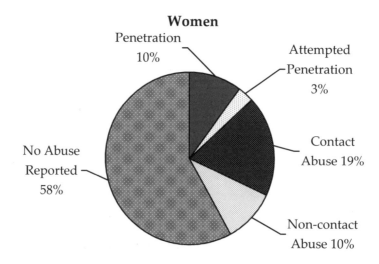

Weighted Prevalence Rates

Since the demographic profile of the SAVI sample differed somewhat from the general population, prevalence rates were recalculated using values weighted to take account of the differences. The weighted values made virtually no difference to patterns of estimates of the prevalence of various forms of sexual violence (see Appendix VII). Thus the actual figures from the SAVI sample can be taken as equivalent to those of a sample weighted for the general population. Because of this, the actual figures obtained in the survey are used in analyses.

RE-VICTIMISATION

As shown in Table 4.6, a significant number of participants experienced re-victimisation. The following figures show the patterns of re-victimisation in men and women, based on their experience of childhood sexual abuse. It is important to emphasise that the patterns described are of associations between child and adult experiences of sexual violence. The data available cannot determine that childhood abuse "causes" adult sexual assault. It is nonetheless very important as child sexual abuse can be seen as a marker of risk for later abuse. Figure 4.4 outlines the findings for women.

The relationship between childhood sexual abuse and adult sexual assault is complex. To clarify, the lowest line in the figure shows the risk of adult sexual assault in women who did not report any childhood abuse. They had a risk of 4 per cent for "other" adult sexual violence, almost 10 per cent for contact, non-penetrative, sexual violence and 3 per cent for penetrative sexual violence. The line links these three figures to summarise the pattern. Turning to women who reported penetrative child abuse, their risks as adults were 2 per cent for "other" sexual violence, 24 per cent for contact non-penetrative sexual violence, and 27 per cent for penetrative sexual violence — a very different pattern. It is notable that risk of adult contact sexual violence is higher in all groups who were abused as children.

Figure 4.4: Risk of Sexual Re-victimisation of Adult Women According to Type of Childhood Sexual Abuse Experience

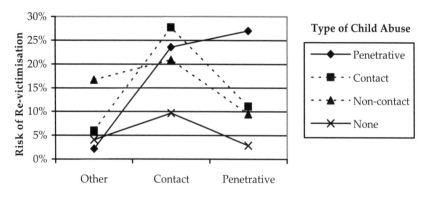

Type of Adult Re-victimisation

Turning to the risk of re-victimisation in men (Figure 4.5), similar patterns emerged, though the absolute risks themselves were generally smaller.

Figure 4.5: Risk of Sexual Re-victimisation of Adult Men According to Type of Childhood Sexual Abuse Experience

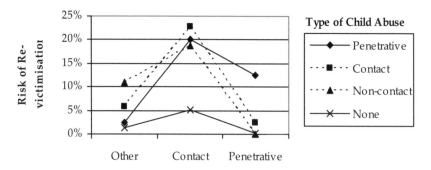

Type of Adult Re-victimisation

Two important patterns emerged. The first was that both men and women who reported sexual abuse of any type as children were considerably more likely to also report it as adults. Second, there was a marked difference between those who reported penetrative sexual abuse as children and those who reported other forms of abuse; those who reported penetrative sexual abuse as children were considerably more likely to report penetrative sexual violence as adults than any other form of adult sexual assault. In women, experiencing penetrative sexual abuse in childhood was associated with a 16-fold increase in the risk of adult penetrative sexual abuse, and a 5-fold increase in the risk of adult contact sexual abuse. For men, the increase in risk was even greater, but the size of the increased risk is harder to assess in men because of the smaller numbers involved. Therefore, confidence intervals were calculated, and the lowest estimates (which can be considered the most conservative) are provided. For men, experiencing penetrative sexual abuse in childhood was associated with a 16-fold increase in the risk of adult penetrative sexual abuse, and at least a 12-fold increase in the risk of adult contact sexual abuse. To emphasise again, it is not possible from the findings here to say that childhood abuse "causes" adult re-victimisation. Childhood sexual abuse is, however, an important marker of increased risk of adult sexual violence.

These findings support a pattern of high levels of re-victimisation in international studies. For instance, a Norwegian study found that 63 per cent of women abused by violent spouses had also been abused in childhood (equivalent levels of child sexual abuse without adult abuse experiences was 10 per cent) (Schei, 1990). A recent London study of over 2,500 women showed that different types of abuse (physical and sexual) co-occurred in childhood and adulthood (Coid et al., 2001). The risk of rape or other sexual assault in adulthood was on average three times higher for those who had been sexually abused as children (i.e. less than age 16 years). Serious sexual assault as an adult was 2.7 times more likely if the woman had experienced serious physical abuse in childhood. These findings highlight the important preventive reasons, as distinct from therapeutic or law enforcement reasons, for encouraging the disclosure of sexual abuse. Taking the high-risk approach used in managing many health conditions may be useful here. A high-risk strategy would target those most at risk of experiencing sexual abuse, i.e. those who have already been abused. Finding and then intervening is a good use of scarce resources in the fight against sexual violence.

In order to work out the pattern of child sexual abuse over the course of childhood, information on the type of abuse and the age at which it occurred is used. Inevitably, some interviewees were unable to say at what age an event had happened. This information was rarely missing for interviewees who had experienced penetrative abuse — only three of 129 persons; 30 persons who had experienced contact or penetrative child abuse (5 per cent) were unable to specify the age, and 116 persons (14 per cent) who had experienced any other form of child abuse were unable to specify the age. For this reason, this analysis will focus only on two aspects of child abuse: penetrative abuse and all contact abuse (including penetrative).

Risk of Child Abuse by Age

Figure 4.6 shows the risk of child sexual abuse by age for men and women.

Figure 4.6: Profile of Penetrative and of All Contact Child Sexual Abuse by Age and Gender of Child

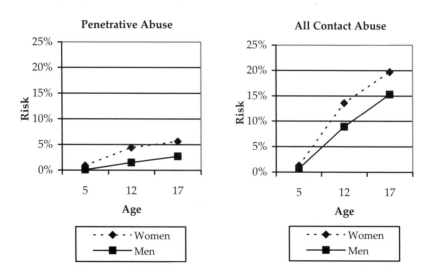

Cumulative risk of penetrative abuse (left) rises more steeply between the ages of 5 and 12 in girls than in boys, and the higher prevalence in girls is mainly due to this increased risk in the pre-teen years. The same holds for all contact abuse, including penetrative abuse, where the gap between the sexes is largely a product of increased risk in the pre-teen years.

The relationship between birth cohort and experience of child sexual abuse was examined. Table 4.8 shows the number of men and women, by year of birth, who participated in the study. One important question concerns whether the level and nature of sexual violence has changed over time. This study allows examination of the experience of child sexual abuse across most of the twentieth century since all of the participants were divided into "cohorts", i.e. groupings by year of birth. The earliest cohort was from 1911–1929 with 201 participants in this older age category (see Table 4.8). The youngest cohort were born between 1970 and 1983. Those born since 1983 would have been too young to take part in the study.

Table 4.8: SAVI Survey Participants Categorised by Year of Birth (birth cohort)

Cohort	Men (n)	Women (n)	Total (n)
1911-1929	87	114	201
1930-1949	329	413	742
1950-1969	674	748	1,422
1970-1983	413	309	722
Total	1,503	1,584	3,087

There was no significant difference between cohorts, either for men or for women, in the experience of penetrative child abuse,[1] and there was no evidence of any trend towards a greater or lesser risk in persons born more recently. However, when *all* forms of contact child abuse are considered (i.e. penetrative and non-penetrative), the pattern is different.

---

[1] Statistical significance: $p = 0.125$ for women and 0.500 for men

Figure 4.7 shows the reported rate of all forms of contact child sexual abuse (filled symbols) and penetrative abuse (open symbols) for men and women born in four periods.

Figure 4.7: The Risk of Penetrative Abuse and All Contact Abuse of Children by Gender and Birth Cohort (per cent reporting)

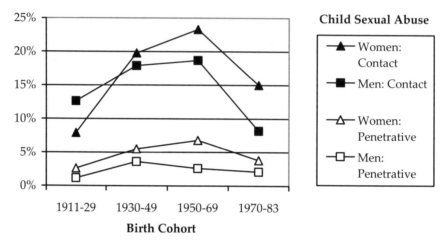

The rate of contact sexual abuse shows a clear pattern. Compared with participants born in 1911–29, those born in 1930–49 and 1950–69 reported significantly higher levels of sexual abuse, with a 2-fold[2] and 2.3-fold[3] increase respectively. However, those born in 1970–83 showed a similar level to those born in 1911–29.[4] The reported rate of penetrative sexual abuse suggested a similar pattern, but the increase in the middle period was not statistically significant. The relative size of the increase was, however, similar, with hazard ratios of 2.4 and 2.5 for the two middle cohorts. The smaller number of cases of penetrative sexual abuse makes it possible that the rise and fall observed reflects chance variation, but the fact that the pattern was similar for all forms of contact abuse

---

[2] Statistical significance: p = 0.0043

[3] p < 0.001

[4] p = 0.537

suggests that there was an increase in penetrative abuse in those born in the mid-century relative to those born earlier and later.

The most interesting question is undoubtedly whether the decline in reported abuse observed in the participants born most recently (1970–83) reflects a decreasing risk of childhood sexual abuse, or may be due to one or more confounding factors, such as differences in willingness to disclose abuse, or a changing perception of what childhood experiences constitute abuse. A number of possible confounding factors can be considered.

Option 1: Younger people are more reluctant to disclose sexual abuse

If this were the reason, then less disclosure to other persons by younger people would be expected. This is not the case. Figure 4.8 shows the rates of disclosure in men and women by cohort of birth. It shows that the proportion of persons who experienced any form of contact child abuse and who told anyone about their experience has risen steadily. The lower incidence of child sexual abuse in the earliest cohort may stem from a reluctance to talk about such experiences, but the latest-born cohort seems to have much less reluctance to talk about what happened to them than participants born in earlier years.

Figure 4.8: Disclosure of Child Sexual Abuse to Others before the SAVI Survey by Gender and Birth Cohort (per cent reporting)

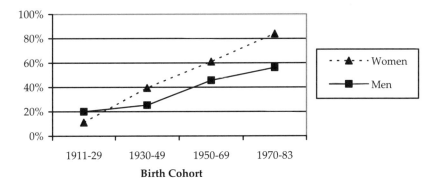

Increased willingness to disclose in younger people was also evident in disclosure patterns to professionals. For example, the proportion reporting to the Gardaí has increased over the period, though the small overall proportion reporting make the trend inconclusive statistically.[5] Figure 4.9 shows the proportion reporting any offence (child sexual abuse or adult sexual assault) in each of the cohorts (child sexual abuse and adult sexual assault were pooled to get a better estimate of the trend; the figures looked similar for each category separately, but numbers were too small to estimate percentages reliably).

Figure 4.9: Disclosure of Child Sexual Abuse or Adult Sexual Assault to Gardaí by Gender and Birth Cohort (per cent reported)

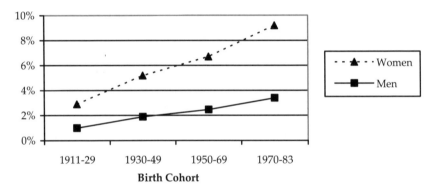

Analysis of data from participants who had not experienced sexual abuse either in childhood or adulthood (data not shown) revealed some interesting patterns. When asked how likely they thought it was that they would disclose such an incident if it happened to them, there was a significant decline in willingness to tell family and to tell a doctor across the birth cohorts; instead, there was a statistically significant increase in the willingness to tell friends and to tell a counsellor[6] by those born later in the century. There was no trend in the proportion who thought that they would tell the Gardaí over time. Overall, there was no significant

---

[5] p = 0.08

[6] All p<0.01

trend across cohorts in willingness to disclose to someone; instead the type of people that participants thought they would disclose to had changed over the years. Taken overall, these results do not suggest a growing reluctance to disclose sexual violence as a plausible explanation for the fall in the proportion of cases in the youngest cohort.

Option 2: Accepted norms for adolescent behaviour have changed

This explanation suggests that children born in the 1970s and 1980s would experience the same events as those born earlier, but that they would not experience them as inappropriate because of a greater acceptance of adolescent sexual exploration. This, again, was not consistent with the data: when analysis of child sexual abuse was limited to cases occurring below the age of 12, the pattern of decline was similar.

Option 3: The decline cannot reflect a genuine decrease in incidence because demand for psychological help by those who have experienced child sexual abuse is rising constantly

The apparent decline is at odds with the increasing demands on counselling services for such abuse. However, it is notable that the proportion of victims of child sexual abuse who attend counselling has risen constantly. Figure 4.10 shows this: more than 20 per cent of men and women from the 1970–83 cohort who experienced contact sexual abuse subsequently sought psychological help. The large increase in the proportion seeking help in recent years, especially in the case of men, may reconcile data on the increasing numbers in therapy but the fall in reported rates of sexual abuse.

Figure 4.10: Attendance at Counselling for Contact Child Sexual Abuse by Gender and Birth Cohort (per cent attending)

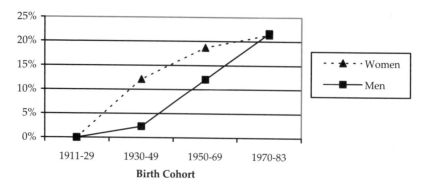

Experience of Adult Sexual Assault

In order to estimate the changing risk of adult sexual assault, the analysis was restricted to sexual violence occurring at or before age 30, since the oldest participants in the most recent birth cohort (1970–1983) were 31 at time of interview. To calculate cumulative risk to age 30, life table methods were used, which take account of the fact that not all participants have been exposed to risk for the same time (the youngest participants have had only a couple of years of exposure to risk of adult sexual assault, while the oldest ones have been exposed to risk for decades). The risk shown in the graph for the 1970–83 cohort, then, is a cumulative incidence — a projection of the risk to age 30, based on the available data; it is *not* a prevalence. The projection is also problematic since a significant percentage of participants were unable to date incidents of adult sexual assault accurately. While only nine persons who reported penetrative sexual abuse did not supply an age, 88 persons who reported contact sexual abuse (24 per cent) did not do so. This was either because the participants were unwilling to discuss the incident in detail, or because they were unsure of the precise timing. These missing ages had to be imputed in order to calculate risk to age 30. Imputation was done on the basis of the participant's sex, birth cohort, and the type(s) of sexual violence they experienced. In all cohorts, the average imputed age was the same as the average age cited by participants who provided this information.

Figure 4.11 shows the proportion of people from each cohort experiencing sexual assault as adults up to and including their thirtieth year. The figures for the earliest cohort are based on relatively small numbers of events, and are subject to a wide margin of uncertainty. Likewise, the figures for the final cohort are probably conservative, as they assume that the risk that the youngest participants will face as they get older will be the same as that experienced by the older members of the cohort; the true cumulative risk will probably be higher. Given these cautions, the increase in risk of adult sexual assault is nonetheless significant over the whole time period, with no evidence of a decline in the most recent cohort.

Figure 4.11: Cumulative Rate (per cent) of Adult Sexual Assault up to Age 30 by Birth Cohort and Gender

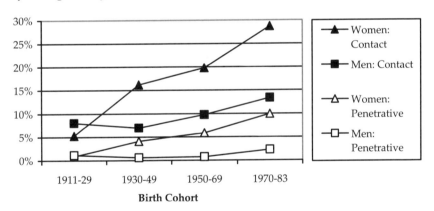

It is probably unproductive to ask what proportion of the observed increase is due to an increase in the "real" risk of sexual violence and how much is due to a change in public perception of what is tolerable sexual behaviour. Unlike child sexual abuse, where the definition hinges on the behaviour of the perpetrator and the age of the child, adult sexual assault is more dependent on the perception by the person being abused that this is being done against their will and constitutes unacceptable behaviour.

What is more important, however, from these findings is that an increasing proportion of adult women and men in Ireland report experiencing events which they construe as sexual violence.

Finally, the increase in adult sexual assault strongly suggests that the decline in the reporting of child abuse is not an artefact of the SAVI Survey methodology, since the same questions were used to elicit experience of child sexual abuse and adult sexual assault. There remains, therefore, the possibility that the decline in child sexual abuse is real. This is supported by a major report from the US Department of Justice, which has noted a 31 per cent overall decrease in substantiated cases of child abuse in the period 1990–1998, with decreases reported in 36 of 47 individual US states for which data were available. This decline is the subject of ongoing research, and it would be premature to say that we know why it is happening, but the fact that it has been observed in data gathered in different populations and in different ways makes it less likely that the decline we have observed in Ireland is an artefact of the SAVI Survey methodology.

The impact of a decline in risk of child sexual abuse on demand for psychological services, if this decline is real, is at present impossible even to guess. Demand for services reflects both recent and older cases, in an unknown mixture dependent on the person's perception of the need for help and the time lag after abuse before a person seeks help. Little is known about how or why either of these factors is changing dynamically, and it will be important for future research to address these questions specifically. Less is known about the pattern of increase in reporting adult sexual assault. The findings here are to be considered with extreme caution since various statistical assumptions have had to be made to deal with a relatively small (in epidemiological terms) sample size. The possibility of diverging patterns of sexual violence, decreasing in childhood and increasing in adulthood, is particularly challenging to explain. Further evidence from international studies is needed to consider patterns across time.

CONTEXT OF ABUSE

Although prevalence figures regarding the number of people who have experienced sexual violence can be useful on their own, their significance can be greatly enhanced when the context of that abuse is considered. Examination of the patterns of abuse situations (e.g. at what age it occurs, how frequently and over what duration of time it occurs, who perpetrates, and where it happens) may yield valuable findings that have implications for both the treatment and prevention of sexual violence.

It is important to note that in many of the following analyses for the survey, the number of *people* relevant to the analysis is counted rather than the number of *episodes* (the term "episode" refers to the number of different abuse situations reported which involved different perpetrators). This method was preferred in many cases where the focus was on how many people were affected, had disclosed, had used services, etc. Again, for clarity in some analyses, only the most serious episode of abuse was used for those who have experienced more than one episode.

Context of Abuse in Childhood (i.e. less than 17-years-old)

Information regarding the pattern of child abuse is presented below. Table 4.9 outlines these characteristics for the SAVI group.

Most sexual abuse in childhood and adolescence occurred in the earlier years of childhood, with 67 per cent of the abused girls and 62 per cent of the abused boys experiencing abuse by age 12, i.e. before or during their primary school years. A higher proportion of girls than boys were abused by age 8 years (29 versus 19 per cent). For many girls and boys (over 40 per cent), abuse was not a once-off event. Many also reported repeated abuse as children which continued over long periods; 58 per cent of girls and 42 per cent of boys abused more than once experienced sexual abuse in childhood that continued for longer than a year.

Table 4.9: Pattern of Child Sexual Abuse for Men and Women Reporting Abuse

	Men % (n)	Women % (n)
Onset of abuse		
0-4 years (pre-school)	1.6 (5)	3.5 (15)
5-8 years (mid-childhood)	17.3 (53)	25.1 (108)
9-12 years (late childhood)	42.7 (131)	38.4 (165)
13-14 years	20.9 (64)	14.9 (64)
15-16 years	17.6 (54)	18.1 (78)
Number of episodes of abuse		
Single experience	56.2 (158)	57.7 (224)
2-3 times	15.7 (44)	13.0 (52)
4-10 times	13.9 (39)	8.0 (31)
More than 10 times	2.5 (7)	1.3 (5)
"Too many to count"[a]	11.7 (33)	19.6 (76)
Duration of abuse [b]		
One week or less	1.4 (1)	4.1 (4)
One 2–3 weeks	9.7 (7)	8.2 (8)
One month	11.1 (8)	3.1 (3)
2–3 months	16.7 (12)	6.1 (6)
4–6 months	12.5 (9)	11.2 (11)
7–12 months/ One year	6.9 (5)	9.2 (9)
1–2 years	23.6 (17)	19.4 (19)
3–5 years	13.9 (10)	23.5 (23)
6–10 years	4.2 (3)	12.2 (12)
More than 10 years	0 (0)	3.1 (3)

[a] Participant indicated that abuse occurred many times and was unable to give an exact number

[b] Duration of abuse was only recorded for abuse that occurred over a period of time (i.e., it does not apply to cases that occurred only once)

Perpetrators of Child Abuse

Information regarding those who perpetrated the abuse is also of importance, especially when considering prevention strategies. This study collected information on who the perpetrator was in relation to the participant. Participants were also asked specifically if the perpetrator was someone who had any authority over them (e.g., teacher, boss). Because a large age difference between the abused person and perpetrator can have greater legal ramifications, the approximate age of the perpetrator was asked of participants who reported child sexual abuse. (For those reporting unwanted adult sexual experiences, the age of the perpetrator was not queried.) The profile of those abusing children is presented in Table 4.10.

In a simple overview, five types of perpetrator each accounted for approximately one-fifth of abuse: family members, neighbours, authority figures, friends/acquaintances and strangers (see Figure 4.12). Perpetrators who were authority figures were reported by 22 per cent of the men and 16 per cent of the women. The particular role they played in these participants' lives as children is analysed in more detail in Table 4.11. Neighbours were identified as the perpetrator for 19 per cent of men and 21 per cent of women, while strangers were identified by 19 per cent and 23 per cent, respectively. Notable differences are found between men and women in the category of "friend"; men were much more likely to identify the perpetrator as a friend (17 per cent) than were women (5 per cent). Gender differences were also notable when examining perpetrators who were family members. Women were much more likely than men to report that the perpetrator was a family member (24 per cent versus 14 per cent). Comparing across all perpetrator groups, a much greater proportion of the perpetrators of abuse in childhood were known by the abused child than unknown.

Table 4.10: Perpetrator Characteristics of Child Sexual Abuse for Men and Women Reporting Abuse

Relationship of Perpetrator to Abused Child	Men % (n)	Women % (n)
Abuser known to the child — family members		
Father	1.0 (3)	3.5 (15)
Brother	2.0 (6)	4.8 (21)
Uncle	4.0 (12)	7.6 (33)
Grandfather	0.0 (0)	2.3 (10)
Other male relative	0.7 (2)	0.7 (3)
Other female relative	0.3 (1)	0.0 (0)
Stepfather	0.0 (0)	0.5 (2)
Mother	0.3 (1)	0.2 (1)
Cousin (male/female)	5.5 (17)	3.4 (15)
Brother-in-law	0.0 (0)	0.5 (2)
Abuser known to the child — non-family members		
Neighbour	18.9 (57)	21.5 (92)
Friend	17.3 (52)	4.9 (21)
Boyfriend	0.0 (0)	1.8 (8)
Authority figure[a]	22.1(66)	16.3 (71)
Acquaintance known > 24 hrs	7.4 (22)	6.1 (26)
Abuser not known to the child		
Acquaintance known < 24 hrs	1.7 (5)	0.9 (4)
Stranger	18.7 (56)	22.9 (98)

[a] Not otherwise listed

Figure 4.12: Comparisons of Categories of Perpetrators of Child Sexual Abuse by Gender of Victim

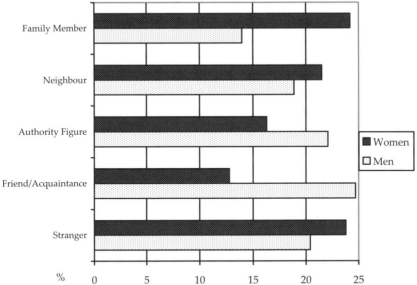

While the gender of the perpetrator is obvious in some categories (e.g., father), it is not obvious in other categories (e.g., neighbour). Therefore the gender of the perpetrator was examined in more detail. Women who reported any type of sexual abuse as children most frequently reported that there was one male perpetrator (95 per cent). Less than three per cent of women reported being abused by more than one man, and less than two per cent reported being abused by a woman (n = 8). Perpetrators of abuse as reported by men followed a slightly different pattern; 78 per cent of men reported abuse by one man, with 14 per cent reporting one female abuser. Additionally, six per cent reported abuse perpetrated by more than one man.

Incest in Childhood

For the purposes of this study, incest was defined using a broad definition meaning contact or penetrative child abuse by any relative, whether blood relative or not. This definition was used to differentiate between abusers inside the family social network and those outside. A narrower definition based on degree of kinship, while it makes some sense if the prohibition of incest is to prevent inbreeding, makes little sense when the argument against incest is based on its adverse effects on the psychological development of the child.

Incest was reported by 5.6 per cent of women and 2.5 per cent of men. It was associated with more severe contact abuse; among interviewees who reported contact abuse, 39 per cent of those who experienced incest experienced penetrative child abuse, while only 18 per cent of others abused did so, a difference which is highly significant statistically ($p = <0.01$). There was no evidence of differing rates of incest across social classes or education groups.

Authority Figures as Perpetrators

Participants were also asked if the person who perpetrated the abuse held any authority over them at the time. Table 4.11 provides descriptions of the roles of those deemed to have been authority figures.

Table 4.11: Profile of Abusers Identified as Being Authority Figures for those Reporting Child Sexual Abuse

Position of Authority[a]	Proportion of Authority Figures		Proportion of All Abusers	
	Men % (n)	Women % (n)	Men % (n)	Women % (n)
Babysitter	19.7 (13)	28.2 (20)	4.2	4.6
Religious minister	9.1 (6)	8.5 (6)	1.9	1.4
Teacher (religious)	18.2 (12)	0.0 (0)	3.9	0.0
Teacher (non-religious)	6.1 (4)	7.0 (5)	1.3	1.1
Boss[b]	6.1 (4)	5.6 (4)	1.3	0.9
Coach/instructor	6.1 (4)	2.8 (2)	1.3	0.5
Other authority figures	34.7 (23)	6.0 (34)	7.5	7.6

[a] Organised from most to least frequently mentioned distinct categories

[b] Note: young people up to 17 years are included in this sample

Combining religious ministers and religious teachers, they constituted the largest single category of authority figures as abusers of boys; 5.8 per cent of all boys sexually abused were abused by clergy or religious. A smaller proportion (1.4 per cent) of girls abused were abused by clergy or religious. For girls, babysitters constituted the biggest group; 4.6 per cent of abusers of girls were babysitters. A similar proportion of boys were abused by babysitters (4.2 per cent). All of these authority groups were more notable by how uncommon, rather than common, they were as perpetrators of sexual abuse against children.

Most child abusers were lone men (89 per cent) with 49 (7 per cent) being lone women. In 30 cases (4 per cent) the abuse was by more than one abuser. Most female abusers (73 per cent) were deemed not to have been in positions of authority. One non-religious female teacher and four babysitters were specified as being abusers in positions of authority. Of the 30 multiple abuser cases, five involved people in positions of authority — one was a religious teacher, three were in a babysitting context and one was unspecified. Most of those abusing as babysitters were lone males (73 per cent) and most were also relatives (58 per cent). Two (of 23) religious ministers/religious teachers were also relatives. One abuser in authority was reported to be a Garda officer.

Juvenile Perpetrators

(A quarter of the perpetrators identified by the participants (25.8 per cent) were juveniles (aged 17 or younger).[7] As it is often difficult to discriminate between "normal" early sexual experimentation and "abnormal" or "abusive" types of activities, previous researchers in this area have made distinctions based solely on the age difference between the perpetrator and the abused. A five-year age difference is a common convention (Murphy, Haynes and Page, 1992), but others (e.g., Kemp, 1998) have noted that a

---

[7] This section referring to juvenile perpetrators includes all minors (i.e., all those aged under 18 years).

"significant maturity difference between the children would be a more appropriate guideline". Several typologies of juvenile perpetrators have been proposed (see Righthand and Welch, 2001, for a review), but most require a thorough examination of perpetrators in order to "classify" them accurately. Individual characteristics of the juvenile (e.g., previous history of aggressive behaviour or sexual abuse) and family characteristics (e.g., parental separation, domestic violence, and highly sexualised environments) are the variables typically investigated.

While it is beyond the scope of this data set to examine various juvenile perpetrator characteristics, it is possible to examine the age differences in more detail. Table 4.12 presents the age category of perpetrators alongside the age category of those they abused (the participants). In almost all cases (184 out of 186), the juvenile perpetrator was older than the abused person.

Table 4.12: Juvenile Perpetrator Age Category with Corresponding Victim Age Category

Age Group of Abused Child/ Adolescent	Perpetrator Age Group			
	4–11 years % (n)	12–14 years % (n)	15–17 years % (n)	Total % (n)
4–11 years	100 (22)	46.3 (25)	38.2 (42)	47.9 (89)
12–14 years	0 (0)	51.9 (28)	30.9 (34)	33.3 (62)
15–17 years	0 (0)	1.9 (1)	30.9 (34)	18.8 (35)
Total	100 (22)	29.0 (54)	59.1 (110)	100 (186)

Pre-adolescent perpetrators (aged under 12 years) had abused others that were in their own age group. However, it is notable that almost 40 per cent of 15-17 year old perpetrators had abused others who were aged under 12 years. This three- to five-year minimum age difference suggests a more abusive-type situation, where developmental and maturity differences may be pronounced. The level or type of sexual abuse perpetrated was also examined (Table 4.13).

*Table 4.13: Juvenile Perpetrator Age Category with
Corresponding Type of Abuse Perpetrated*

Type of Child Abuse Perpetrated	Perpetrator Age Group			
	4 –11 years % (n)	12-14 years % (n)	15-17 years % (n)	Total % (n)
Non-contact	52.2 (12)	35.2 (19)	23.2 (25)	30.3 (56)
Contact	39.1 (9)	50.0 (27)	63.0 (68)	56.2 (104)
Penetrative	8.7 (2)	14.8 (8)	13.9 (15)	13.5 (25)
Total	100 (22)	100 (54)	100 (110)	100 (185)

Over all the age groups, juvenile perpetrators were more likely to engage in contact abuse than other types of abuse (56 per cent); however, quite serious forms of abuse (penetrative) were also perpetrated (13 per cent). When examined by age of perpetrator, the youngest (aged 4–11) had the lowest proportion of contact and penetrative abuse (39 per cent and 9 per cent, respectively). However, there was no significant difference between the 12–14 and 15–17 age groups in the breakdown of types of abuse; approximately 60 per cent was contact and 14 per cent was penetrative. The relationship of the juvenile perpetrator to the abused was also examined, and the results indicated that 20 per cent of them perpetrated against someone within their own family network, with no differences by age group. A synthesis of two surveys of confirmed child sexual abuse in Ireland (reported to health boards or other authorities) found 21 per cent of perpetrators were juveniles aged 15 years or younger. An additional 16 per cent were between ages 16 and 20 (O'Reilly and Carr, 1999). The proportion of abusers of children who were themselves juvenile is a particular concern as it mirrors findings elsewhere. For instance, the recent national guidelines on Child Protection and Welfare estimate juvenile or "teen" perpetrators constitute one-third of child sexual abuse. Detailed discussion of the management of juvenile perpetrators is beyond the scope of this report. Irish writers such as Olive Travers have addressed means of dealing with juvenile offenders which encourage more focus on prevention and rehabilitation (Travers, 1998).

Other Context Factors Associated with Child Sexual Abuse

In order to gain a better understanding of the context and situational factors surrounding child sexual abuse, participants were asked a series of questions regarding the abuse they reported. Prior to asking these questions, the interviewer explained and assured the participant that "the abuser is always responsible for what has happened". Participants then had a list of factors read to them and asked if they thought any of the factors could be associated with their abuse. Because these questions are quite sensitive, interviewers were instructed to use their discretion in determining how much information about the experience they should try to elicit from the participant. Tables 4.14 and 4.15 list some of the main contextual and situational variables that were reported by those participants who indicated that they had experienced child sexual abuse. Figures shown in the tables represent each factor as a proportion of all those abused, e.g. percentage of overall group who reported "being left alone" was a factor. These figures should be interpreted with caution, as not all participants were willing to speak about the factors surrounding their experience.

Table 4.14: Location of Child Sexual Abuse by Men and Women Reporting Abuse

Location of Abuse	Men % (n)	Women % (n)
In participant's home at the time	13.9 (39)	29.1 (113)
In abuser's home	19.3 (54)	24.2 (94)
Private residence; garden (outdoors)	0.4 (1)	1.5 (6)
Public place, outdoors	32.1 (90)	30.4 (118)
School/college	15.7 (44)	2.1 (8)
Work setting	5.7 (16)	3.9 (15)
Car	4.6 (13)	0.3 (1)
Car park	0.4 (1)	1.0 (4)
Hotel	0.0 (0)	6.4 (25)

Almost a third of cases of childhood abuse reported by participants occurred outdoors or in a public place. Women were more likely to experience abuse in childhood in their own homes (29.1 per cent) than in the homes of their abuser (24.2 per cent). Conversely, men were more likely to report having been abused in their abuser's home (19.3 per cent) than in their own (13.9 per cent). Boys were eight times more likely than girls to experience abuse at school. On the other hand, 25 girls had experienced abuse in a hotel, whereas no men reported the same.

Table 4.15: Context of Unwanted Sexual Experiences for those Abused as Children

Situation/Context	Men % (n)	Women % (n)
Items prompted by the interviewer		
Being left alone	27.1 (76)	40.2 (156)
Away from home	10.7 (30)	6.4 (25)
Alcohol was involved:		
Only participant drinking	0.8 (2)	0.5 (2)
Only perpetrator drinking	6.0 (17)	8.0 (31)
Both drinking	3.6 (10)	1.3 (5)
Having lessons/tutoring	2.9 (8)	1.3 (5)
Babysitting	0.4 (1)	2.6 (10)
On holidays	1.4 (4)	1.0 (4)
Items raised spontaneously by participants		
Hitch-hiking*	1.4 (4)	0.3 (1)
Taking a lift* (i.e. in a car)	1.1 (3)	1.0 (4)
Sharing a bed or bedroom*	2.5 (7)	0.5 (2)
In hospital*	1.1 (3)	0.3 (1)
Sexual experimentation*	3.2 (9)	1.5 (6)

Note: For both the location of abuse and the context of abuse, participants could have indicated that episodes of abuse happened in more than one place, thus percentages sum to more than 100 per cent.

Participants were given a list of situational variables and asked if they felt that they had any bearing on their experience of abuse as a child (Table 4.15). Over a third of participants felt that the fact that they were alone made them more vulnerable to abuse. The fact that their abuser was drinking was also seen to be a prominent factor of the abuse for 6 per cent of men and 8 per cent of women. Despite being directly asked, very few participants reported experiencing abuse at a party (n = 3), on a date (n = 1) or in a situation where drugs were being used (n = 3). Several situations were raised spontaneously by participants, including sexual experimentation (cited by 3.2 per cent of men and 1.5 per cent of women) and hitch-hiking (1.4 per cent of men and 0.3 per cent of women).

Participants were also asked to describe what their abusers did to gain compliance in the context of abuse (Table 4.16).

Table 4.16: Actions by Perpetrators to Control Children they Abused

Controlling Strategies	Abused as Children	
	Men % (n)	*Women % (n)*
Physical force	10.6 (30)	17.4 (67)
Bribery	16.0 (45)	17.6 (68)
Specific threats	6.2 (17)	7.6 (29)
Other pressure	13.2 (36)	10.8 (41)

Bribery was reported most often as being the controlling strategy used in an abusive situation. Methods of bribery included offering sweets, money, cigarettes or treats. One woman recalled an incident when she was eight when a workman in his forties asked her to touch him while offering her sweets and telling her that he had chosen her "because she was special". Most participants who reported bribery felt that it was a means of perpetuating abuse. More women than men reported experiencing physical force during an experience of abuse in childhood (17.4 per cent compared to 10.6 per cent). The extent of this force ranged from being pinned down, to being bitten, slapped and thumped.

Participants were asked if they had experienced any physical injuries or other physical health-related consequences as a result of abuse. Only 13 men and 16 women reported having sustained physical injuries due to abuse. Of these, three needed first aid or GP care and a further two needed hospital attention. No participants reported either becoming pregnant or contacting a sexually transmitted disease due to child sexual abuse. Four women, however, did report experiencing gynaecological problems as a result of the abuse.

Of interest was the question of whether or not those who experienced childhood abuse thought that their abuser was perpetrating against other children as well. A third of both men and women abused as children now believed that their abuser was also abusing other children at the time of their abuse (Table 4.17). The potential for children to protect other children, as well as themselves, by being empowered to tell is clear from these figures. Of concern is the fact that 13 people believed their abuser may still be actively abusing other children. Participants were reminded, in a sensitive manner, that this was a very serious concern if it was a possibility. They were encouraged to consider contacting the authorities if they had relevant information and asked if they would like the telephone number of the relevant contact person in their health board area. Three of 13 took the details offered.

Table 4.17: Awareness of Abuse of Others by the Child Abuse Perpetrators

	Answered "Yes"[a]	
	Men % (n)	*Women % (n)*
Belief that other children were being abused at the time?	35.1 (93)	36.7 (136)
Belief that other children are being abused now?	3.8 (10)	0.8 (3)
Willing to take health board number concerning reporting abuse (of those believing abuse may be ongoing)	20.2 (2)	33.0 (1)

[a] In many cases participants felt they could not answer the question. "Yes" percentages were calculated from the overall sample who answered each individual question.

Another context which may be considered as significant when considering the abuse of children is the location in which they were raised. The study asked if participants had been in residential care settings ("in care") during childhood. Thirty-nine people (13 boys and 26 girls, or 1.3 per cent of the whole sample) experienced residential care during childhood. While it is unknown if they were in that care setting at the time of abuse, 53.8 per cent of these reported some type of sexual abuse as children. Considering details of the context of abuse of these individuals, all but one of these cases of abuse happened outside the period of care. The evidence thus suggests that it is quite likely that the sexual abuse experienced by these children was a contributing factor in the decision to place them into residential care rather than a consequence of that care.

Context of Sexual Assault as an Adult (17 years or older)

As with childhood abuse, it was felt that a more detailed description of the pattern of abuse, including the context in which sexual assault occurs in adulthood may be of use in prevention and education efforts (Table 4.18).

While the vast majority of the cases of unwanted sexual experiences were reported as being once-off or single events (80 per cent of women, 76 per cent of men), a smaller, but significant number were reported as occurring more than once with the same perpetrator(s) (20 per cent of women, 24 per cent of men). Some participants reported that the abuse had occurred so many times that they were not able to give an exact number, and were not pushed to do so by the interviewers. Eight per cent of women and almost four per cent of men reported this type of multiple abuse from the same perpetrator. As only a fifth of adults had experienced more than a single episode of sexual assault, only small numbers gave details of the duration of the abuse. Of these participants, almost half of women (46 per cent) and over a third of men experienced abuse over a period of one year or longer (3.1 per cent lasting over 10 years).

Table 4.18: Pattern of Unwanted Sexual Experiences as an Adult Reported by Men and Women

	Men % (n)	Women % (n)
Number of episodes of abuse		
Single experience	75.7 (103)	80.3 (257)
2–3 times	14.7 (20)	5.9 (19)
4–10 times	5.1 (7)	5.0 (16)
More than 10 times	0.7 (1)	0.3 (1)
"Too many to count"[a]	3.7 (5)	8.4 (27)
Duration of Abuse		
One week or less	1.4 (2)	4.1 (4)
2–3 weeks	9.7 (3)	8.2 (1)
One month	11.1 (2)	3.1 (3)
2–3 months	16.7 (2)	6.1 (2)
4–6 months	12.5 (1)	11.2 (5)
7–12 months/ One year	6.9 (0)	9.2 (2)
1–2 years	23.6 (3)	19.4 (2)
3–5 years	13.9 (1)	23.5 (6)
More than 10 years	0 0 (0)	3.1 (3)

[a] Participant indicated that abuse occurred many times and was unable to give an exact number

Two women disclosed abuse that was ongoing at the time of the interview. One participant, an older woman, reported still being abused in her home by a man who was now her ex-partner. This man involved her in a variety of unwanted sexual acts, including intercourse, by using bribery and threats. She reported experiencing a wide range of psychological effects, including diminished self-esteem such that she now works in a menial job despite being professionally qualified. She was in therapy at the time of the survey but had told no one else about her experience of abuse. The second participant who reported ongoing abuse was being abused by her husband for the last 20 years. Her husband uses physical force and has bruised, beaten and raped her. She reported experiencing extensive psychological effects, including an eating disorder. She had told a friend about the abuse almost ten years after it started; she said she took so long to tell because she thought this was not unusual as her mother had also been beaten up by her husband. She had not sought professional help. She was given details for a priority appointment with a counselling service by the interviewer.

Perpetrator characteristics for adult abuse are outlined in Table 4.19 (and Figure 4.13). In the case of both women and men who experienced sexual violence, the abuser was more often known to the abused person than a stranger (70 per cent versus 30 per cent for women and 62 per cent versus 38 per cent for men). Almost one quarter (23.6 per cent) of perpetrators of violence against women as adults were intimate partners or ex-partners. This was the case for very few (1.4 per cent) abused men. Most perpetrators of abuse against men were friends or acquaintances (42 per cent). While most abuse was perpetrated by persons known to adults, the risk of sexual assault by a stranger was greater for adults than for children.

Table 4.19: Perpetrator Characteristics of Unwanted Sexual Experiences as an Adult Reported by Men and Women

	Men % (n)	Women % (n)
Relationship of abuser		
Spouse/Partner	0.7 (1)	4.4 (15)
Boyfriend/Girlfriend	0.0 (0)	16.5 (56)
Friend	21.8 (31)	11.8 (40)
Male relative	0.0 (0)	4.1 (14)
Ex-partner	0.7 (1)	2.7 (9)
Neighbour	4.9 (7)	3.8 (13)
Acquaintance known less than 24 hrs	6.3 (9)	8.9 (30)
Acquaintance known more than 24 hrs	20.4 (29)	15.0 (51)
Co-worker	4.9 (7)	6.8 (23)
Stranger	31.7 (45)	21.2 (72)

Perpetrators of adult sexual abuse are broken down by gender of victim in Figure 4.13.

Figure 4.13: Comparisons of Categories of Perpetrators of Adult Sexual Assault by Gender of Victim

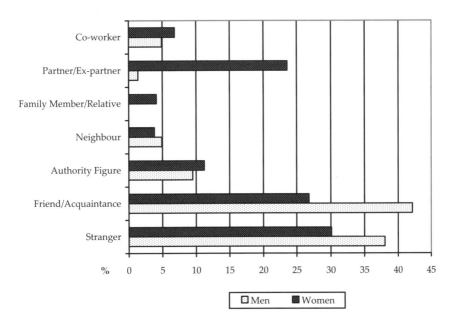

Participants were asked if the perpetrator was also a person in a position of authority over them. For those who were identified as such (Table 4.20), the largest category for women was "boss" (this represented 4.5 per cent of all abusers). For men the abuser was identified as "boss" in 21.4 per cent of cases (2.0 per cent of all abusers). Religious ministers were identified as the abuser in 17.5 per cent of cases for women and 7.1 per cent for men (they represented 2.0 per cent of all abusers of women and 0.7 per cent of men). Five women (i.e. 12.5 per cent of authority figure abusers) were abused by members of the Gardaí.

Table 4.20: Profile of Abusers Identified as Being Authority
Figures for those Reporting Adult Sexual Abuse

Position of Authority[a]	Proportion of Authority Figures		Proportion of All Abusers	
	Men % (n)	Women % (n)	Men % (n)	Women % (n)
Boss	21.4 (3)	40.0 (16)	2.0	4.5
Religious minister	7.1 (1)	17.5 (7)	0.7	2.0
Garda (police)	0.0 (0)	12.5 (5)	0.0	1.4
Doctor	7.1 (1)	0.0 (0)	0.7	0.0
Landlord	7.1 (1)	0.0 (0)	0.7	0.0
Teacher (non-religious)	0.0 (0)	2.5 (1)	0.0	0.2
Other authority figures	57.1 (8)	27.5 (11)	5.4	3.1

[a] Organised from most to least frequently mentioned distinct categories

As in the section regarding child sexual abuse, participants were asked about the contextual and situational factors surrounding the reported sexual abuse. Table 4.21 lists the main factors reported by those who had experienced unwanted adult sexual experiences.

Abuse of adults mostly occurred outdoors. Alcohol was involved for approximately half of all those involved; in one third of cases, both abuser and abused had been drinking. Where only one party was drinking, the perpetrator was the one drinking in the majority of cases (84 per cent of female and 70 per cent of male abuse cases).

Table 4.21: Context of Unwanted Sexual Experiences as an Adult Reported by Men and Women

	Men % (n)	Women % (n)
Location of abuse		
Your home	5.1 (7)	20.2 (67)
Their home	16.1 (22)	14.2 (47)
Garden	0.0 (0)	0.3 (1)
Public place/outdoors	24.1 (33)	23.9 (79)
School/college	3.7 (5)	0.3 (1)
Work setting	7.3 (10)	7.3 (24)
Car/car park	11.7 (16)	11.8 (39)
Hotel	6.6 (9)	1.2 (4)
Context or situation		
Relationship was breaking up	2.2 (3)	3.9 (13)
On holidays	2.2 (3)	2.4 (8)
Hitch-hiking	2.9 (4)	0.6 (2)
Taking a lift (i.e. in a car)	0 (0)	0.6 (2)
At a party	7.3 (10)	9.4 (31)
On a date	1.4 (2)	6.0 (20)
In a disco/pub/ nightclub	2.2 (3)	1.2 (4)
Alcohol was involved (total)	52.6 (72)	45.3 (150)
Only participant drinking	5.8 (8)	3.0 (10)
Only perpetrator drinking	13.9 (19)	16.3 (54)
Both	32.8 (45)	26.0 (86)
Drugs		
Only participant using	1.4 (2)	0.9 (3)
Only abuser using	0 (0)	1.8 (6)
Both	2.9 (4)	0.6 (2)

Ireland does not appear to differ in these statistics from those provided in other national studies which have clearly documented alcohol involvement in cases of sexual violence. Greenfeld (1998), in an analysis of crime statistics from a variety of sources in the US, found that in over a third of the cases of rape or sexual assault (of persons over the age of 12), the perpetrator was reported to have been using alcohol at the time. In another analysis of US crime statistics, this time using the 1992–1994 National Crime Victimisation Survey, Brecklin and Ullman (2001) found 60.9 per cent reported that their perpetrator used either alcohol or drugs at the time of the offence. They found that alcohol use just prior to the assault was associated with assault by a stranger, as was being in riskier situations (e.g., at night, outdoors). Other studies have explored the role that alcohol may play in increasing the risk of assault. Ullman, Karabatsos and Koss (1999) examined data from a national sample of college women and results suggested that "a drunk or drinking victim may be targeted by the offender who sees an opportunity to commit sexual assault without engaging in other coercive behaviours" (p. 620). Alcohol may also contribute to sexual violence through multiple pathways, including effects on cognitive and motor skills, beliefs about its effects on sexual behaviour and aggression and stereotypes about those who drink (Abbey et al., 2001). While it is clear that the victim is not to blame in these situations, prevention programmes need to "incorporate information about the associations of alcohol use, situational factors, and rape outcomes" (Brecklin and Ullman, 2001, p. 19).

Comparisons of SAVI Prevalence and Perpetrator Findings with Other Studies

The only large-scale survey data in Ireland with which to compare the SAVI survey data was conducted in 1993 by Irish Marketing Surveys, on behalf of ISPCC. A brief pencil-and-paper questionnaire on experiences of child sexual abuse was completed by 1,001 adults. Results of this survey indicated that 15 per cent of women and 9 per cent of men reported contact sexual abuse in childhood. Contact abuse occurred once in 39 per cent of cases, twice in 47 per cent and more often in 14 per cent. They estimated, based on these figures, that one in seven Irish women and one in ten men had experienced contact sexual abuse during childhood. In 1993, that constituted approximately 288,000 adults. The SAVI figures indicated a higher prevalence (20 per cent) contact abuse for girls versus 15 per cent and 16 per cent contact abuse for boys versus 9 per cent. This is not surprising considering the different method-ologies used. Participants in the SAVI survey were asked an ex-tensive range of questions in a completely anonymous (telephone survey) setting while those in the ISPCC study completed a brief questionnaire and returned it (albeit in a sealed envelope) to an interviewer. Both differences (level of contact and numbers of questions) increase the likelihood of reporting in SAVI. It is internationally accepted that more extensive survey formats provide greater opportunities for people to reveal private and distressing aspects of their lives.

In terms of the context of abuse, the ISPCC data revealed that most perpetrators were aged 16 or above (86 per cent). A third of those reporting contact abuse said the abuser was related to them. No fathers were reported with 1 per cent of abusers reported to be stepfathers. Most commonly cited abusing relatives were brother/ brother-in-law (9 per cent), uncle (9 per cent) and cousin (9 per cent). Most commonly cited non-relatives were neighbours (27 per cent), male strangers (20 per cent), schoolmate/student (6 per cent), friend of parent (6 per cent) and religious teacher (4 per cent). Non-religious teachers were reported as abusers in one per cent of cases. The participants reported that the abuse usually stopped because as a child they avoided the abuser (49 per cent), con-fronted them (13 per cent), told an older person (7 per cent) or left home (4 per cent). In some situations the abuser "just stopped" (17 per cent) or moved on to another person (12 per cent). Two per cent of those abused continued to experience abuse after age 16.

The SAVI data presented so far also allows considerable com-parison with similar international studies. Comparisons with other studies were somewhat easier to make for child sexual abuse. Table 4.22 outlines comparisons with US and UK data. The US study is a national telephone study of 4,023 adolescents (aged 12–17 and conducted in their homes following parental consent). It assessed levels of child sexual abuse (Kilpatrick and Saunders, 1997). The UK study was a large student sample (n = 1,224) of those

aged 16–25 and asked about sexual abuse (by self-report questionnaire) up to age 18 (Kelly, Regan and Burton, 1991). Since SAVI
participants are adults of every age and, by study definitions, are
all already at age 18 and describing abuse before age 17, there are
some difficulties in comparisons. The US study had adolescents
(aged 12–17) reporting abuse at a time when many have not "completed" the period of age risk they describe (to age 18). The UK
study also has some overlap; the youngest students have not yet
reached age 18 years — the cut-off point about which they are reporting. Thus, the following comparisons are made with caution.

*Table 4.22: Comparisons of International Child Abuse
Prevalence Rates with SAVI Findings*

	Abuse of Boys		Abuse of Girls	
Type of Abuse	*SAVI* %	*Other* *Country* %	*SAVI* %	*Other* *Country* %
US Study (1997)				
Any sexual assault *	13.5	3.4	14.8	13.0
Penile penetration	3.0	0.5	2.0	3.3
Object/finger penetration	0.6	0.6	4.4	2.7
All penetration	2.7	1.1	5.6	6.0
UK Study (1991)				
Any contact abuse	16.2	20.4	20.4	27.0
Force/Rape	2.7	4.4	5.6	5.1

* Contact abuse and attempted penetration and oral sex excluding penile and
object/digital penetration

A total of 8.1 per cent of the US sample reported at least one sexual assault prior to the interviews with 42 per cent of the group
reporting more than one experience. About a third (20 per cent)
reported being abused before age 11 years with just over one-
third (36 per cent) identifying strangers as the perpetrators. Next
most common was friends (20 per cent) with fewer family members mentioned. These figures, and those in Table 4.3, portray

quite different experiences for Irish adults who have been sexually abused as children and contemporary American adolescent experiences as children. Most notable is the higher level of overall sexual assault noted in the Irish male sample. Levels of very serious sexual abuse (penetration) were similar for girls in the Irish and US groups with less penetrative abuse of boys in the US group.

Although both studies were similar in the use of telephone surveys, the US male group was interviewed in young adulthood. This important difference should be considered in the context of some other important methodological differences when comparing these data. Firstly, the US study was as reported by adolescents, speaking by telephone from their own homes and with parental permission. Selection biases in which parents allowed access and the willingness of teenagers to disclose sensitive or embarrassing information on the telephone in the family home may have prevented the reporting of some episodes. Secondly, adolescents may not construe or remember cases of abuse at the time but may define these as abuse later in life. They may also be less able, in terms of emotional maturity or considerations about social identity, to report such experiences while they are still adolescents. These matters may be particularly salient for adolescent boys. Furthermore, apart from embarrassment, some children may have been in abusive home situations where they were unable for fear of their own safety to report abuse. In the SAVI Survey, the aim was that interviews with adults were conducted in such a way that others in the household were not told the nature of the survey by the researchers and that the participant was alone when taking the interview call.

Finally, the US group were reporting on a childhood lived in the 1980s and 1990s, while the childhood of the SAVI participants span most of the twentieth century. If, as Finkelhor (1998) suggested, and the SAVI data support, there is a possibility of a real reduction in the overall incidence of child sexual abuse in the latter decades of the twentieth century, differences across groups in rates, particularly in rates of less serious forms of contact abuse, can explain differences in the findings of the two studies. Such speculation is made cautiously given the complexity of the data under discussion.

Prevalence rates in the UK, with a somewhat older target sample, appear to some extent higher than SAVI data with the exception of force and rape of girls. It is not clear what effects student status and report format (telephone versus self-report) had on disclosure rates. Regarding adult sexual violence, the role of intimate partners in abuse affecting women in SAVI is replicated in many international studies. Equally, the absence of this group as a risk to men in the SAVI study is replicated elsewhere. A US study of 16,000 randomly selected adults found prevalence rates of attempted or completed penetrative abuse to be 7.7 per cent for women and 0.3 per cent for men (Tjaden and Thoennes, 2000). Using a wider definition of sexual abuse, a random sample of Norwegian women reported prevalence rates of 10 per cent for violent sexual abuse and an additional 7 per cent for non-violent abuse (Schei, 1990). Similar figures were found in a New Zealand study (Mullen, Romans-Clarkson, Walton and Herbison, 1988). In the broadest summary of comparisons, there is certainly little comfort in Irish figures on child sexual abuse relative to these other countries.

PSYCHOLOGICAL CONSEQUENCES OF SEXUAL VIOLENCE

As discussed earlier, a limited number of questions pertaining to psychological consequences were asked of participants who reported any form of sexual abuse. The focus was on post-traumatic stress disorder (PTSD) as one of the hallmark disorders of serious sexual abuse. Post-traumatic disorder was selected for study as there is already a considerable literature on the subject, though most of it derives from clinical settings rather than population studies. Post-traumatic stress disorder has well-defined diagnostic criteria which are easier to elicit than those of many other psychiatric disorders as sufferers usually have considerable insight into their condition and its causes. The symptoms involve re-experiencing the traumatic event (as thoughts, memories or dreams), persistently avoiding situations which are associated with the trauma, and a numbing of general responsiveness (impaired relationships with people, for instance, or loss of interest in activities), and persistent symptoms of increased arousal (easily startled, irritable, etc.).

Strictly speaking, PTSD requires exposure to some threat to life or physical integrity, and so it is possible that, for instance, experiences reported such as indecent exposure might not qualify (though sexual assault is specifically mentioned in the diagnostic guide). However, it might also be argued that if an event brings about the characteristic psychological reactions which constitute PTSD, the threat involved in the situation must have been traumatic, whether it constituted a physical danger or not. In strict psychiatric terms, a psychological reaction to an event which is not life-threatening is called an adjustment disorder. Likewise, if a person is exposed to a life-threatening event, but their reaction does not meet the full criteria PTSD, they would strictly be classified as adjustment disorder also. In this report, we are adopting a simpler approach: all those who report the symptoms of PTSD as a result of an adverse sexual experience are classified as having PTSD, regardless of the physical threat inherent in the experience, and all those who partially met the criteria for post-traumatic stress were classed as "sub-syndromal" post-traumatic stress disorder.

It is easier to link PTSD with sexual experiences than it is to link problems such as depression or anxiety, since the criteria demand that symptoms are linked specifically to the threatening experience.

Because psychological consequences can have a cumulative or compounding effect for people who experience more than one episode of sexual abuse or assault during their lifetime, participants who had multiple experiences were not asked to differentiate between the events in terms of consequences. For example, someone who experiences PTSD as the result of child sexual abuse, and who is raped later in life as an adult, may well experience more severe symptoms of PTSD after the subsequent abuse. This discrimination was also not made for the questions regarding the participant's uptake of psychological or counselling services. Thus, each participant was asked only one set of questions about any psychological consequences experienced or therapy undertaken, regardless of the number of episodes of sexual abuse that they reported. This has to be borne in mind in the presentation of results, as statistical analysis indicates that some, but not all, of the reported rates of psychological problems in persons who experience adult sexual violence are attributable to their prior experience of childhood sexual violence.

In this study, the PTSD Checklist — Civilian Version (PCL-C) (Andrykowski, 1998) was used to measure the prevalence of PTSD among those who reported any form of sexual abuse. This measure has been used in a telephone methodology previously and is mainly used as a screening measure. The measure consists of 17 items that mirror the criteria specified in the Diagnostic and Statistical Manual, version four, revised edition (DSM-IV-R), and cover Criteria B, C, and D of the diagnosis. Of the remaining criteria, criterion A specifies that there has been exposure to a significant threat. Criterion E specifies that the reaction must last at least a month; this criterion is met by all those who are classified as currently suffering from PTSD, as none had experienced sexual violence less than a month from interview. The only criterion not included, criterion F, specifies that the disorder should result in distress or impairment to the person's function in social, occupational or other important areas of function. Clearly, rating this is beyond the scope of a telephone interview. Despite these limitations, the data provided in this study give some indication as to the possible prevalence of PTSD among those who reported some form of sexual abuse in the broader community.

Participants were asked to indicate if they experienced any of the symptoms listed specifically as a result of the unwanted sexual experience that they reported, in order to ensure that they experienced the symptoms as a result of their experience and not some other trauma. Those individuals who have a specific combination of symptoms from all three categories of criteria are given the designation of meeting the "full" criteria in this study. Individuals who did not meet the full criteria, but met two of three categories of criteria, were described as having "sub-syndromal" PTSD.

A distinction was also made between those who currently reported having PTSD symptoms and those who met the above criteria in the past, but not currently (i.e., symptoms have remitted). They were described here as those with "past PTSD".

Note that the PCL-C as used in this study cannot definitively determine whether or not a participant meets the full DSM-IV-R criteria for PTSD, as Criteria E and F (see above) were not assessed. A full assessment of each participant by a trained professional would be necessary to validate these results. Before participants were asked about specific symptoms related to PTSD that they may have experienced as a result of abuse, a simple question about the overall effect the abuse had had on their life was asked.

Overall Effects

All participants who indicated that they had an unwanted sexual experience, either as an adult or a child, were asked how the experience affected their life "overall", ranging from "not at all" to "extremely" (Table 4.23).

Women were more likely than men to rate the overall effects of their experiences as having affected them "a lot" or "extremely" (19 per cent versus 9 per cent of men). Those who experienced abuse both as a child and as an adult were more likely to say that it affected their lives significantly (26 per cent) as compared to those who experienced their abuse only as a child (11 per cent) or as an adult (14 per cent). As expected, the type of abuse experienced also greatly influenced how much participants rated their experience as having affected their lives. Of those who experienced the most serious form of abuse, penetrative, almost one in ten (39 per cent) said it affected them "a lot" or "extremely".

Table 4.23: Overall Effects of Lifetime Sexual Abuse and Violence

	Overall Rating of Effects of Abuse		
	Not at All/ A Little % (n)	*Moderate Amount* % (n)	*A Lot/ Extremely* % (n)
Gender			
Women	70.5 (379)	10.2 (55)	19.3 (104)
Men	81.9 (249)	9.2 (28)	8.9 (27)
Timing of abuse			
As a child	80.2 (368)	8.5 (39)	11.3 (52)
As an adult	78.2 (111)	7.8 (11)	14.1 (20)
Both as child and adult	60.0 (138)	14.4 (33)	25.6 (59)
Type of abuse			
Non-contact abuse	90.4 (141)	5.1 (8)	4.5 (7)
Contact abuse	82.6 (346)	7.9 (33)	9.6 (40)
Attempted penetration	73.0 (46)	14.3 (9)	12.7 (8)
Penetrative abuse	44.1 (86)	16.9 (33)	39.0 (76)

The fact that 70 per cent of women and 82 per cent of men said their experience affected them only a little or not at all appears to be related to the type of abuse experienced. For instance, 90 per cent of those experiencing non-contact abuse reported little effect. In addition, therapists who work in this area say that those who have undergone any kind of therapy are more likely to report more effects as they become aware of more aspects of their lives that have been influenced by their experiences. Alternatively, many actively try to deny or minimise the impact on their lives as a coping strategy: "It must not have impacted on my life because I have successfully married, have a good job, family, etc."

The previous Irish ISPCC survey (Irish Marketing Surveys, 1993) also considered people's perceptions of the impact of abuse on them. In terms of their perceptions, 35 per cent of those experiencing contact abuse felt it had no real effect, 25 per cent reported being upset but getting over it quickly, 19 per cent reported effects that lasted a long time but have now been resolved and 21 per cent reported lasting effects. Interestingly, effects were quite similar for those experiencing non-contact abuse with, for instance, 16 per cent reporting a lasting effect on them. The findings of the two studies were quite similar.

Post-traumatic Stress Disorder (PTSD)

The percentage of participants who reported experiencing symptoms of PTSD as measured by the PCL-C (and as defined above) are given in Table 4.24. This table also examines PTSD by gender, the timing of the abuse, the type of abuse and the time elapsed since the abuse occurred.

Past PTSD

Of the women who answered the questions about PTSD (n = 556), approximately 14 per cent reported a number of symptoms which would have met the criteria of full PTSD at some point in their lifetime but not currently. An additional 11 per cent met the criteria for sub-syndromal PTSD, yielding a total of 138 women (25 per cent) who have experienced a significant number of symptoms. Sixteen per cent of men who had been abused reported similar PTSD in the past.

Current PTSD

Almost six per cent of women and three per cent of men reported a cluster of symptoms that met the full criteria for current PTSD. An additional 11 per cent of women and six per cent of men met sub-syndromal criteria. While a large number of participants did not meet either category of PTSD, this was not very surprising given the fact that research indicates that in half the cases of PTSD, symptoms remit, with complete recovery within three months.

Table 4.24: The Presence of Post-traumatic Stress Disorder (PTSD) in the Past or Currently by Various Dimensions of those Abused as Children or Adults

	Past PTSD		Current PTSD	
	Full Criteria % (n)	*Sub-syndromal % (n)*	*Full Criteria % (n)*	*Sub-syndromal % (n)*
Gender				
Women	13.7 (76)	11.2 (62)	5.8 (32)	11.2 (62)
Men	7.4 (23)	9.0 (28)	3.2 (10)	6.4 (20)
Timing of abuse				
As a child	8.1 (38)	9.2 (43)	2.3 (13)	7.9 (37)
As an adult	8.0 (12)	11.3 (17)	2.7 (4)	8.7 (13)
Both as child and adult	20.6 (49)	12.2 (29)	10.5 (25)	13.0 (31)
Type of abuse				
Non-contact abuse	2.5 (4)	5.0 (8)	0.0 (0)	1.2 (2)
Contact abuse	6.3 (27)	10.5 (45)	2.1 (9)	8.1 (35)
Attempted penetration	14.7 (10)	11.7 (8)	2.9 (2)	13.2 (9)
Penetrative abuse	29.0 (58)	14.5 (29)	15.5 (31)	17.5 (35)
Time elapsed since abuse				
Less than 1 year	12.5 (1)	12.5 (1)	0.0 (0)	12.5 (1)
1-2 years	25.0 (10)	12.5 (5)	10.0 (4)	12.5 (5)
3-5 years	13.2 (5)	10.5 (4)	5.3 (2)	10.5 (4)
6-10 years	14.3 (5)	14.3 (5)	2.9 (1)	8.6 (3)
11-20 years	11.3 (17)	12.6 (19)	4.6 (7)	13.3 (20)
More than 20 years	10.1 (60)	9.3 (55)	4.6 (27)	8.3 (49)

Factors which predicted the occurrence of PTSD, both in the aftermath of the event and subsequently, were examined. In both cases, the severity of PTSD (none, sub-syndromal or full) was related to the severity of the sexual abuse, with a markedly higher risk in those who experienced penetrative abuse, in childhood or adulthood. The severity of PTSD also decreased with the time elapsed since the sexual violence: for penetrative child abuse, for example, this decrease corresponded to a predicted prevalence of full or sub-syndromal disorder in 54 per cent of the women who had reported PTSD and 39 per cent of the men at five years after the event. This declined to a 43 per cent and 29 per cent risk 25 years after the event. It must be stressed that these are extrapolations, and that the prevalence of PTSD was much lower for non-penetrative forms of abuse. Nonetheless, the figures underline the long-lasting after-effects of sexual violence. Men were significantly less likely to report PTSD than women at comparable levels of abuse. Men who had recently experienced contact sexual violence were as likely to suffer from post-traumatic stress disorder as women, but the risk fell more sharply with time since the event.

Figure 4.14 shows the predicted risk of current PTSD (either full or sub-syndromal) as a function of the time that has passed since the incident and the type of sexual violence — child or adult. In each case, sexual violence was defined as contact violence, including rape. The predicted risk is for those who experience childhood sexual violence alone or adult sexual violence alone. Predicted risk was higher in persons who were victimised as both children and as adults, but it was not possible to calculate a single measure of "time since event". Psychosocial effects other than PTSD are discussed later in the chapter.

Comparisons were also made with the extent of abuse experienced. As expected, those with less serious forms of abuse were less likely to meet the criteria for PTSD. Again, if examined critically, it is quite possible that many participants would not have met the very first criteria of PTSD, that is, that there is a threat to the physical integrity of the individual and feelings of intense fear, hopelessness or horror. For example, it seems much less likely that a participant who only experienced someone exposing

themselves (and nothing else) would meet this first criteria, as this experience does not involve risk to physical integrity.

Figure 4.14: Risk of Experiencing PTSD by Time and Type of Abuse

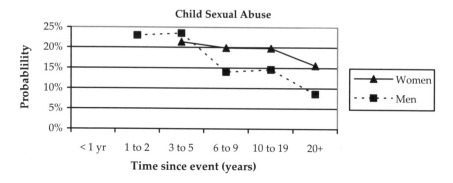

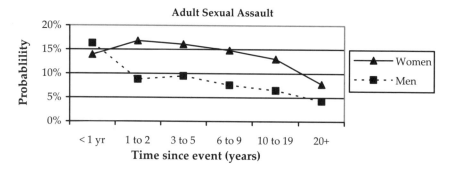

PTSD as a Consequence of Incest

Persons experiencing incest in childhood were more likely to meet full or partial criteria for PTSD. Even adjusting for the severity of the abuse, risk of PTSD for those experiencing incest are at minimal double that of similar acts of sexual violence perpetrated by non-family abusers. The predicted risk at ten years from the time of abuse is presented in Table 4.25.

Table 4.25: Predicted Level of PTSD at Ten Years for those
Experiencing Various Types of Abuse (% PTSD)

PTSD Prevalence in:	Women		Men	
	Contact	*Penetrative*	*Contact*	*Penetrative*
Incest	45%	71%	33%	60%
Other forms of abuse	19%	42%	13%	31%

Overall, for each category of abuse, the presence of incest roughly doubles the risk of experiencing post-traumatic stress disorder.

Comparisons with other Research on PTSD

Kilpatrick and Saunders (1997) reported that almost 30 per cent of US adolescents who were sexually abused had at some point experienced PTSD with almost 20 per cent still experiencing PTSD symptoms when interviewed. These figures were set against a level of PTSD in non-abused adolescents of 6.2 per cent (ever experienced it) and 3.6 per cent (still experiencing it). The SAVI figures are somewhat lower than these but reflect PTSD levels of those abused both as adults and children.

Other Psychological Effects

Since PTSD symptoms are only one type of many possible outcomes from sexually abusive situations, participants were also asked in an open-ended format if they experienced any other after-effects of their experiences. A total of 190 people took the opportunity to share other consequences of their experiences. A content analysis of their responses was conducted. Four main themes were identified: effects on their personal identity; effects on their interpersonal relationships; other symptoms of mental health difficulties; and effects on their knowledge or awareness of sexual abuse issues. An outline of these effects by gender and timing of abuse is presented in Table 4.26.

Table 4.26: Spontaneously Reported Psychosocial After-effects of Sexually Abusive Situations

	Gender		Timing of Abuse		
	Men	*Women*	*As a Child*	*As an Adult*	*Both as Child and Adult*
	% (n)	% (n)	% (n)	% (n)	% (n)
Effects on personal identity					
Self-esteem	4.7 (3)	11.9 (16)	2.4 (8)	0.9 (1)	5.7 (10)
Blames self/guilt	4.7 (3)	5.9 (8)	1.8 (6)	2.8 (3)	1.1 (2)
Effect on interpersonal relationships					
Trust issues	6.3 (4)	18.5 (25)	4.1 (14)	2.8 (3)	6.3 (11)
Relationship difficulties	9.4 (6)	12.6 (17)	2.9 (10)	2.8 (3)	5.7 (10)
Difficulties with sexuality	15.6 (10)	10.4 (14)	3.2 (11)	4.7 (5)	4.6 (8)
Mental health difficulties					
Depression/ withdrawal	3.1 (2)	7.4 (10)	1.1 (4)	1.9 (2)	3.4 (6)
Avoidance behaviours	3.1 (2)	3.7 (5)	1.1 (4)	0 (0)	1.7 (3)
Anxiety/ Hyper-vigilance	31.3 (20)	38.5 (52)	14.4 (49)	11.3 (12)	5.1 (9)
Somatic symptoms	3.1 (2)	5.2 (7)	0.9 (3)	1.9 (2)	2.3 (4)
Residual fear/ wanting revenge	4.7 (3)	7.4 (10)	1.8 (6)	1.9 (2)	2.9 (5)
Alcohol/drug problems	6.3 (4)	4.4 (6)	1.1 (4)	0 (0)	3.4 (6)
Awareness or knowledge					
Effects on parenting style	21.9 (14)	12.6 (17)	6.8 (23)	0.9 (1)	3.4 (6)
Sensitivity to issues/awareness	25.0 (16)	9.6 (13)	3.8 (13)	6.6 (7)	5.1 (9)
Learning experience	17.2 (11)	5.2 (7)	2.6 (9)	4.7 (5)	2.3 (4)

Some of the qualitative accounts of these experiences are provided below.

Effects on Personal Identity

Examples of statements that participants gave in this category include:

> "I was just a very nervous child. I just switched off . . . blanked everything . . . made light of everything. I had a very poor self-image — worthless."

> "I dress differently — completely covering my body with long clothes now and have always done so . . . unaware until now the reason why."

One man admitted that he was still angry with himself for not disclosing because he felt that other children were abused after him by the same perpetrator.

Effects on Interpersonal Relationships

Participants cited various effects on their interpersonal relationships. One woman thought that it made her sexually aware at a very young age and that had further consequences for her when she was older — that she "knew too much". A male participant said he "doesn't like to be too huggy with the guys; doesn't like to be physical with men". One woman said she lost friends because she withdrew so much into herself. Another said:

> "Subconsciously it may have affected me . . . (I) reacted to people later on without being fully aware of those reactions."

Intimate relationships seemed to be particularly affected:

> "It took a long time for me to have any sex with (my) husband, or become more intimate."

Another said:

"My husband completely rejected me . . . blamed me to the point where he insisted on separate sleeping quarters."

A young woman explained that she wants to "get over it". She wants another relationship, but is "terrified to go out on dates".

Mental Health Difficulties

Again, there was much variation in this category. One participant said they could not swallow food and had stomach problems. Another described panic attacks and stress which he believed was "not warranted" for situations in which he experienced it. One participant said that after the rape, they abused alcohol "to get away from it". Lastly, one woman described how it:

"Affects everything you do, your whole life. . . . (I'm) angry and depressed . . . betrayed, let down, cheated, deprived . . . just about everything."

Increased Awareness or Knowledge

A small number of participants felt that they had learned, or even gained from the experience. One man said that as a result of his experience, he talks to his children about potential dangers. Another man said it made him "more aware of his instincts — (he) gets out of situations which make him feel uncomfortable". One participant said that for her, it "made me grow up and take control". This is consistent with some recent literature which finds that most people find some degree of positive change or personal growth as a consequence of sexual violence (Frazier, Conlon and Glazer, 2001).

Mental Health and General Well-being Indices

While not providing a detailed comparison of mental health issues for those who had or had not experienced sexual abuse over their lifetime, a number of brief checks of well-being differences were made. A general quality of life assessment, scores on a mental health inventory, and proportions of those using psychiatric medications or hospital services in the past were assessed.

Regarding quality of life, a single summary question was asked, "In general, how would you rate your quality of life?" There was a significant relationship between previous abuse experience and current quality of life (Table 4.27).

Table 4.27: Mental Health Indices by Experience and Level of Abuse

	Type of Abuse			
	No Abuse	*Non-contact Abuse*	*Contact Abuse*	*Attempted or Actual Penetrative Abuse*
General quality of life (Mean, SD)[a]	4.4 (1.5)	4.5 (1.5)	4.4 (1.6)	4.1 (1.6)
Mental health (MHI-5)[b] (Mean, SD)	16.3 (2.8)	15.7 (2.9)	15.3 (3.2)	14.7 (3.6)
Ever received medication for anxiety (%)	7.1	11.9	13.2	36.8
Ever received medication for depression (%)	8.9	13.5	15.7	49.8
Ever been a psychiatric hospital inpatient (%)	2.2	4.6	5.4	16.9

[a] Scores range from 1–5; 1 = very poor to 5 = very good

[b] higher scores = better psychological functioning

All participants were asked about their mental health over the last month using an abbreviated form of the Rand Mental Health Inventory (MHI-5). This consists of five items rated on a six-point scale, ranging from "none of the time" to "all of the time" (scores range from 0–30). The MHI-5 is a general measure of well-being and serves as an indicator of a wide range of psychological distress. The MHI-5 score profile is also outlined in Table 4.27 (higher scores indicate better psychological functioning). Self-rated general quality of life was lower in women than men, and declined with age. Given that, only one group of victims of sexual abuse emerged with significantly lower self-rated quality of life: those who had experienced penetrative sexual violence. MHI-5 scores were lower for all those who had experienced sexual violence, with a graded effect visible: the more serious the violence the person had experienced, the poorer their score. This was especially true for those who experienced incest. This effect was independent of the participant's sex and age.

Likelihood of having received a prescription medication for anxiety was higher in women and increased with age. Adjusted for age, there was an increased risk in all categories of sexual abuse except non-contact adult sexual assault. Likewise, likelihood of having had an antidepressant prescribed was higher in women and rose with age. Adjusted for age, there was an increased risk associated with contact and penetrative abuse, both in childhood and adulthood. Finally, likelihood of admission to a psychiatric hospital or unit was associated with contact sexual violence, both in childhood and adulthood.

DISCLOSURE OF SEXUAL VIOLENCE TO OTHERS

Of all the participants who were sexually abused as children, 41.2 per cent had never told anyone about this abuse. Of all who were sexually assaulted as an adult, just over a third (34.2 per cent) had never before disclosed the abuse. Overall, 57 per cent of men and 42 per cent of women did not tell anyone about their experience(s) of sexual violence before the SAVI interview. The type of abuse experienced and the first person who was told about the experience is summarised in Figure 4.15.

Figure 4.15: First Disclosure of Child Sexual Abuse or Adult Sexual Assault by Gender and Person Told

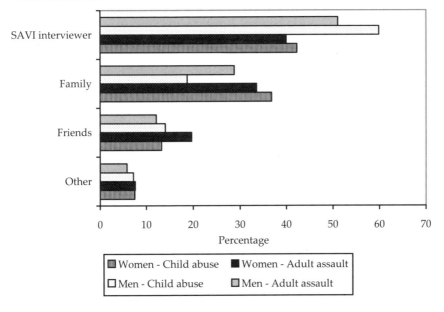

The most remarkable finding from questions on disclosure was that almost half of all instances of abuse (47 per cent) had not been told to another person before the survey, i.e., over 500 cases of abuse in a sample of just over 3,000 people had never been spoken of publicly before. The finding is both shocking and humbling. It is shocking in that for every six persons spoken to in the general public there was an average of one disclosed and one undisclosed instance of abuse. It is also humbling and reassuring that many people felt willing and able to report abuse in the context of an anonymous survey. As discussed elsewhere, all were offered contact details of services where relevant and a sizeable minority accepted details concerning specific clinical services. When asked why they had decided to share their previously undisclosed experience of abuse, the majority of participants said that it was because they were asked and wanted to help with the survey. As one participant said, "no one ever asked before and it has been on my mind a long time". Another participant explained that she was "tired of abuse in Ireland being hidden".

Levels of non-disclosure were somewhat higher for child sexual abuse (49.6 per cent versus 43.2 per cent). Thus, one in two cases of child sexual abuse reported to the interviewers had never been previously described to others. The results also showed lower levels of disclosure by men for both child and adult forms of sexual violence.

Of those who previously disclosed abuse to others, over half (of both children and adults) first told an immediate family member with over a quarter telling friends. Few participants chose a professional as the focus of their initial disclosure. Fifteen per cent of men and 25 per cent of women reported having to tell more than one person before they found someone to help them following an experience of child sexual abuse. Similarly, 26 per cent of men and 22 per cent of women who were abused as adults needed to tell more than one person before they got help.

Because the high level of non-disclosure may have serious implications for service provision, a more detailed analysis of the data was undertaken. The next table (Table 4.28) depicts levels of disclosure by present age of participant. With the exception of men reporting adult abuse (who had a varied pattern), older people were less likely to disclose abuse in general. The greatest age and gender contrast was between young men and women, with women approximately twice as likely to disclose both child and adult abuse. Over 60 per cent of young adult men who had been abused had told no one about their experiences.

Because disclosure may be related to the severity of abuse experienced, this possible relationship was examined more closely (Table 4.29). In this table, the percentages reflect the numbers of women and men who *did tell* at least one other person about their abuse.

The level or extent of abuse does not appear to have an effect on whether or not the participants ever disclosed their experience to someone else. One exception to this, however, is that men who had experienced attempted penetration as adults were less likely

(25 per cent as compared to approximately 50 per cent of all other categories) to tell about their experience.

Table 4.28: Non-disclosure of Sexual Violence by Gender and Present Age

Never Disclosed Abuse	Present Age			
	18-29 *% (n)*	*30-49* *% (n)*	*50-69* *% (n)*	*70 +* *% (n)*
Child abuse				
Men	55.3 (26)	52.9 (74)	71.2 (57)	82.4 (14)
Women	22.4 (11)	38.1 (84)	55.1 (65)	59.1 (13)
Adult abuse				
Men	61.5 (16)	40.0 (26)	62.2 (23)	54.5 (6)
Women	35.1 (20)	34.4 (56)	48.5 (47)	69.2 (9)

Table 4.29: Disclosure (whether the participant ever told anyone about the abuse) by Type of Abuse

Type of Abuse	Child Abuse		Adult Assault	
	Men *% (n)*	*Women* *% (n)*	*Men* *% (n)*	*Women* *% (n)*
Abuse — not otherwise specified	n/a	n/a	52 (41)	66 (81)
Child pornography	19 (40)	25 (12)	n/a	n/a
Indecent exposure	46 (70)	62 (146)	n/a	n/a
Contact abuse	40 (181)	57 (203)	47 (124)	58 (206)
Attempted penetration	43 (22)	64 (32)	25 (9)	62 (20)
Penetration/Oral sex	43 (40)	56 (89)	67 (13)	58 (97)

For those who had never disclosed abuse, the reasons chosen not to do so were of interest, as they may yield information useful for public education and awareness programmes. Reasons spontaneously given by the participants are outlined in Figures 4.16 (childhood) and 4.17 (adulthood). Note that participants could give more than one reason why they did not ever disclose the abuse.

For those reporting child sexual abuse, the most frequently cited reason for not disclosing this abuse was feelings of embarrassment or shame. Feeling that the abuse was "too trivial" to tell anyone else about it was the next most often cited reason. Men who were abused as children were more likely to give this reason than were women who were abused as children. (The feeling that the abuse was too trivial as a reason for non-disclosure is examined in more detail below.) Of particular concern are those that felt "nobody would believe them" and they "didn't know who to turn to".

Figure 4.16: Reasons Child Sexual Abuse Was Not Disclosed to Others by Gender

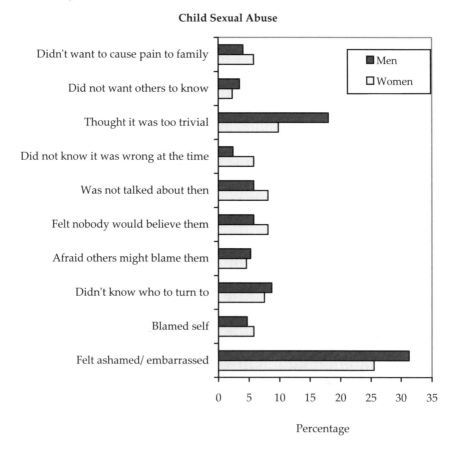

Figure 4.17: Reasons Adult Sexual Assault Was Not Disclosed to Others by Gender

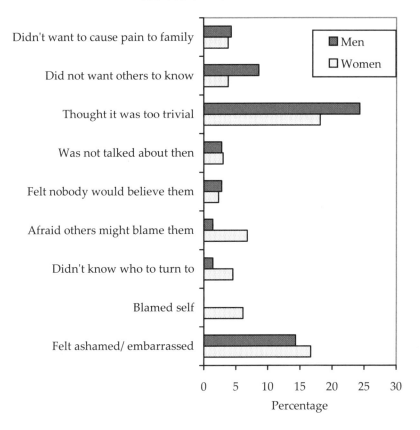

Adult Sexual Assault

Although the percentage of adults who did not disclose their sexual assault to anyone also cited shame and embarrassment as the reason for not doing so, the percentage was lower than for those abused as children. Those assaulted as adults were also more likely to report that they didn't want anyone else to know. While a small percentage of women said that they did not disclose their experience because they blamed themselves, no men gave this reason. However, the reason cited over and above all the other reasons for non-disclosure was because they thought their experience was too trivial. On looking in more detail at the types of abuse described by participants as "too trivial", it is perhaps not surprising that 22 per cent of cases of adult sexual assault and 40 per cent of cases of child sexual abuse which were not reported were categorised as non-contact abuse (e.g. indecent exposure). However, the majority of cases not reported because it might be seen as too trivial involved some type of physical contact (78 per cent of the adult assaults considered trivial and 52 per cent of the child abuse considered trivial). Sexual abuse involving physical contact includes a very wide range of experiences and it is impossible to make any judgements on the effects that it may have on a person, especially considering the fact that individuals have different perceptions of what is and is not acceptable. However, it is harder to reconcile the fact that a small number of people (5 reporting adult sexual assault and 5 reporting childhood sexual abuse) who experienced the most serious forms of abuse (attempted penetration and penetration) said they did not disclose their abuse to anyone because they felt that it was too trivial. Therefore, the stated reason for not disclosing as too trivial cannot always be taken at face value. Men were more than twice as likely than women to explain their non-disclosure of abuse as being due to its trivial nature.

Some individual comments from those interviewed serve to illustrate the challenges to disclosure. Shame was a key factor. The following statements are from those who were abused as children:

> "I have three children of my own . . . if they ever knew, I'd die."

> "I didn't go to a counsellor because if my mother ever knew it would destroy her." (woman abused by her father as a child)

Lack of trust was another challenge:

> "I wouldn't talk to friends about it, I don't trust people."

Others felt that it might adversely affect important relationships. For instance:

"I'd like to be closer to my husband than I am. I'd rather not tell him . . . I'd be afraid it would pull us apart."

In some situations, people made the judgement that there was nothing they or others could do:

"I believe she (mother) knew and there was nothing she could do." (woman abused by her father as a child)

"I didn't tell anyone because it was going on all round me. No one would have cared." (man abused as a child by fellow pupils in boarding school)

"The only way to survive was to grow up and stand up to them. We had no choice. No one believed us." (man abused as a child with friends, from aged 8–13 years, by older group of boys, aged 15–18)

Some individuals felt that the event was too trivial to bring up, simply stating that there was "no trauma" or "I felt no need" (man abused as a boy of ten by his 30-year-old neighbour).

In other situations, disclosing to others, in particular reporting to authorities, was seen in the following way:

"It takes too long and only reminds people of what happened."

Data from the ISPCC survey in 1993 indicated that, regarding disclosure to others, only 30 per cent told at the time of the abuse with a further 30 per cent telling later. Thus, 40 per cent reported not telling anyone else about the abuse. Of the 76 per cent who gave reasons for not telling at the time, 24 per cent reported it was because they felt ashamed, guilty, dirty or to blame, with another 24 per cent fearing they would be punished or otherwise get into trouble. A fifth (19 per cent) did not fully understand what was going on at the time while 18 per cent were afraid they would not be believed. Of those reporting abuse, 6 per cent were aware that other siblings were being abused and 14 per cent felt that children outside their family were. Most (80 per cent) reported that they did not know.

Professional Services Utilised and Participant Satisfaction with Those Services

One of the main aims of the study was to gain insight into the utilisation of professional support services by those who are sexually abused or assaulted. Participants were asked about whether they sought help from professionals. If they did use services, they were asked specific questions about the services they received. The questions regarding services focus on the participants' interactions with the professionals and, in particular, those aspects which have been shown to cause additional distress to the person if not handled appropriately (Campbell et al., 1999). This additional distress to the victim by professionals has been called "secondary re-victimisation".

Gardaí and Legal System

Disclosure rates to Gardaí were strikingly low. Of those who disclosed adult sexual assault, one man (of 98 assaulted — 1 per cent) reported to Gardaí as did 19 women (of 244 — 7.8 per cent). Regarding childhood abuse, this was reported for 10 (of the 178 — 5.6 per cent) men and 28 (of 290 — 9.7 per cent) women. Thus the majority of those who experienced sexual abuse or assault did not report it (these figures are somewhat higher than disclosure rates in the 1993 ISPCC survey where 1 per cent told Gardaí). Police reporting rates internationally are also low. For instance, a US study of over 4,000 women found an 8.5 per cent prevalence of child sexual abuse (defined as rape) with 11.9 per cent of these having ever reported to police or other authorities (Hanson, Resnick, Saunders et al., 1999).

Figure 4.18 depicts the number of SAVI participants who reported to the Gardaí by the various categories of sexual violence over their lifetime (data on women and men combined). The numbers decline steeply from those who disclosed some form of abuse to a SAVI interviewer for the first time to those who said that they had disclosed to at least one other person at some point in their lives before this survey, to those who had reported the abuse to the Gardaí.

Figure 4.18: Disclosure of Lifetime Sexual Violence to SAVI Survey Interviewers Only, to Others and to Gardaí by Type of Abuse

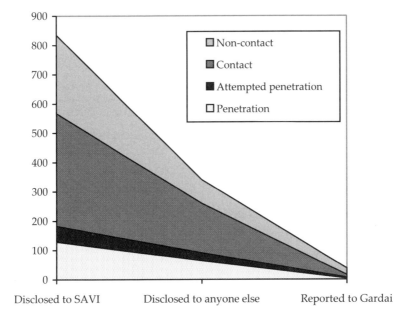

Reasons people chose to report or not report their experiences to the Gardaí may be of use in determining future public education programmes. One explanation for not reporting may be that the person did not believe their experience to be serious enough to be reported to the Gardaí. Table 4.30 presents the types of abuse (that occurred either in childhood or adulthood) that participants reported to the Gardaí. (Note that the percentages represent the number who indicated that they reported their experiences to the Gardaí out of all who reported some form of abuse.)

While one might expect that the more serious forms of sexual violence, such as penetrative abuse, are more likely to be reported to the Gardaí than the less serious forms, this appears to be the case only for those assaulted as adults. Approximately 8 per cent of those who experienced penetrative abuse (or assaults meeting the legal definition of rape or rape under Section 4) as adults reported to the Gardaí (compared to 3 per cent of cases of penetrative child sexual abuse). The type of abuse with the greatest proportion being reported to the Gardaí for child sexual abuse was indecent exposure (10 per cent of cases reported) — what might be considered a much less serious form of abuse. The reasons for this discrepancy are unclear. Overall, a very small proportion of abuse experiences were reported to the Gardaí.

Table 4.30: Types of Sexual Violence Reported to the Gardaí

Abuse Category	Child Abuse % (n)	Adult Assault % (n)
Abuse — not otherwise specified[a]	n/a	4.1 (5)
Child pornography	0 (0)	n/a
Indecent exposure	10.2 (22)	n/a
Contact abuse (no penetration)	2.3 (9)	1.8 (6)
Attempted penetration	5.6 (3)	0 (0)
Penetration/ Oral sex	3.1 (4)	8.2 (9)
Total	4.6 (38)	3.3 (20)

[a] This category was created to account for any unwanted sexual experiences in adulthood which participants reported in an open-ended question and which did not definitively fit into any of the other categories

Participants who did not report to the Gardaí were directly asked in an open-ended question about why they chose not to disclose their abuse (Figure 4.19). Note that those who already had told the interviewer that they had not disclosed their abuse to anyone else in the past were not asked if they reported their experiences to the Gardaí. Therefore, the percentages reflect only those who said that they reported their experiences to at least one other person. (For reasons why participants did not disclose their experiences to anyone ever, see earlier in the section on disclosure.)

Figure 4.19: Spontaneous Reasons Given for Non-disclosure to Gardaí by Child or Adult Sexual Violence

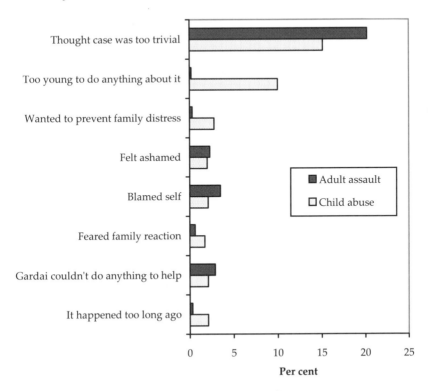

The most common reason for non-disclosure of child sexual abuse to Gardaí was the perceived seriousness of the abuse (15 per cent); 13.5 per cent of men and 16.2 per cent of women thought the case was too trivial to be reported to the Gardaí. The next most common reason was age (too young to do anything about it) (10 per cent); 8.4 per cent of men and 11 per cent women. Women were also more likely to report they felt ashamed, blamed themselves or feared family reactions and publicity. For adult assault, the most widely cited reason for non-disclosure was also the low perceived severity of the abuse (20 per cent). A feeling that the Gardaí "couldn't do anything to help" was another common reason. While the reason "too trivial" could be taken at face value, it was possible to examine the type of abuse reported to the SAVI study for those who gave this reason. Surprisingly, a number of those who experienced penetrative abuse gave this reason (21 per cent of those who experienced penetrative abuse as a child and 12 per cent of those who experienced penetrative abuse as an adult).

While many chose not to report to Gardaí, a small number of participants did choose to report their experiences. Participants who reported their experiences to the Gardaí were asked a number of questions about their experiences. Figures 4.20 and 4.21 give the proportions of participants who had positive, neutral or negative experiences with different aspects of the Gardaí services. However, not all those who reported to the Gardaí were able to rate all aspects of this experience. Therefore, percentages were calculated from the total of people who responded to each individual item, as not all participants answered all nine items. Samples for each item vary, ranging from 11 to 16 people for adult abuse and 13 to 26 people for child abuse.

Over half of all participants who reported an experience of sexual abuse (in either child or adulthood) to the Gardaí were satisfied with the overall quality of the service they were given. Participants were satisfied with how seriously the Gardaí treated their situation (89 per cent of those abused as children and 69 per cent as adults) and that they were not made feel responsible in any way for the abuse (93 per cent child and adult combined). However, approximately half of those abused as adults did not feel that they were given satisfactory information about further services that can help people who have experienced abuse. A significant minority of both adults (31 per cent) and children (17 per cent) were dissatisfied with the Gardaí's sensitivity to their feelings. These findings add to those of the detailed study of law enforcement services for 20 women in a number of EU countries, including Ireland, who had been raped (Bacik et al., 1998). They summarised evidence of increasing satisfaction with police services to those who have been abused over the past two decades. This is undoubtedly as a result of increased training in this area for police staff. The data here highlight the need for further attention, in particular to the provision of information about police investigations or procedures and about other services. Protocols to ensure this information is covered in a clear, comprehensive and up-to-date manner are necessary.

Figure 4.20: Satisfaction Ratings of Aspects of the Services Received by the Gardaí for those who Experienced Child Sexual Abuse

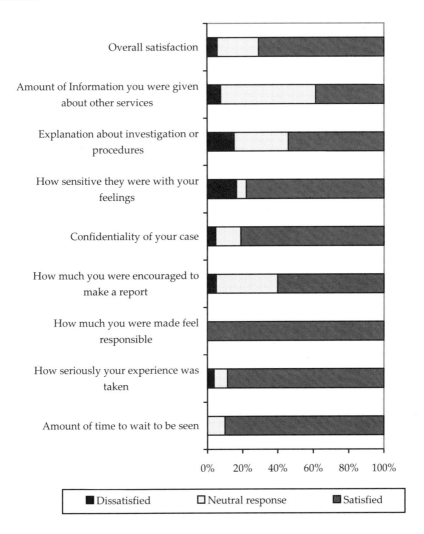

Figure 4.21: Satisfaction Ratings of Aspects of the Services Received by the Gardaí for those who Experienced Adult Sexual Assault

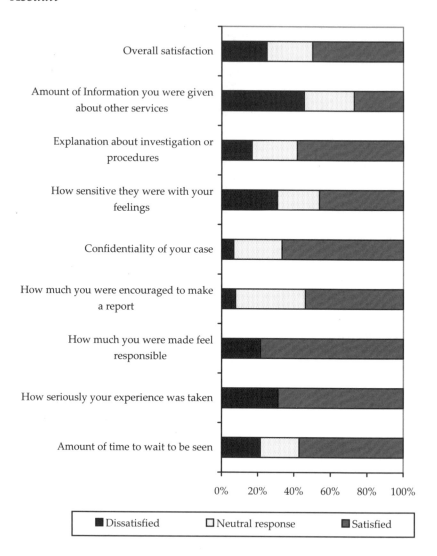

The SAVI data on experiences with the legal system (beyond re-porting to the Gardaí) should be treated with caution since the numbers of participants who were able to comment on these ex-periences were so small (there were only six court cases for child sexual abuse with four convictions and two court cases with one conviction for adult sexual assault).

Therefore, additional data about the legal system in Ireland is presented here to supplement the SAVI data. The DRCC annual report (2000) recorded 177 cases being reported to the Gardaí by their clients in 2000 with 14 of these cases going to court. These resulted in 11 convictions. Eight were for child sexual abuse. A quarter of these cases (26 per cent) were dropped with almost half still being processed.

The Garda annual report statistics for the year 2000 (Garda Síochána, 2000) provide a useful profile of the level and nature of sexual offences. The total number of sexual assault offences recorded by Gardaí in 2000 was 549 (a 1 per cent decrease on 1999 figures). This overall number appears to be reasonably constant since the mid-1990s (sexual assaults numbered 561 in 1995, 516 in 1996 and 524 in 1997) (Leon, 2000). Sexual offences constituted 1 per cent of all reported crimes. While figures seemed similar to 1999, the numbers of more violent crimes (aggravated sexual assaults) increased by 33 per cent, i.e. from 9 to 12 cases. This was in line with a substantial increase in all forms of violent assault in 2000. Figures for incest also increased by 38 per cent from 13 cases in 1999 to 18 in 2000. It is difficult to evaluate the significance of changes with such small numbers in particular categories such as aggravated sexual assault or incest. The year 2000 profile of cases, criminal procedures and convictions is presented in Table 4.31.

Of all the cases that were reported to the Gardaí, 73 per cent of offences were considered "detected". For detected offences, criminal proceedings were commenced in 130 (32 per cent) cases. All cases were concluded by the time of reporting; there were 27 convictions, i.e. 20.8 per cent of those taken to criminal proceedings and 6.7 per cent of those cases where an offence was detected by Gardaí. The attrition rate (i.e. the difference between the number of complaints reported to the Gardaí and number of prosecutions) is thus 95.1 per cent. Attrition is often described as the difference between the number of cases occurring and prosecutions. In this instance, the former figure is unknown. The number of reports made to the Gardaí are the only possible starting point in the analysis here. Figure 4.22 depicts this attrition for the various types of sexual offences reported. (Note that when viewed alongside Figure 4.18, the number of participants who said that they did not report to the Gardaí from SAVI data, this high attrition rate appears even more stark.) Previous analysis of Garda figures using specific categories of sexual offence have identified much lower attrition rates, e.g. 25.9 per cent for sexual assaults (Leon, 2000). Meanwhile the Cork and Kerry Rape Crisis Centre in-depth analysis of 8 cases found that of six who approached the Gardaí, four were referred to the Director of Public Prosecutions and to court (Leane et al., 2001). There was one conviction from a guilty plea.

Table 4.31: Sexual Assault Offences: Numbers Reported to Gardaí and Convictions Achieved in the Year 2000

Type of Sexual Offence	Offence Reported to the Gardaí			Offence Detected by Gardaí	Criminal Procedure Commenced	Court Conviction*
	Male	*Female*	*Total*			
	n	*n*	*n*	*n*	*n*	*n*
Rape of female	–	238	238	180	51	2
Rape (section 4)	21	31	52	39	11	3
Buggery	23	0	23	18	4	0
Incest	2	16	18	18	1	0
Unlawful carnal knowledge	0	15	15	14	9	4
Aggravated sexual assault	3	9	12	9	2	1
Gross indecency	3	0	3	3	2	1
Sexual offences involving mentally impaired person	1	2	3	1	0	–
Total	141	408	549	401	130	27

* Results of cases dealt with on indictment (i.e. referred to Director of Public Prosecution) or summarily (not referred) were combined. In this report, all cases were reported as concluded.

There are a few caveats to the attrition rates offered here. First, the cases noted under court convictions may be unrelated to the cases reported to the Gardaí in 2000, as the process from reporting to court proceedings typically takes many months and often more than one year. Second, assuming that a small, but significant, number of cases reported to the Gardaí were perpetrated by juveniles, one would not expect these cases to come before adult court proceedings. Outcomes for juvenile offences differ significantly from adults, such as commitment to reformatory schools. As O'Malley (1996) points out, a more "comprehensive set of annual criminal justice statistics to replace the present fragmented and incomplete system" needs to be put in place in order to get "an accurate picture of crime and punishment in Ireland." (p. 378).

Figure 4.22: Attrition Rate from Reported Sexual Offences to Gardaí to Conviction (data from Garda Síochána annual report, 2000)

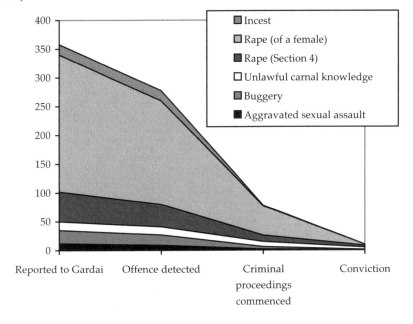

Medical Professionals

Only 17 participants reported child abuse and 21 reported adult assault to medical professionals. These low levels of contact with
medical professional appear typical from previous research. For
instance, only 26.2 per cent of a national sample of US women
raped as adults received medical care following the incident (Resnick, Holmes, Kilpatrick et al., 2000). Reporting the crime to police
and fear of STDs were major factors influencing receipt of medical
care. More women who were physically injured sought care (42
per cent) yet this proportion was even a minority of those who
were physically injured. These authors emphasise the importance
of developing a "post-rape health care" strategy for all those who
have been raped because, even in the absence of physical injury,
there are concerns about sexually transmitted diseases and, for
women, pregnancy.

Figures 4.23 and 4.24 show satisfaction levels with the quality
of service received by those SAVI participants who approached
medical professionals. As with experiences with the Gardaí, not
all of these participants remembered enough about the experience
to rate the services or were willing to elaborate on this experience.

Figure 4.23: Ratings of Aspects of the Services Received from Medical Professionals for those who Experienced Child Sexual Abuse

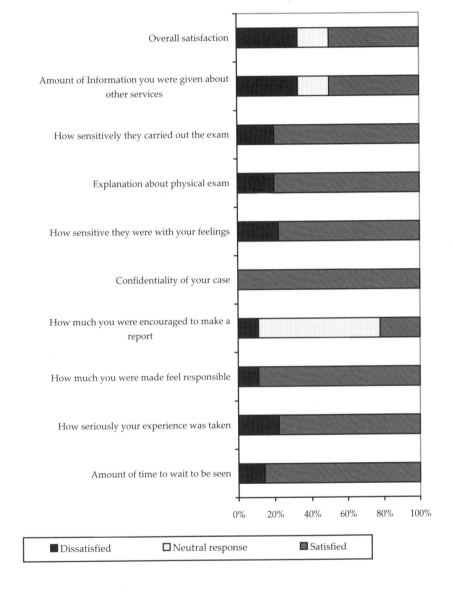

Figure 4.24: Ratings of Aspects of the Services from Medical Professionals for those who Experienced Adult Sexual Assault

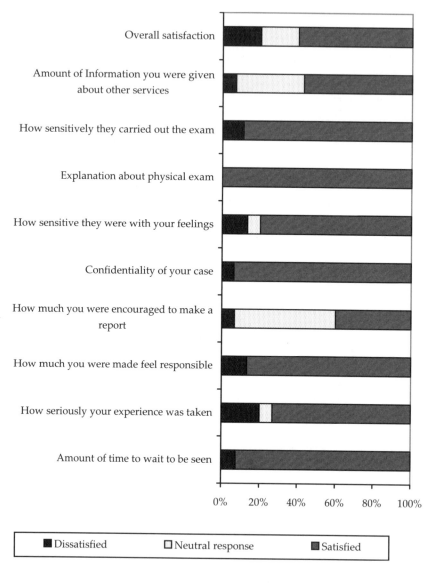

Those who reported child sexual abuse to medical professionals were less satisfied with the overall experience than those who had reported adult sexual assault (33.3 per cent dissatisfied as compared to 20 per cent). Most of the participants who had reported sexual violence to a medical professional were satisfied with time waiting to be seen and almost all were satisfied with the confidentiality of their case. However, a significant minority (11 per cent who reported child abuse and 13 per cent who reported adult sexual assault) felt that medical professionals made them feel responsible for their experience of sexual violence. Almost a quarter (22 per cent who reported child abuse and 20 per cent who reported adult sexual assault) felt that their case was not taken seriously. Explanations about, and the conduct of, physical examinations were also a source of dissatisfaction for one in five cases of child sexual abuse, but were less problematic for adults. These findings build on those of a recent EU report (Bacik et al., 1998). Women reported anger and distress with treatment by medical staff. While general guidelines are in place for doctors dealing with sexual violence (e.g. American Medical Association, 1992), there are few specialist services (e.g. one specialist unit in Ireland at the Rotunda Hospital, Dublin). It should be noted that while only one of the 29 SAVI participants had used this specialist service, she rated all aspects of that service very highly. Without specialised training, however, doctors may feel reluctant to deal with the subject because of lack of experience in the area. For instance, a recent study of "domestic" violence in Ireland found that 39 per cent of 1,692 women in relationships had experienced partner violence (Bradley, Smith, Long and O'Dowd, 2002). Only 12 per cent of those who had experienced violence had been asked about it by doctors. Previous reports such as the *Report of the Task Force on Violence Against Women* (Department of Health, 1997) have called for specialised units in each health board area to address this particular issue.

Counselling/Psychological Professionals

A total of 83 participants from the SAVI sample went for counselling (63 women and 20 men). Figure 4.25 gives the relative proportion according to gender of the type of abuse (whether child, adult or both) that led to counselling being sought.

Figure 4.25: Type of Abuse (child, adult or both) of SAVI
Participants Attending Counselling by Gender

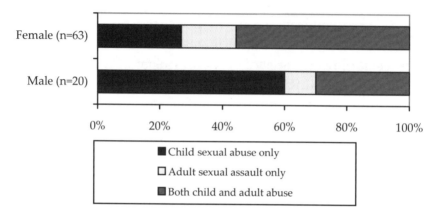

Over half of the women attended for abuse which was
experienced both as a child and adult. A similar proportion of
men attended for child abuse only.

Figure 4.26: Ratings of Aspects of the Services Provided by
Counselling Professionals

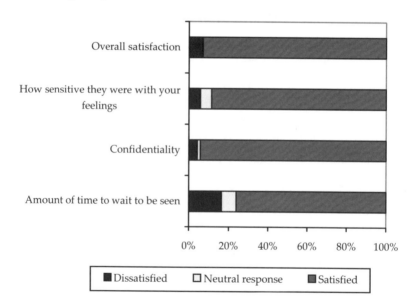

The majority (93 per cent) of participants were satisfied with their experience of going to counselling. In particular, they were satisfied with the confidentiality with which their situation was treated. However, 16 per cent were not satisfied with the amount of time that they had to wait to obtain counselling.

Of particular interest was whether those who experienced incest were more likely to go to counselling. Of those who reported experiencing incest 25 per cent sought counselling, whereas only 10 per cent of those who experienced sexual violence other than incest did so. Table 4.32 below shows the predicted probability of seeking counselling (only counting those where the event happened at least ten years previously).

Table 4.32: Pattern of Use of Counselling Services for those Experiencing Various Types of Abuse (% counselling)

	Women		Men	
Sought counselling for:	*Contact Abuse* %	*Penetrative Abuse* %	*Contact Abuse* %	*Penetrative Abuse* %
Abuse by non-family member	16	31	12	24
Incest	32	53	25	44

It is clear that help-seeking was considerably higher in those who had experienced incest. Thus it appears that counselling services see a higher proportion of clients with intra-familial sexual abuse than that which prevails in the general public.

Use of Health Board Services

Only two participants knew about and could evaluate their contacts with child sexual abuse services in the health boards. This did not allow meaningful evaluation here. This type of evaluation, to be most useful, would need to include the parents of children seen for sexual abuse and accounts from children themselves, as children, experiencing the service. Detailed analyses of the profile of child sexual abuse cases presenting to health boards in both the

Republic of Ireland and Northern Ireland have been conducted and reviewed elsewhere (O'Reilly and Carr, 1999). A project is currently underway to evaluate the experience of services to adults for child sexual abuse by the National Counselling Service (a joint group of the Irish health boards). Research focusing on children's experiences of the services they encounter are very challenging but uniquely worthwhile in this area. CARI (Children at Risk in Ireland) have done some work with a US psychothera- pist, Dr Annie Rogers, to bring the voice of the child to the fore in describing child sexual abuse. Similarly, Ferguson and O'Reilly (2001) interviewed a small number of children about their experi- ence of health boards in child protection cases. Some feedback was very positive while other feedback showed how confusing and uninformed children can be in these settings.

This section dealt with disclosure to professionals and subse- quent experiences of service delivery. In terms of barriers to dis- closure and service access, it is important to consider the views of the general public concerning their willingness to disclose if they ever experienced sexual violence themselves and whether there are preferred patterns of disclosure across family, friends and pro- fessional contacts. This was considered in a hypothetical way in this study.

Other dimensions of interest to assess in the public sample were their attitudes to sexual violence and their perceptions of its prevalence. Finally, they were asked if they had been exposed to a range of experiences which could constitute sexual harassment. Views on likelihood of disclosure of a future experience of sexual violence were considered next.

Views on Likelihood of Probable Disclosure in the Event of Experiencing Sexual Violence

Participants were asked how likely they would be to tell friends, family, a doctor, the Gardaí and a counsellor if they themselves were unfortunate enough to be sexually assaulted at some future point (Table 4.33). They rated their probable disclosure on a five-point scale ranging from "definitely would tell" to "definitely would not tell". If they answered "uncertain", "probably not" or "definitely not", they were encouraged to explain their reasons. Some participants gave multiple reasons, while others felt that the question was too hypothetical to be able to give an exact reason.

Table 4.33: Likelihood of Disclosing in the Event of Future Sexual Abuse

	Family % (n)	Friends % (n)	Gardaí % (n)	Doctor % (n)	Counsellor % (n)
Definitely not/ Probably not	16.5 (501)	28.8 (870)	14.5 (434)	7.5 (226)	13.4 (403)
Uncertain	11.1 (339)	12.5 (379)	12.6 (377)	6.0 (181)	11.8 (356)
Probably would/ Definitely would	72.3 (2,194)	58.7 (1,775)	72.9 (2,186)	86.6 (2,625)	74.9 (2,260)

Probable Disclosure to Family

Twenty-eight per cent of participants felt that they would have reservations about telling family members. Of these participants, more than a quarter (27 per cent) cited shame and embarrassment as the reason. Fear of worrying or hurting family members accounted for 11 per cent and 6 per cent felt that their family would not understand or be supportive of them. Another ten per cent said that they would prefer to deal with matters themselves.

Probable Disclosure to Friends

Many participants (41 per cent) said that they definitely or probably would not tell, or were uncertain about telling friends if they were abused. Of these, a quarter of participants cited embarrassment as the main reason (similar to those citing this as a barrier for family); 10 per cent stated lack of trust and fear of gossip and 10 per cent said that they would fear ridicule and not being believed by friends. About a fifth of participants felt that they would prefer to deal with the matter themselves without involving friends.

Probable Disclosure to Gardaí

Over a quarter (27 per cent) of participants expressed reservations about telling the gardaí if they were sexually abused. Negative perceptions of the gardaí accounted for 21 per cent of reasons given; the most frequently stated being a lack of trust. Some of those expressing reservations (18 per cent) did not see gardaí as suitable and would see it only as a last resort. Five per cent said that they would not see the point in going to the gardaí as they felt that nothing would be done. Another 5 per cent of participants said that they would prefer not to get the legal system in general involved, with some of these participants stating that the legal system was for criminals, not victims. About 10 per cent cited personal reasons for not disclosing to the gardaí, ranging from being afraid to feeling uncomfortable speaking about the issue with the gardaí to fearing the risk of stigma. Nine participants noted that friends had had poor experiences with gardaí in the past. A further five said that the fact that they have family members employed in the gardaí would be off-putting. Another group (17 per cent) felt that they would prefer to deal with the matter themselves. Nine per cent of participants said that they would consider going to the gardaí, but only if the incident was very serious or violent.

Probable Disclosure to a Doctor

Very few (less than 15 per cent) felt that they would not go to a doctor if they experienced sexual abuse. A common reason cited by those who felt they would not go was negative perceptions of doctors, such as lack of trust, fear that it would not be confidential and thinking that their doctor would be insensitive (13 per cent). A substantial number (6 per cent) felt that they were too close to their doctor to talk of such matters. Another 5 per cent of participants cited personal matters, such as embarrassment and awkwardness, as the main reason for not considering going to a doctor if abused, while 5 per cent felt that they would rather deal with things alone. A number of participants (23 per cent) felt that they would not automatically go to a doctor if they had been sexually abused and felt that it would be largely dependant on the situation and the physical and emotional severity of the abuse. A small number felt that they would only disclose to a doctor if they were directly asked whether they had been abused.

Probable Disclosure to a Counsellor

Almost a quarter of the participants were "uncertain" or would "probably or definitely not" go to a counsellor. The most common reason given was that they would choose instead to talk about the matter with someone else (21 per cent). A minority (15 per cent) of participants reported negative attitudes towards counsellors, such as not trusting them (22 participants) and having had poor experiences in the past (n = 18). Lack of knowledge about counsellors (for example, what they do and where they are based) accounted for approximately one-tenth of participant reluctance to receive counselling if they were ever abused. Other reasons included wanting to keep it private (6 per cent), embarrassment or feeling uncomfortable (4 per cent) and not feeling that they would need to get this help (10 per cent). Seven per cent of participants felt that their decision to see a counsellor would depend on how serious the experience of abuse had been.

Influence of Age and Gender on Willingness to Disclose

Public perceptions of the likelihood of disclosure were examined by gender (Figure 4.27) and age of the participants (Figure 4.28) and by experience of abuse (both timing and severity) (Table 4.34).

Both men and women reported that they were least likely to disclose to friends and most likely to disclose to a doctor (in the event of an experience of sexual abuse). Men were more likely to believe they would not disclose to all categories of others. This gender difference was particularly notable for disclosure to family and friends; over 40 per cent of men believed they would not tell friends if they were sexually abused. This suggests the likely stigma that they expect would be attached to such disclosure. Patterns by age were less clear. Younger people were less likely to expect they would tell family members and doctors and more likely to expect they would tell friends than were others. Those over age 70 were least likely to tell counsellors or friends.

Figure 4.27: Profile of Probable Non-disclosure in the Event of Being Abused by Gender

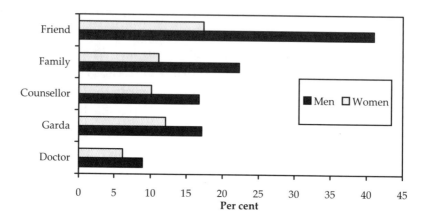

Figure 4.28: Profile of Probable Non-disclosure in the Event of Being Abused by Current Age Group

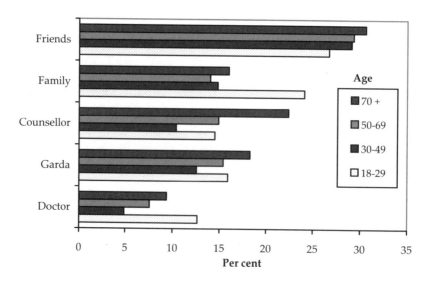

Likely disclosure by previous experience of sexual abuse and the timing of first abuse is considered in Table 4.34. The most notable pattern is the relatively high probability of non-disclosure of abuse to friends; highest for those who have not been abused and next for those who have been abused in childhood. Conversely, those abused as adults appeared more reluctant to disclose subsequent abuse to family members.

Table 4.34: Reluctance of Public to Disclose a Future Event by their Previous Abuse History and Timing of Abuse

		Timing of First Abuse	
Unwilling to Disclose to:	*No Abuse % (n)*	*Childhood % (n)*	*Adulthood % (n)*
Family	16.1 (314)	16.8 (147)	19.8 (38)
Friend	31.8 (620)	24.5 (214)	17.9 (34)
Doctor	7.3 (143)	7.1 (62)	10.4 (20)
Counsellor	13.7 (268)	12.3 (107)	13.6 (26)
Gardaí	13.7 (286)	14.1 (123)	13.2 (25)

Level of abuse and reluctance to disclose is presented in Table 4.35. It shows that willingness to disclose to family and doctors was somewhat lower for those experiencing serious penetrative abuse. When information on anticipated and actual disclosure to professionals was combined, actual reporting for those abused was dramatically lower than anticipations of disclosure by the whole sample (i.e. 5 per cent actual versus 87 per cent anticipated disclosure to doctors; 7 per cent versus 73 per cent to Gardaí and 12 per cent versus 75 per cent to counsellors). Some people qualified their views on willingness to disclose to doctors by saying they would attend and tell doctors if they deemed it medically necessary.

Participants were asked if they would know where to go/who to go to if they experienced sexual violence at a future stage in their life. Overall, almost three-quarters (72.4 per cent of participants) said that they would. However, almost a fifth of females

(18.7 per cent) and 36.8 per cent of males felt that they would not know where to go if they were in this situation. Of those who said that they would know where to go, almost a tenth cited their doctor and a similar number said that they would go to the Gardaí. Just over 5 per cent (n = 113) felt that they would go to the Rape Crisis Centre while 79 participants said that they would contact a counsellor or psychologist if they were sexually abused. Other frequently cited sources were social services (n = 37) and the Rotunda Sexual Abuse Treatment Unit (n = 24). Quite a few participants (n = 37) felt that, while they did not know there and then where they would go if they were sexually abused, in the event of it happening they would use the telephone directory to find emergency/help-line numbers.

Table 4.35: Reluctance of Public Disclosure by Severity of Lifetime Experience of Abuse

Unwilling to disclose to:	No Abuse (n = 1,955)	Non-contact Abuse (n = 257)	Contact Abuse (n = 537)	Attempted or Actual Penetration/Oral Sex (n = 274)
	% (n)	% (n)	% (n)	% (n)
Family	16.1 (314)	16.7 (43)	16.9 (91)	19.0 (52)
Friends	31.8 (620)	26.5 (68)	21.8 (116)	23.4 (64)
Doctor	7.3 (143)	5.4 (14)	6.7 (36)	12.0 (33)
Counsellor	13.7 (268)	12.9 (33)	12.5 (67)	12.0 (33)
Garda	14.8 (286)	13.8 (35)	13.2 (70)	15.7 (43)

Comparisons of Sexual Violence Profiles from SAVI Population Data and Sexual Abuse Service Use Data

Uptake figures are not available for sexual abuse services nationally. Some comparisons with accessible data were made to consider if there were obvious differences between self-referred abuse and those reporting abuse as a result of a random survey (Table 4.36).

Table 4.36: Comparison of SAVI Profile of Abuse with Abuse as Presented to Selected Sexual Abuse Treatment Agencies: Crisis Telephone Callers and Attenders at Counselling Services

	SAVI	DRCC [a]		CARI	
Type of Contact	%	*7/98–6/99* %	*7/99–6/00* %	*1/99–12/99* %	*1/00–12/00* %
Crisis Line Callers					
Type of abuse reported:					
Child sexual abuse	78	57	56	–	–
Adult abuse/ rape	8	40	41	–	–
Both	14	3	3	–	–
Gender distribution					
Female	55	79	81	–	–
Male	45	21	19	–	–
Counselling Service Clients					
Adults	n/a	(n = 697)	(n = 704)	n/a	n/a
Families		n/a	n/a	(n = 244)	(n = 263
Children only		n/a	n/a	(n = 99)	(n = 86)
Gender distribution					
Female	76	87	85	74[b]	70[b]
Male	24	13	15	26[b]	30[b]
Pregnancy (of those at risk, by age, gender and contraception practices	UC (n = 8)	16 (n = 21)	15 (n = 19)	n/a	n/a

[a] Data recalculated from DRCC annual report figures to exclude sexual harassment cases.

[b] Percentages of male and female (*child*) clients — as available in CARI annual report.

UC: Unable to calculate: since SAVI did not collect information on contraceptive practice, it is not possible to estimate those who could become pregnant as a consequence of rape.

The profile indicates that the majority of abuse experiences in SAVI occur in childhood while adult sexual assaults are more represented in the DRCC client crisis telephone caller profile. This may reflect levels of disclosure or the perceived profile of DRCC as a service organisation for adults (in comparison to other telephone services dedicated specifically to child care). Women also constituted a higher proportion of the DRCC telephone crisis counselling client group than was represented in the SAVI population data. Gender patterns were repeated in terms of the clients who attended for counselling sessions at the DRCC. In terms of the proportions of men and women experiencing abuse versus attending counselling, one in four (24 per cent) of those abused were men in SAVI while about half of that, one in eight, were the proportion of men attending DRCC counselling. DRCC service uptake figures for men reflected those reported in SAVI; men being less likely to attend services following sexual violence.

Calls made to CARI (Children At Risk in Ireland), a service which deals mainly with child sexual abuse, also show a gender difference with most clients being female. CARI figures are not directly comparable with SAVI or DRCC since they reflect child client attendance.

It is not possible to draw inferences about the prevalence of pregnancy as a consequence of sexual abuse from SAVI. However, the fact that eight such pregnancies were reported was notable. One in seven female DRCC clients who could become pregnant did report pregnancy as a consequence of sexual violence.

PUBLIC PERCEPTIONS OF SEXUAL VIOLENCE

Estimating the Prevalence of Sexual Violence

Participants were asked to estimate the level of sexual violence in Irish society today by various categories. Table 4.37 shows the median estimates alongside the prevalence rates obtained in the SAVI study.

The table shows the median estimates made by participants of the prevalence of various types of sexual violence. The median, or 50th percentile, is the value at or below which half the estimates lie. Half of those interviewed estimated the percentage of women raped as adults at 19 per cent or less.

Table 4.37: Public Perceptions of the Prevalence of Sexual Violence Compared to Levels Obtained in SAVI Survey

Prevalence Category	Median Value Estimated by Public %	Results of this Survey %	% Who Under-estimated	% Who Over-estimated
Percentage of women raped or sexually assaulted as adults	19.0	20.0	29.3	16.4
Percentage of men raped or sexually assaulted as adults	7.5	9.0	33.6	20.1
Percentage of girls raped or sexually assaulted by a non-family member	15.0	15.0	30.8	21.2
Percentage of boys raped or sexually assaulted by a non-family member	10.0	14.0	41.0	14.5
Percentage of girls experiencing incest*	10.0	5.6	16.0	46.0
Percentage of boys experiencing incest	8.0	2.5	14.0	54.0
Percentage of child sexual abuse perpetrated by children or adolescents	30.0	26.0	17.6	9.6

* Incest is defined widely here: sexual relations between members of the same family including parents, grandparents, siblings, step-parents, foster-parents, aunts, uncles and cousins

On first inspection, public perceptions of levels of sexual violence were broadly in line with the SAVI Survey findings in general. In the case of incest, however, public estimates of its frequency were considerably higher than those obtained from the survey, even though a broader definition of incest was used than the strictly legal one (one which is probably more in line with common perception of incest). Population estimates of the prevalence of incest were twice as high for girls as that reported with estimated levels almost three times higher than reported for boys.

The data were examined to see what proportion of people were seriously wrong about the prevalence of sexual violence. "Seriously wrong" was defined as underestimating the true figure by at least half, or overestimating it by at least twice.

The most frequent pattern was of underestimation; about a third of those interviewed underestimated the prevalence of rape and child sexual abuse by non-family members by at least a half. While overestimates were less common, taken together with underestimates, they show that about 50 per cent of those interviewed were seriously wrong about the frequency of sexual violence, either because they overestimated or underestimated it.

The Relationship between Participant Gender and Over- or Underestimation

In all estimates of the prevalence of sexual abuse and rape, women were significantly more likely to overestimate than men; typically, four times as many women overestimated as men (data not shown). Men were more likely to underestimate then women; typically twice as many men as women underestimated. All these differences were statistically significant. Only in the case of estimating the percentage of child sexual abuse perpetrated by children or adolescents did the two sexes come close to the same pattern of errors, although women tended to overestimate slightly more often than men.

The initial impression of agreement given in the table gives way, on examination, to the more salutary finding that a substantial proportion of participants were seriously wrong about the prevalence of sexual violence, with women more likely to over-estimate and men more likely to underestimate the extent of the problem.

The percentages of sexual abuse cases coming to the attention of police and resulting in court convictions were also considered by comparing general population estimates and actual percentages as identified in the SAVI survey (Table 4.38).

Table 4.38: Public Perceptions of Reports to Gardaí and Court Outcomes with SAVI

Prevalence Category	Estimated by Public %	Results of this Survey %
Percentage of women who report their experience to Gardaí	33.5	7.1
Percentage of men who report their experience to Gardaí	15.8	2.6
Percentage of court cases that result in guilty verdict	45.9	*

* These numbers were very small (eight cases and five convictions), so they may be misleading.

Here the public substantially overestimate the proportion of cases of sexual violence that are reported to the Gardaí; for women, the overestimates are almost five-fold and for men they are six times the actual levels. While it is possible to calculate estimates of conviction rates from SAVI (five of eight cases or 62 per cent), these bear little relationship to national Garda figures (see Table 4.31 where 20.8 per cent of court cases resulted in conviction in the year 2000). From this, the public also overestimated court convictions. Overall, the public perception is of a much greater proportion of cases coming forward and being successfully convicted than is the reality as seen from SAVI and official Garda statistics.

In terms of patterns elsewhere, studies with a more detailed focus on sexual violence (as distinct from crime), show higher levels of abuse reported but with no change in proportions reporting to police. Thus, two large studies of reporting of child sexual abuse showed rates as low as 3 per cent (Finkelhor and Dzuiba-Leatherman, 1994) and 15 per cent (Kilpatrick and Saunders, 1997). SAVI population estimates that women are more likely to report than men is also borne out by information on those sexually abused in SAVI and by international data.

Public Attitudes to Sexual Violence

Respondents were asked if they agreed or disagreed (or were uncertain) with statements concerning general beliefs about sexual violence (Table 4.39). A number of points are important in interpreting this table. Firstly, all percentages refer to those participants agreeing with the relevant statement. Secondly, statistically significant differences in the percentages of men and women endorsing items are signified by asterisks. Those without asterisks were endorsed by similar percentages of men and women. Beliefs were categorised by whether they focused on the abused person or the perpetrators, or beliefs concerning causes, consequences and reporting of sexual violence. Finally, items in the table were labelled either true or false. This broad categorisation is for illustrative purposes rather than being a definitive way to classify such statements. Public awareness campaigns may wish to focus both on increasing the population's knowledge about facts (e.g. "most perpetrators are known to those they abuse") and on increasing the population's understanding that broad generalisations or stereotypes may be unhelpful (e.g. the belief that "men are less affected by the experience of sexual assault than women").

Overall, the SAVI sample expressed an understanding of rape "myths" and misconceptions. For example, the following levels of agreement were expressed regarding statements such as "a raped woman is usually an innocent victim" (85 per cent) and "a date rape can be just as traumatic as rape by a stranger" (92 per cent). However, it seems that common rape myths still prevail in a significant minority of the Irish public. Almost a third (29 per cent) of participants felt that "women who wear short skirts or tight tops are inviting rape" and 40 per cent felt that "accusations of rape are often false".

Table 4.39: Agreement with a Series of Beliefs about Sexual Violence

	Men % Agree- ment (n)	Women % Agree- ment (n)
Beliefs about victims of sexual violence		
A woman can be raped by her husband (*True*)[a]	91.9 (711)	94.7 (734)***
Men can be raped (*True*)	90.6 (657)	91.1 (730)
A raped woman is usually an innocent victim (*True*)	85.6 (663)	84.6 (657)
Rape victims are usually young and attractive (*False*)[a]	28.1 (218)	11.9 (92)***
A man who is sexually assaulted by another man must be homosexual or have been acting in a gay manner (*False*)	24.7 (180)	20.2 (162)
A person being raped could stop the rapist if they really wanted to (*False*)	10.4 (76)	4.4 (35)***
Beliefs about perpetrators of sexual violence		
Most rapes are carried out by someone known to the victim (*True*)	82.9 (604)	81.8 (658)
Women sometimes sexually abuse children (*True*)	73.6 (568)	73.1 (565)
Men who sexually assault other men must be gay (homosexual) (*False*)	40.8 (316)	26.9 (209)***
Child abuse is mostly committed by strangers (*False*)	11.8 (91)	6.6 (51)**

Table 4.39 cont'd

	Men % Agree- ment (n)	Women % Agree- ment (n)
Beliefs about the causes of sexual violence		
The reason most rapists commit rape is to control and dominate another person (*True*)	60.9 (470)	71.2 (553)***
The reason most rapists commit rape is overwhelming sexual desire (*False*)	46.6 (339)	34.0 (273)***
Women who wear short skirts or tight tops are inviting rape (*False*)	30.2 (220)	27.4 (220)
Beliefs about the consequences of sexual violence		
A date rape can be just as traumatic as rape by a stranger (*True*)	92.0 (667)	93.0 (748)
Men are less affected by the experience of sexual assault than women (*False*)	40.5 (313)	30.1 (234)***
Sexually experienced people are less traumatised by rape (*False*)	23.8 (173)	18.3 (147)*
Beliefs about reporting sexual violence		
Accusations of rape are often false (*False*)	42.3 (327)	37.9 (294)
Accusations about having been sexually abused as a child are often false (*False*)	24.1 (175)	17.3 (138)***
If a rape victim isn't visibly upset by the experience, it probably wasn't a rape (*False*)	16.2 (125)	16.5 (128)
When a woman says "no" to sexual advances, she really means "yes" (*False*)	7.3 (53)	3.4 (27)***

[a] Statements rated as false are either clearly untrue or deemed unhelpful by professionals in this area because they either blame the victim or are used as rationalisations by the public to decrease their perceptions of their own risk.

* $p < .05$; ** $p < .01$; *** $p < .001$.

Significant differences between males and females were found for 12 out of 20 items. Men showed themselves to be significantly ($p <$ 0.001) more accepting of rape myths, particularly regarding males and sexual violence, such as "men who sexually assault other men must be gay" and "men are less affected by the experience of sexual assault than women". This gender difference can also be seen in attitudes towards motivation for rape. Men were significantly more likely ($p = <0.001$) to agree that "the reason most rapists commit rape is overwhelming sexual desire" and that "rape victims are usually young and attractive". Another rather worrying group of attitudes held by significantly more men than women ($p = <0.001$) were the beliefs that "a person being raped could stop the rapist if they really wanted to" and that "when a women says no, she really means yes".

Other surveys of rape attitudes have also found men to be significantly more accepting of rape myths (Burt, 1980; Williams, Forster and Petrak, 1999; and Ward, 1988). These rape myths tend to be more doubting and critical of victims and less harsh on the perpetrators of sexual violence.

Attitudes Concerning the Education of Children about the Risk of Abuse

Participants were asked whether they themselves had been told about the risk of sexual abuse as a child. The vast majority (88.4 per cent) said they had been told nothing. Of those who had, the mean age that abuse was discussed was nine years and over two-thirds (70 per cent) were told by their mother. Participants were then asked whether they had discussed the matter of sexual abuse with their own children (if they had any). Over half of participants with children had spoken about sexual abuse with them (55.2 per cent) and almost a third of those who had not discussed it said that it was because their children were still too young. Furthermore, the majority of participants (86.2 per cent) who had spoken to their children on the matter reported having felt fairly or very confident in their ability to do so. This suggests that the Irish population may have become more open to discussing sexual abuse. Of those participants who had chosen not to speak to their children about sexual abuse, almost a fifth (19.5 per cent) felt that sexual abuse was unlikely to occur in their own family or community. Approximately 10 per cent felt that there was no need as it was already covered at school. A further 10 per cent felt that there was no need to discuss sexual abuse with their children as it did not happen in "those days" (i.e. in the past when their children were growing up).

Attitudes towards the Media

Participants were asked if they felt that media coverage was damaging or beneficial, or if they felt it had no effect (see Table 4.40). They were also asked to explain their answers.

Table 4.40: Attitudes towards Media Coverage of Sexual Abuse and Violence

Attitude to Media	% (n)
Somewhat damaging/Very damaging	17.3 (500)
No effect	6.7 (193)
Somewhat beneficial/Very beneficial	76.0 (2,191)

The majority (76 per cent) of participants felt that the media coverage of sexual abuse and violence was either somewhat or very beneficial. Men and women did not differ significantly in their views. The main reason (stated by 60.3 per cent of participants) was that coverage increases the public's awareness of the problem and educates people as to what is happening. As one participant put it, "forewarned is forearmed". Some participants also felt that the media can help victims (5.2 per cent) although very few felt that it deterred perpetrators (1.3 per cent). Almost a fifth (17.3 per cent) of participants felt that media coverage was damaging or very damaging. The main explanation for this was that there is too much exposure (6.8 per cent), which could make people "immune . . . and desensitised" to the subject. Participants also felt that media coverage could be damaging, in that it encourages perpetrators (3.3 per cent), "it might tempt someone into abusing a child", while 3.5 per cent felt that it is damaging to the abused person and their family. A further 69 participants (2.4 per cent) thought that the current media coverage on sexual abuse was not appropriate viewing for young people or a general audience. Under a tenth of participants felt that media coverage had no effect, with 113 (3.9 per cent) participants saying that this was due to there being too little coverage.

The role of the media has been addressed in other studies in Ireland and elsewhere. The power of the media has been addressed in terms of changing both policy and attitudes. One description of their power in this regard is "Legislation by Tabloid" (Goddard and Saunders, 2001). Detailed analysis of sexual abuse coverage in Ireland has been reported (McDevitt, 1998) as has an analysis of media representations of particular types of abuse, e.g. abuse by clergy (Breen, 2000).

SEXUAL HARASSMENT

Traditionally, researchers have defined and investigated sexual harassment as a form of discrimination which takes place in a work or educational setting. This tradition is mainly due to the fact that the term sexual harassment first emerged in a legal context where women sought legal recourse for the negative consequences of trying to work or study in an atmosphere of intense sexual pressure or innuendo. While these strict definitions of sexual harassment have been expanded (e.g., to include men) and refined both in the courts and in psychological research, a broader view of sexual harassment as behaviours that fall along the continuum of sexual abuse and violence has also emerged. Viewed in this way, sexual harassment exists both within and outside the context of work, with discrimination being only one of the possible consequences of such experiences. In this study, sexual harassment has been examined both broadly (i.e., as a sexually offensive experience which can happen in any context) and in the traditional manner (i.e., as a sexually offensive experience which occurred in the context of a work or educational environment). The items used to study these experiences have been used previously, and are a subset of the items which form the Sexual Experiences Questionnaire (SEQ-DoD) (Fitzgerald et al., 1999). Previous researchers have recommended that a recent time frame be used in conjunction with these items; therefore, only sexual harassment which was experienced in the previous 12 months was queried. Thus, the incidence rather the prevalence of sexual harassment has been examined in this study.

A small but significant number of both men and women reported incidents of a sexually harassing nature in the past year. Some form of sexual harassment was experienced at least once during the last 12 months by 16.2 per cent of women and 12.6 per cent of men. Women were more likely than men to experience almost every type of sexual harassment examined in this study (Figure 4.29). The experience most frequently reported by women and men during the last 12 months was someone making crude and offensive remarks, either publicly or privately to them (12.8 per cent and 9.8 per cent, respectively). Alternatively, the experience of having someone threaten them with some sort of retaliation for not being sexually co-operative was reported by the least number of women and men (both at 1 per cent).

As not all of the items can be viewed as having the same impact on the person who experiences them, if a participant indicated that they did experience one of the above items, they were asked how distressing the incident was to them (Figure 4.30).

Figure 4.29: Incidence of Sexual Harassment in the Last 12 Months by Gender

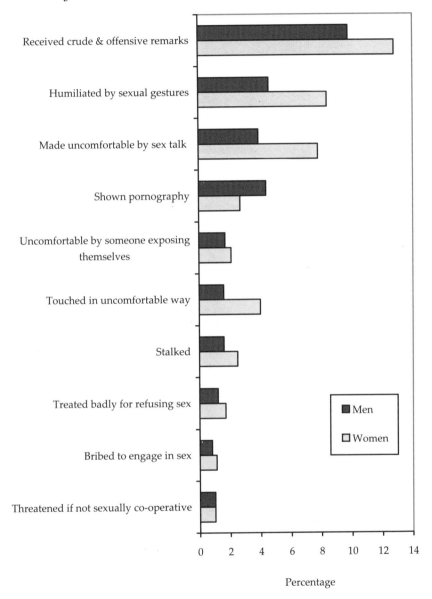

Percentage

Figure 4.30: Level of Distress Reported by those who Experienced Sexually Harassing Behaviours

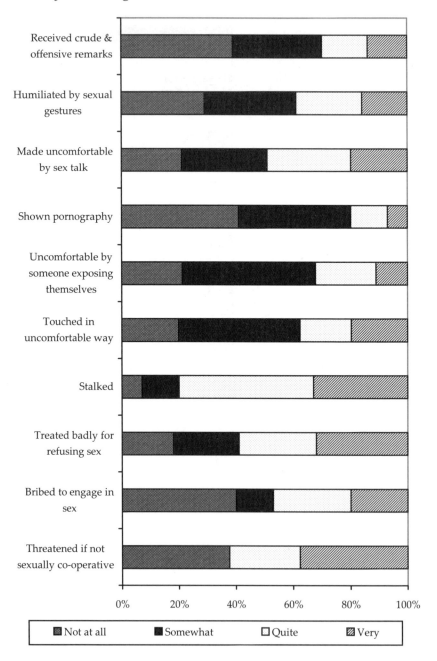

Figure 4.30 indicates the levels of distress experienced by participants. For example, "shown pornography", which was described to participants as having someone who "displayed, used or distributed pornographic or suggestive materials to you or in your presence in an offensive manner" was rated by very few of those who experienced it (7 per cent) as "very" distressing. This can be contrasted to those who reported experiencing stalking. Stalking was defined by interviewers as being "actions like following you, waiting for you without your approval, writing or talking to you against your wishes, or implying threats". While only 12 men and 19 women reported having experienced "stalking" in the last 12 months, very few (7 per cent) rated it as "not at all distressing", while the majority (80 per cent) rated it as "quite" or "very" distressing.

Sexual Harassment in the Workplace or in an Academic Setting

As previously described, researchers have traditionally limited their examination of sexual harassment to the workplace, and more recently, to the academic setting. Where participants reported sexual harassment by their "superior", "boss", "co-worker", "fellow employee", or "teacher" they were included in the following analyses. A total of 46 women (2.9 per cent) and 40 men (2.6 per cent) of the SAVI sample indicated that they experienced at least one form of sexual harassment by someone within their work environment. To further explore whether or not these experiences of sexual harassment (legally defined) impacted on their work, participants were asked how much the experiences affected their work. Of those who responded, 27 per cent indicated that it affected their work "somewhat" to "very", as opposed to those who said "not at all" (73 per cent). This may partly explain why very few indicated that they informed their employer about the situation (15 per cent of those women describing workplace harassment and 12.5 per cent of men). Reasons cited for not informing their boss or another person in authority were given by 40 participants. Nine indicated that they did not find the situation serious enough to do anything about it. Six reported dealing with the situation in their own way (e.g., "dealt with (it) myself — didn't want to get him in trouble"). Five indicated that it was embarrassing, but considered the experiences to be more like jokes than harassing behaviours. Three participants indicated that they "didn't like to talk about it" or didn't "want to cause trouble", while another four reported that they feared they would come across as "petty" or would not be taken seriously. Of perhaps the most concern were the three who indicated that the person doing the harassing was the most senior person in the work environment. As one participant explained, this "person is in charge of the office — the most senior in the chain".

In a recent report on workplace bullying in Ireland (Task Force on the Prevention of Workplace Bullying, 2001), much lower percentages of women and men were found to have experienced sexual harassment in the workplace. They found 0.4 per cent of women and 0.08 per cent of men experienced sexual harassment over a six-month period. Assuming the incidence rate would remain the same over a 12-month period (i.e., doubling the figures to compare with the SAVI results), this yields figures of 0.8 per cent and 0.16 per cent for women and men, respectively. While these figures remain much lower than those found in the SAVI study, one explanation is that the methodologies of the two studies are significantly different. While both were conducted with members of the general public over the telephone, the study on workplace bullying used a definition of bullying as a gating question. That is, if the respondent indicated that "yes" they had experienced bullying according to this definition, they were then asked a series of questions about that experience in more detail. It was after the respondent described the incident that the interviewer then categorised their experience, with one possible category being sexual harassment. The SAVI study methodology differs in that it asked multiple behaviourally specific questions. Thus, participants had a number of opportunities to indicate that they experienced some form of sexual harassment.

Queries about two additional experiences related to sexual harassment (outside of the workplace) were included: obscene phone calls and sexual "jokes". Participants were asked if they experienced either of these types of incidents in their lifetime (as opposed to over just the last 12 months). Obscene phone calls from strangers were experienced by 26 per cent of the sample, while obscene phone calls from someone known to the participant were experienced by a fewer number (9 per cent). If a participant indicated that they had received these types of calls, they were asked to indicate the total number they received in the past year. While the majority (65 per cent) did not receive any in the past year, 17 per cent reported that they had received at least one, while nine people indicated that they received at least 50. When asked how distressing these phone calls were to them, the majority reported that they were "quite" or "very" distressing (55 per cent).

Previous literature has documented the potentially abusive nature of many initiation rituals that are sexual in nature. These initiations or "jokes" often occur in school or other group settings. An open-ended question was asked about lifetime experiences of this nature and 101 participants (3.2 per cent) reported that such an incident had happened to them. A similar number of women and men reported these experiences (49 and 52 respectively). Participants were asked to briefly describe the event and these events were later categorised. Eleven described events that occurred on pre-wedding occasions, i.e. stag or hen nights, where participants felt uncomfortable with the situation which usually consisted of having to watch or touch a stripper or play with sex toys. An extreme example of this type of experience was being stripped and tied to a lamp-post. Strippers at birthday parties also caused discomfort to five participants. Uncomfortable situations at work parties (such as being prompted to act in a sexually explicit way) happened to a further five participants. Feeling embarrassed by sexually explicit suggestions or jokes was cited by six participants, while nine participants said that they had felt peer pressure to do sexual things that they felt uncomfortable with, such as during games like spin the bottle. Other initiation-type rituals that seemed to happen at school were described. These included other boys grabbing one participant's testicles and older girls ganging up on the younger girls in the changing room. Ten participants said that they would prefer not to describe what had happened to them, suggesting the potentially upsetting nature of such events. All participants who reported these types of events were asked how distressing the incident was to them at the time. A total of 43 per cent said the experience was "quite" or "very" distressing, while only 29 per cent found it "not at all" distressing. Women appeared to be more likely than men to find the situation "quite" or "very" distressing (56 per cent versus 35 per cent, respectively). These finding indicate the very real distress that friends and co-workers may unwittingly inflict on others in the name of "harm-less fun".

SURVEY PARTICIPATION EFFECTS

As described in the Introduction, the SAVI study was the first national telephone survey conducted on such a sensitive and difficult topic in Ireland. Not only is sexual violence difficult to discuss, but professionals agree that those who have experienced sexual abuse or assault may be quite vulnerable to unprompted events such as a survey. As clearly expressed in the WHO (1999) document, it is for that reason that research in these sensitive areas must not be carried out at the expense of those who participate. Indeed, the safety and well-being of participants was of paramount importance throughout this research project. Although the results of the feasibility study suggested that the methodology was acceptable, because the sample was small (n = 73), it remained largely unknown if the ethical and safety considerations put in place were not only adequate, but also put the safety and potential needs of the participants first.

While the effects of such an undertaking can never be entirely known, a small amount of data was collected for the purpose of monitoring and examining the effects of this type of study on both the general public and the researchers involved in its completion. The evidence for the survey's effects on those involved with it is presented below.

Effects on the Participants

Utilisation of the Freephone

As previously discussed, the freephone was set up for a variety of reasons. In order to examine how this number was used by both the participants and those who chose not to participate, a record was kept of these calls and included such information as when they called, their gender, and their stated reason for calling the freephone number. The total number of calls that were recorded during the three-month period of interviewing was 172. A small percentage of callers (7.5 per cent) hung up immediately upon hearing the greeting (i.e., that they had reached the freephone number at the College of Surgeons) so no information could be ascertained from these calls. Slightly more women than men used the number (55 per cent versus 45 per cent, respectively). For those calls where the reason for the call was recorded, the vast majority used the freephone to verify the study (62 per cent). The next most often given reason was to re-contact the interviewer to alert them that they either needed to re-schedule a previously scheduled interview, or were available to take part in the interview right then. Less common reasons for calling the freephone number were to query how their phone number was obtained or to say that they did not want to take part in the survey (both at 3 per cent). Of particular interest was the number of people who might use the freephone to complain or object to the study. Only 10 calls were made to the freephone for this purpose. Of these, one was a Garda phoning to say he had received a complaint, and wanted to confirm that an authentic study was being conducted.

Results of the Follow-up Calls

All participants were asked if they would be willing to be re-contacted for a follow-up call after participating in the survey. (For a detailed explanation of the purpose of a follow-up call, see the Methods section in Chapter 2.) Follow-up calls were made to 71 per cent of the SAVI sample (see Table 4.41). If the participant specifically stated that they would prefer not to be called back (typically stating that they were too busy), a call was not attempted. This accounted for 301 (9.6 per cent) of the sample. When this was the case, the participant was encouraged to take note of the freephone number if, on reflection, they had anything to add or query. The remaining participants who did not receive a follow-up could not be contacted. Interviewers attempted to call a participant back three times if s/he had not disclosed abuse and six times if s/he had.

Table 4.41: Follow-up Telephone Calls Made Two to Three Days after the Survey

Final Outcome of Call	Number of Participants
Completed follow-up calls	2,206
Recontact not successful	613
Asked not to call back	301
Total	3,120

When asked at this follow-up call, a small number of people reported being upset by the interview (2.9 per cent). A further six participants indicated that they were worried, with six indicating that they felt "down" (i.e. negative or depressed feelings) immediately following the interview as a result of the questions asked. However, all of these participants reported feeling "ok" or better at the time of the follow-up call.

Other Evidence of Effects of the Survey on Participant Well-being

As described in the section on ethical and safety issues, all interviewers were trained to monitor the participant's distress during an interview. While the number of times that an interview was stopped and then continued (because the participant wished to complete the survey) was not recorded, there were only two occasions in which an interviewer felt serious concern about a participant during the course of the interview. One person (a young woman) spontaneously reported that she currently had suicidal ideation. The interviewer immediately stopped the interview and assessed the seriousness of these statements (as outlined in a standard safety protocol developed before the study). The participant admitted that she had these feelings from time to time, but had never acted on them in the past. The interviewer then explored with the participant what strategies she might use to cope with these feelings in the short term, and where she might go to get further help for herself. She agreed to contact a help-line she had often used in the past, and agreed to be re-contacted by the interviewer for a follow-up call. On re-contact the following day, she stated that she was feeling better and confirmed that she had made an appointment with her doctor. Four people contacted for the survey later contacted the Dublin Rape Crisis Centre to record concerns or distress about having discussed such sensitive issues. Some commenced therapy with DRCC as a consequence of this while in one case reassurance of the authenticity and confidentiality of the study was provided.

Participant Referrals

All those who reported an experience of abuse were given a national freephone number for sexual abuse services and were asked if they wanted contact details of their local services for abuse. Interviewers made the decision that it was appropriate to pass on these referrals to 429 participants; however, 315 declined to take the numbers offered. Of the people who took numbers offered, most were referred to sexual abuse services in their locality with a small number being referred to other specialist services such as AWARE (a service for depression). A number of people also took service numbers for someone other than themselves (e.g., a participant who experienced no abuse themselves, but had a friend or family member who had been abused and whom they thought could use a service).

Willingness of Participants to Participate in Possible Future Studies

Because of the unique value of the SAVI Survey sample — the first large random sample of the Irish adult population agreeing to participate in a study on lifetime experiences of sexual violence — each individual was asked about their willingness to participate in subsequent studies when contacted for the follow-up call a few days after the main interview. The question to participants was phrased as follows:

> "Sometimes when we put all the information on studies like this together, we may wish to get back to a group of people for a follow-up study. We've no plans for this at the moment, but would you be willing to be contacted again at a future date if this were to happen? You could of course say no at that time if I didn't suit you. What do you think? Yes__ No__"

Of those contacted at follow-up (n = 2,206), 1,781 (81 per cent) agreed to be re-contacted about future studies. This indicates a high level of acceptance of a quite general request, and provides further evidence that the survey was not upsetting or intrusive to many.

Effects on the Interviewers

Reactions to the Process of Interviewing

At the end of each survey, the interviewer was given a chance to rate how the interview had gone (from "very difficult" to "very smoothly") and to note how she was feeling (from "not upset at all" to "very upset"). A small number of interviews (3.5 per cent) were rated by the interviewer as being difficult or very difficult. In ten cases, interviewers said that the interview had left them feeling upset in some way. This was a surprisingly low number considering the sensitive, and at times traumatic, nature of the calls. The low amount of distress felt by the interviewers may be attributable to the presence of other members of the SAVI team at all times during interviewing. On analysing the statements in the section concerning the interviewer's feelings at the end of the survey, it appears that discussing the call with a SAVI team member afterwards helped immensely in managing any feelings of distress due to the nature of the call.

Indirect and Anecdotal Information

All interviewers stayed with the project until the end of the survey period. This staff retention rate was notable given the short contract period and half-time research positions.

The role of interviewer in a telephone survey of sexual abuse is a multi-faceted one: it incorporates the strange combination of working as a salesperson (to gain maximum participation), a confidant (to ensure a high level of trust in order to allow the participant to be honest) and a neutral researcher (to ensure that the final results are not biased in any way). It was perhaps this final role that proved to be the most difficult for many of the SAVI interviewers. The nature of working in the area of sexual abuse means that a person will come across emotional, and sometimes traumatic, stories. In these situations it could prove difficult to keep a neutral viewpoint and distance. Furthermore, many of the SAVI team came from a counselling background and at times felt that it was difficult to remain a "professional and impartial collector" (Morton-Williams, 1993). They reported that in these situations it was helpful to remember the value of the work in that the information gathered would benefit the wider public (even if it did not directly benefit the participant). Counselling, if needed by the participant, had to be directed elsewhere. Interviewers indicated that it was particularly tough to end a call when a participant who was upset after disclosing abuse was adamant that he or she did not want outside help. As one interviewer put it:

> "I feel I want to help but cannot and should not as she does not want help."

Follow-up calls gave the interviewer a chance to "check in" with the participant again and proved to be invaluable if an interviewer was worried about a person.

Interviewers admitted that the experience was emotionally draining at times. They found that having the support of the rest of the SAVI team on a daily basis did a lot to alleviate this. However, they also felt the experience was quite rewarding. They reported that the most rewarding part of the job was gaining the trust of the members of the public who spoke to them. The fact that so many people told them deeply intimate stories of their life (when they had often told no one else) left many of the interviewers feeling genuinely grateful for having had the chance to take part in the study.

Overall, the various measures put in place appear to have ensured a believable, valid and safe survey for those contacted and those participating and working on the project.

SURVEY RESULTS SUMMARY POINTS

Study Population

- Over 3,000 randomly selected Irish adults took part in the study (n = 3,118). This represented a 71 per cent participation rate of those invited. For a telephone survey, and on such a sensitive topic, this very high participation rate means that the findings can be taken as broadly representative of the general population in Ireland. The information available can therefore provide important and previously unavailable information on the extent and nature of sexual violence in Irish society.

Prevalence of Sexual Violence

Child Sexual Abuse (defined as sexual abuse of children and adolescents under age 17 years)

- **Girls:** One in five women (20.4 per cent) reported experiencing contact sexual abuse in childhood with a further one in ten (10.0 per cent) reporting non-contact sexual abuse. In over a quarter of cases of contact abuse (i.e. 5.6 per cent of all girls), the abuse involved penetrative sex — either vaginal, anal or oral sex.

- **Boys**: One in six men (16.2 per cent) reported experiencing contact sexual abuse in childhood with a further one in fourteen (7.4 per cent) reporting non-contact sexual abuse. In one of every six cases of contact abuse (i.e. 2.7 per cent of all boys), the abuse involved penetrative sex — either anal or oral sex.

Adult Sexual Assault (defined as sexual violence against women or men aged 17 years and above)

- **Women**: One in five women (20.4 per cent) reported experiencing contact sexual assault as adults with a further one in twenty (5.1 per cent) reporting unwanted non-contact sexual experiences. Over a quarter of cases of contact abuse in adulthood (i.e. 6.1 per cent of all women) involved penetrative sex.

- **Men**: One in ten men (9.7 per cent) reported experiencing contact sexual assault as adults with a further 2.7 per cent reporting unwanted non-contact sexual experiences. One in ten cases of contact abuse in adulthood (i.e. 0.9 per cent of all men) involved penetrative sex.

Lifetime Experience of Sexual Abuse and Assault

- **Women**: More than four in ten women (42 per cent) reported some form of sexual abuse or assault in their lifetime. The most serious form of abuse, penetrative abuse, was experienced by 10 per cent of women. Attempted penetration or contact abuse was experienced by 21 per cent, with a further 10 per cent experiencing non-contact abuse.

- **Men**: Over a quarter of men (28 per cent) reported some form of sexual abuse or assault in their lifetime. Penetrative abuse was experienced by 3 per cent of men. Attempted penetration or contact abuse was experienced by 18 per cent, with a further 7 per cent experiencing non-contact abuse.

Characteristics of Sexual Abuse and Violence in Childhood and Adulthood

- Overall, almost one-third of women and a quarter of men reported some level of sexual abuse in childhood. Attempted or actual penetrative sex was experienced by 7.6 per cent of girls and 4.2 per cent of boys. Equivalent rape or attempted rape figures in adulthood were 7.4 per cent for women and 1.5 per cent for men. Hence girls and women were more likely to be subjected to serious sexual crimes than boys and men. Levels of serious sexual crimes committed against women remained similar from childhood through adulthood while risks for men were lower as children than for girls and decreased three-fold from childhood to adult life.

- Of those disclosing abuse, over one-quarter (27.7 per cent) of women and one-fifth (19.5 per cent) of men were abused by different perpetrators as both children and adults (i.e. "revictimised"). For women, experiencing penetrative sexual abuse in childhood was associated with a sixteen-fold increase in risk of adult penetrative sexual abuse, and in a five-fold increase in risk of adult contact sexual violence. For men, experiencing penetrative sexual abuse in childhood was associated with a sixteen-fold increase in the risk of adult penetrative sexual violence, and an approximately twelve-fold increase in the risk of adult contact sexual violence. It is not possible to say that childhood abuse "causes" adult revictimisation. Childhood sexual abuse is, however, an important marker of increased risk of adult sexual violence.

- Most sexual abuse in childhood and adolescence occurred in the pre-pubescent period, with two-thirds (67 per cent) of abused girls and 62 per cent of abused boys having experienced abuse by twelve years of age.

- In four of ten cases (40 per cent), the experience of child sexual abuse was an ongoing, rather than a single, abuse event. For many of those who experienced ongoing abuse (58 per cent of girls and 42 per cent of boys), the duration of abuse was longer than one year.

- A third (36 per cent) of those who had experienced sexual abuse as a child now believe that their abuser was also abusing other children at the time.

Characteristics of Perpetrators and Context of Sexual Violence

- Most perpetrators of child sexual abuse (89 per cent) were men acting alone. Seven per cent of children were abused by one female perpetrator. In 4 per cent of cases more than one abuser was involved in the same incident(s).

Perpetrators of Child Sexual Abuse

- **Girls**: A quarter (24 per cent) of perpetrators against girls were family members, half (52 per cent) were non-family but known to the abused girl and a quarter (24 per cent) were strangers.

- **Boys**: Fewer family members were involved in child sexual abuse of boys. One in seven perpetrators (14 per cent) was a family member with two-thirds (66 per cent) non-family but known to the abused boy. One in five (20 per cent) were strangers.

- In sum, in four-fifths of cases of child sexual abuse, the perpetrator was known to the abused person.

- The perpetrator was another child or adolescent (17 years old or younger) in one out of every four cases.

Perpetrators of Sexual Violence against Adults

- Almost one-quarter (23.6 per cent) of perpetrators of sexual violence against women as adults were intimate partners or ex-partners. This was the case for very few (1.4 per cent) abused men. Instead, most perpetrators of abuse against men were friends or acquaintances (42 per cent). The risk of sexual assault by a stranger was higher for adults (representing 30 per cent of assaults on women and 38 per cent of assaults on men) than for children.

- Alcohol was involved in almost half of the cases of sexual assault that occurred as an adult. Of those who reported that alcohol was involved, both parties were drinking in 57 per cent of cases concerning abuse of women, and in 63 per cent of cases concerning abuse of men. Where only one party was drinking, the perpetrator was the one drinking in the majority of cases (84 per cent of female and 70 per cent of male abuse cases).

Psychological Consequences of Sexual Violence

- Approximately one in three (30 per cent) women and one in four (18 per cent) men reported that their experiences of sexual violence (either in childhood, adulthood or both) had had a moderate or extreme effect on their lives overall.

- A quarter (25 per cent) of women and one in six (16 per cent) men reported having experienced symptoms consistent with a diagnosis of post-traumatic stress disorder (PTSD) at some time in their lives following, and as a consequence of, their experience of sexual violence.

- Those who had experienced sexual violence were significantly more likely to have used medication for anxiety or depression or to have been a psychiatric hospital inpatient than those without such experiences. For instance, those who had experienced attempted or actual penetrative sexual abuse were eight times more likely to have been an inpatient in a psychiatric hospital than those who had not been abused.

Disclosure of Experiences of Sexual Violence

- Almost half (47 per cent) of those who disclosed experiences of sexual violence in this study reported that they had never previously disclosed that abuse to others. Thus in a study of over

3,100 adults, almost 600 people disclosed instances of abuse for the first time to another person.

- Older people were generally less likely than other age groups to have disclosed to others in the past with one exception: most (60 per cent) young men who had experienced child sexual abuse had told no-one prior to the study.

- Most people who disclosed sexual violence did so to friends (71 per cent) or family members (43 per cent). Family members were more likely to be told in the case of child sexual abuse.

- The most common reason people gave for not telling about their abuse as children was because of feeling ashamed or blaming themselves. A quarter of both men and women who had experienced child sexual abuse reported these as the reasons for not telling. These reasons were uncommon for those who had experienced sexual violence as adults. A fifth of adults had not disclosed abuse because they thought that what had happened to them was too trivial to tell others.

- Disclosure of abuse to professionals was strikingly low. Regarding experiences of adult sexual assault, only one man (of 98 abused, i.e. 1 per cent) and 7.8 per cent of women (19 of 244) had reported their experiences to the Gardaí (i.e. 6 per cent overall of those abused). Patterns were similar regarding experiences of child sexual abuse. Ten men (of 178) and 28 women (of 290) reported their experiences to the Gardaí (i.e. 8 per cent overall of those abused). Disclosure to medical professionals was 6 per cent for adult sexual assault and 4 per cent for child abuse while disclosure to counsellors/therapists was 12 per cent; 14 per cent of women and 8 per cent of men disclosing to counsellors/therapists.

- Regarding client evaluation of services received from professionals, overall satisfaction with services received was greatest for counsellors and therapists at 81 per cent. About half (56 per cent) of those who reported to the Gardaí were satisfied overall with the service they received with little differences for child or adult abuse. Those who received help from medical professionals were mixed in their ratings, with those who received services for adult sexual assault being almost twice as satisfied with the services they received than those with experiences of child sexual abuse (60 per cent versus 33 per cent).

- Lack of information from the Gardaí and medical personnel was the main source of dissatisfaction with these services. Specifically, Gardaí were seen to provide inadequate explanations of procedures being undertaken, and medical personnel were seen as needing to provide more information regarding other available services and options. With regard to counselling services, time waiting to get an appointment was the major source of dissatisfaction.

- Legal redress for sexual crimes, as reported in this study, was the exception rather than the rule. Of 38 individuals who reported child sexual abuse to the Gardaí, six cases (16 per cent) resulted in court proceedings with four guilty verdicts. Of 20 people reporting adult sexual assault, two court cases (10 per cent) were taken with one resulting in a guilty verdict.

Public Perceptions of Sexual Violence

The perceptions of all the participants were taken to represent the "public" perception of sexual violence in Irish society today.

Perceptions of Prevalence of Sexual Violence

- Estimates of the prevalence of adult sexual assault and most types of child sexual abuse by the participants indicated that about half of those interviewed were quite inaccurate about the frequency of such events, either because they overestimated or underestimated them. Underestimation was more common, with a third underestimating the prevalence of rape among adult women and men, and child abuse by non-family members. However, participant estimates regarding the prevalence of incest were substantially higher than those reported in the present study.

- Participants significantly overestimated the number of cases reported to the Gardaí (estimated 34 per cent women and 16 per cent men; actual percentages 10 per cent women and 6 per cent men) while correctly signalling the gender difference of men being less likely to report than women. Estimates of the likelihood of getting a conviction in court cases were similar to actual reports although actual reports relate to such small numbers that conclusions need to be drawn with caution.

Perceptions of Probability of Disclosure

- When asked to judge whether they would tell others if they themselves were sexually abused, over a quarter of study participants said that they would be unlikely to tell family members. More (41 per cent) felt they probably would not tell friends. Regarding professionals, over a quarter (27 per cent) felt they would be unlikely to tell the Gardaí and almost a quarter were uncertain or thought they would not go to a counsellor. However, most (85 per cent) felt they would disclose to a doctor, some with the added qualification that they would only if medically necessary. Men were more likely to think they would not disclose to all groups except doctors.

Perceptions of Service Access

- Over a quarter of the group (27.6 per cent) reported that they would not know where to go to get professional help for sexual violence if they needed it. Men were significantly less likely than women to be able to identify where they could go for help and young adults of both sexes (those aged 18–24) were less likely than others to know where to seek help. Half of young men (i.e. under age 30) reported that they would not know where to find professional support or services.

Public Beliefs about Sexual Violence

Beliefs about sexual violence were assessed with attitude statements about common rape beliefs.

- Some reported attitudes reflected more accurate views and views which are more supportive to those who are affected by sexual violence. For instance, almost all (92 per cent) agreed that "a date rape can be just as traumatic as rape by a stranger"; 85 per cent agreed that "a raped woman is usually an innocent victim" and 91 per cent disagreed that "child sexual abuse is usually committed by strangers". On the other hand, four in ten (40 per cent) of study participants felt that "accusations of rape are often false".

- Men were significantly more accepting of "myths" about sexual violence than women, particularly with regard to motivation for rape and sexual violence committed against men. Specifically, 47 per cent of men (versus 34 per cent of women) agreed that "the reason most rapists commit rape is overwhelming sexual desire" and 41 per cent of men (versus 27 per cent of women) agreed that "men who sexually assault other men must be gay (homosexual)".

- Attitudes towards media coverage of sexual violence were predominantly positive with three-quarters (76 per cent) believing coverage was beneficial.

Sexual Harassment

- Some form of sexual harassment was experienced at least once during the last 12 months by 16.2 per cent of women and 12.6 per cent of men. Being stalked in a way that was frightening to them was reported by 1 per cent of the participants.

Section III

MARGINALISED SUB-GROUPS

The aim of this overall project was to examine sexual violence in Irish society. The major emphasis has been on the community-dwelling general population, in part because they represent the majority and in part because there has been little opportunity to study them in the past. It is of course acknowledged that many subgroups in society who will not be reached by landline telephones may differ from the general population in either their risk of sexual violence or their use of services because of aspects of their subgroup identity. The aim of this section of the report was to highlight possible differences in risk, the particular challenges of disclosing sexual violence and seeking services for some more vulnerable groups in our society. The coverage is not intended to be exhaustive. Rather it aims to help the reader appreciate some of the complex challenges to face policy makers and service providers in attempting to meet the awareness-raising, prevention and management needs of such groups in a holistic approach to managing sexual violence. The groups included were homeless women and their children, Travellers, women in prostitution, people with learning disability, prisoners and patients in psychiatric settings. While the sub-study on homeless women provides an in-depth exploration of sexual violence in their lives, the issues raised for each of the other groups deserve further exploration in order to understand more fully the challenges facing these groups. The groups described were considered for the present study by means of differing methodologies and levels of involvement. The reasons for this included both pragmatic concerns and the awareness that there are differing perspectives on abuse in marginalised groups. Each of the groups included and the methods used are briefly introduced below.

In the sub-study of homeless women, the women were consulted directly. One-to-one interviews with such a vulnerable group requires extensive skill and resources, including time. An extensive study was possible by combining the research concerns of the SAVI Study with a larger project on the health needs of homeless women. This sub-study was an assessment of the level of lifetime sexual violence experienced by 100 homeless women and their children in Dublin. Interviews were conducted in the context of a wider health status evaluation of these women who were housed in temporary local authority and private settings. For homeless women some of the research concerns were about a background featuring sexual abuse as a precursor to homelessness while other concerns were about their vulnerability to abuse as a consequence of homelessness. Concerns for their children were also a focus of this study.

The second sub-study addressed the particular challenges of dealing with sexual violence as a marginalised cultural group in society. The study was conducted by speaking with those associated with a representative organisation for Travellers — Pavee Point. Women from the Travelling community participated in a focus group to discuss the particular challenges of managing sexual violence for women and men in their community. The next sub-study addressed challenges for prisoners in managing sexual violence. As with the homeless women, sexual violence as an issue may be a precursor to criminal activity and to prison. It may also be a concern as a risk of prison life itself. In this third group, contact with prisoners was not considered appropriate by the research team as the limited time and resources available could not do justice to the complexity and seriousness of the issues involved. Thus the issue of sexual violence and the prison population was considered with a wide range of prison service personnel, from management through professional to chaplain and frontline staff. The focus was on their perceptions of problems and of possible solutions.

A vulnerable group by virtue of the lifestyle they live are women in prostitution. Here, social attitudes to abuse and to prostitutes and prostitution may converge to make for a very challenging environment in which to protect women from, and support them through, sexual violence. Consideration of this issue involved speaking with a representative of an outreach organisation and surveying a group of staff and volunteers who provide a night-time outreach programme for women involved in prostitution. This is somewhat different to the approach to professionals taken with the prison group.

People with a learning disability were also considered in terms of the challenges of sexual violence. Here, the international and Irish literature reflecting problems and management initiatives was considered in association with discussions involving a small number of key professionals in the area in Ireland. The challenges are both to create a safe environment for those with learning disability while also seeking not to restrict their choices or legitimate rights to interpersonal relationships in a singular pursuit of safety as the highest priority. A guidelines-based approach was the main focus here — if and where they exist, how they developed and where they are used.

The sixth and last group addressed were individuals who have serious mental health problems. A review of international literature was combined with discussions with health professionals concerning the level of enquiry, recording and management of sexual violence in psychiatric settings. The reported complexities of getting information on sexual violence from or about this group highlight some of the dilemmas in managing vulnerable groups and sensitive issues in a system combining health and legal challenges.

Overall, it is hoped that coverage of these exemplar groups will raise awareness and highlight some of the challenges to an informed and inclusive approach to managing sexual violence. For some groups, the higher level of risk than in the general population provides an added impetus to addressing support and management issues for these and other vulnerable groups not directly examined in this study. Tackling sexual violence requires commitment at many levels to address the varied contexts and vulnerabilities to abuse itself and to provide support and redress tailored to meet those same particular contexts and vulnerabilities.

Chapter 5

HOMELESS WOMEN AND THEIR CHILDREN: VULNERABILITY TO SEXUAL VIOLENCE

INTRODUCTION

This sub-study was part of a wider project concerned with the health of homeless women and their children in Dublin.[1] Homeless women have additional problems that distinguish them from homeless men and non-homeless women. They face a very high risk of physical and sexual attack from intimates, acquaintances and strangers (Goodman et al., 1991). The lifetime violent victimisation of homeless women is seen as so high that it amounts to a normative experience. The majority of women in Goodman's study, for instance, were abused both as children and adults. Levels of gynaecological problems are high (Breakey et al., 1989) with pregnancy rates almost twice that of settled women. A 1992 survey in the UK called "4 in 10" highlighted the level of sexual violence in the pre-homeless experience of young women (Hendessi, 1992). Forty per cent of 53 women reported a history of sexual abuse under the age of 16. The authors noted that the rates were very similar to rates reported in the nineteenth century. The

[1] This separate sub-study was conducted by a research team from the Royal College of Surgeons in Ireland: Mary Smith (Project researcher) and Hannah McGee (Director) (Health Services Research Centre) and William Shannon (Professor of General Practice) in association with Tony Holohan (specialist in Public Health Medicine at the ERHA). It was funded by a Health Research Board project grant with additional support from the ERHA.

"Counted In" study (Williams and O'Connor, 1999) indicated that women constitute a minority of the homeless population in Dublin (approximately 36 per cent). Nonetheless, they constitute a significant number of individuals, many of whom are also responsible for children in homeless settings. Very little evidence is available on this group; for instance, in a study examining the physical and dental health of over 200 homeless people, only 22 women were represented (Condon, 2001). The overall aim of this study was to assess the physical and psychological health status of the Dublin population of homeless women. As part of the health and social services needs assessment, sections on women's health issues and on physical and sexual violence as health concerns for women and their children were included. Key questions were to establish the prevalence of abuse or fear of abuse in this group, and the possible role of abuse in homelessness, as well as service attitudes, use and needs.

METHODS

Sample

The population targeted was homeless women who had presented themselves to the Eastern Region Health Authority (ERHA) as homeless, and who were then provided with emergency accommodation in bed and breakfast (B&B) settings and hostels for homeless persons. Those sleeping rough, a minority of the population of homeless women according to the Counted In report (Brookoff et al., 1997), or those not accessing ERHA services, were omitted. The Homeless Persons Unit estimated that the B&B to hostel accommodation ratio for women was 2:1. The study aimed to recruit women from B&Bs and hostels in these proportions to help reflect the overall profile of these women. Providers of accommodation were asked by letter from the ERHA to allow the researchers access to their residents in order to invite them to participate.

Procedure

Co-operation for identifying the women accessing homeless services through the ERHA was provided by Charles Street, Homeless Persons Unit who made available addresses of hostels and of
B&B owners providing emergency accommodation for homeless
women and their children (and partners in some instances) for the
study. Forty B&B establishments (34 separate owners) indicated
that they accommodated homeless women at the time of the
study. All but one agreed to co-operate with recruitment (i.e. provided names, allowed access or offered to distribute recruitment
literature). This amounted to 267 names to which invitations were
issued. Invitation was by letter to named residents, or by general
advertisement and opportunistic recruitment of a group in residence during a given period of time. Prospective participants
could indicate their willingness by returning a freepost acceptance
form to the project, or by agreeing in person when the researcher
visited the establishment.

A total of 67 were interviewed (25 per cent participation rate)
from the B&B population. A further 25 women responded to the
invitation to participate with 4 refusing, 16 agreeing but failing to
show up or be interviewed for various reasons and 5 responding
too late to fit within the time-frame of the study. All participants
were given full details of the project, confidentiality and anonymity were assured, and informed written consent to participate was
acquired. The women were offered a token of £10 in consideration
of the time taken (interviews lasted on average 1 hour) and were
interviewed with due regard for their privacy and willingness to
discuss certain topics in varied settings. Interviews were conducted from January to October 2000.

Hostel accommodation: The main hostels providing accommodation for this population were asked for their co-operation by
letter from the Homeless Persons Unit. Four hostels were targeted; one private, one ERHA funded and two run by religious
orders. Three agreed to participate by providing names, allowing
access or offering to distribute recruitment literature (these had a
combined capacity of about 60 beds). One hostel, which had the

largest capacity of about 100 beds, did not want to participate. As with the B&B residents, potential participants indicated their willingness by responding to the recruitment literature by freepost, or by agreeing in person to interview on the day. A total of 33 women were interviewed — a participation rate of about 50 per cent of the residents at the time. When the interviewer reached the sexual violence section of the larger interview, it was prefaced with a repeat of the clarification to women that they could continue to participate or not as they felt appropriate. For those with children, they were cautioned in advance that reports of sexual abuse concerning their children could be subject to reporting to the authorities if the cases were not already known to them.

The Sample

The numbers achieved reflect the 2:1 distribution estimated by the Homeless Persons Unit of B&B to hostel dwellers.[2] The lack of participation of one of the hostels, with the largest (and anecdotally the most "difficult" or deprived) group of women was unfortunate. Their absence, alongside the absence of those "sleeping rough" (estimated at about 40 women), may mean that the results do not reflect the details of the lives of what are likely to be the most vulnerable women.

Measures

The study involved interviews with the participants using a schedule that included demographic details, history of homelessness, self-reported health status, access to health care, use of and satisfaction ratings with services, standardised measures of psychological well-being and quality of life, and histories of domestic violence, sexual violence, alcohol and illicit drug use. The sensitive nature of the study required interviewing by a skilled researcher. One researcher, an experienced nurse researcher, con-

---

[2] Figures gathered by Simon Outreach in conjunction with Focus Ireland and Dublin Corporation, *Irish Times*, 29 November 2000.

ducted all interviews. The study was approved by the Research Ethics Committee, Royal College of Surgeons in Ireland.

RESULTS

Forty-nine of the 100 women interviewed had suffered some form of serious sexual violence, either assault or abuse in their lifetime. The term sexual assault was used here to describe all forms of unwanted/uninvited sexual acts that involved contact but not penetration. Verbal or emotional abuse, harassment, threats, "stalking" etc. of a sexual nature were not accounted for in the figures. Seven of the 49 women, while acknowledging they had suffered some form of sexual violence, opted not to provide further details — mostly because they became very upset. Two of these women acknowledged they had been raped; the extent of the abuse experienced by the remaining five is not known. Most women for whom details are known had been victims of rape at least once in their lives. Of those who indicated they had been raped, six also indicated "revictimisation" or separate instances of sexual assault (i.e. considered separate because the incident(s) involved a different perpetrator).

Sexual Violence: The Role of Homelessness

Table 5.1 describes the profile of sexual violence by accommodation status at the time of abuse. In Table 5.1 each woman is counted only once and is assigned to the most serious category of abuse experienced. This table outlines that most women (32 of 49, 65 per cent) were abused before they became homeless. This relates partly to age of abuse, as seen later. When asked directly, 14 women said the sexual violence they had experienced either directly caused, or significantly contributed to, their becoming homeless. Three of these women were the targets of physical, as well as sexual, violence from partners and had become homeless as a direct result of leaving the violent relationship; the remaining 11 had been abused as children in the family home; 4 by their fathers and the remainder by other relatives, all before the age of 13 years.

Table 5.1: Types of Sexual Violence Experienced by
Accommodation Status at Time of Abuse

Type Abuse	Not Homeless % (n)	Homeless % (n)	Both Homeless and Housed % (n)	Unknown % (n)	Total % (n)
Rape	69 (22)	67 (6)	100 (3)	—	63 (31)
Sexual assault	28 (9)	33 (3)	—	—	24 (12)
Assault*	3 (1)	—	—	100 (5)	13 (6)
Total % (n)	65 (32)	17 (9)	6 (3)	10 (5)	10 (49)

* Details not complete as participant "prefers not to talk about it"

Of those women first abused as adults, eight indicated that a period of homelessness preceded sexual assault — five were raped (two by strangers, two by a relative and one by someone known to the abused women) and three were sexually assaulted (each by a stranger, a partner and a relative). One woman, raped in adulthood by a stranger while homeless, had not experienced sexual violence before becoming homeless.

Sexual Violence: Location Where Abuse Took Place

Women were asked to indicate where the abuse took place. There were multiple locations and instances for some, particularly for those women who had been assaulted by more than one perpetrator. For some women, particularly those who suffered rape and/or sexual assault as children, the details reported mostly pertain to the more serious crime of rape. Because of the sensitive and distressing nature of the topic, limited probes were used to separate out the details of all instances of abuse where a complex or lengthy history existed. Table 5.2 outlines the information available; discrepancies between the numbers reporting any abuse (n = 49) and the totals outlined are because some women reported many events and details and some withheld details.

Table 5.2: *Age of Women by Location of Sexual Abuse*

	Age When Instances of Abuse Occurred				
Location of Abuse	< 8 yrs	8–12 yrs	13–14 yrs	15–17 yrs	18+ yrs
Home of the abused	11 (6*)	6 (2*)	2 (2*)	—	7 (2*)
Home of the perpetrator	2	3	1	1 (*1)	3
Neutral place	—	—	1	1	1
On the street	—	—	—	—	8 (7**)

* Indicates abused and perpetrator are known to have shared the same home at the time — e.g. of 11 cases under the age of 8, in the abused person's home, the perpetrator also lived there in 6 cases.

** Indicates numbers responsible who were strangers. In 3 instances the perpetrator was the customer soliciting the woman who was engaged in prostitution

Sexual Violence: Perpetrators

The perpetrators of rape and sexual assault against these women are outlined in Figure 5.1. Some women were abused by more than one perpetrator. All but one of the perpetrators was male; there was one instance of abuse by an adult female. This occurred when the woman was a child in care — her carer was the perpetrator. In half of the rape cases (15 of 31) the abuse was perpetrated by relatives.

There was more than one perpetrator or episode in some instances; in total, 55 perpetrators were identified by 42 women.

Figure 5.1: Relationship of Perpetrator to Abused Woman

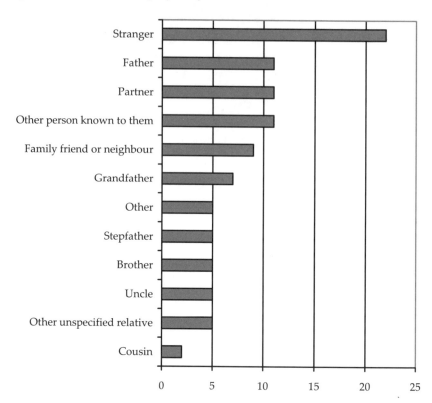

Percentage of Sample

Age at Onset of Sexual Violence

The age when abuse first began is outlined in Figure 5.2. The ages for some women "who did not want to talk about it" or began to give information and then stopped, are missing.

Only five women said the rape or assault they experienced was a single incident; 20 women endured sexual violence for an average of 5.4 years (SD: 4.5; Range 1–20 years). The remainder who indicated a timeframe estimated the period for which they experienced abuse to have been throughout their complete childhood or adulthood — one woman said "all my life".

Figure 5.2: Age at which Abuse Occurred (single events) or Started (ongoing abuse)

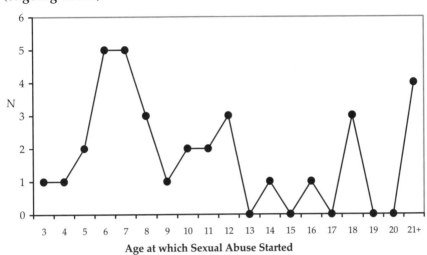

Age at which Sexual Abuse Started

Disclosure of Sexual Violence

Women were asked if they had ever disclosed what had happened to them. Less than a third of the women (31 per cent) had disclosed at the time of the abuse (Table 5.3).

Table 5.3: Disclosure of Sexual Violence to Others

Time of Abuse	Told at the Time % (n)	Did Not Tell Until Later % (n)	Never Told % (n)
Childhood	54 (7)	48 (13) (as child) 26 (7) (as adult)	50 (1)
Adulthood	46 (6)	26 (7)	50 (1)
Total % (n)	31 (13)	64 (27)	5 (2)

In this study, two of the 49 women had not disclosed previously. All women disclosing abuse were given information on available services, as in the main SAVI study.

Sexual Violence: Responses to Seeking Help

Seeking professional help and availing of it were not necessarily immediate. Indeed, in most cases, it involved a considerable time lapse. The professional services sought in Table 5.4 include seeking medical help.

Table 5.4: Professional Services Sought and Provided for Sexual Violence

	% (n)
Needed and got medical attention	32 (15)
Needed but did not look for professional help	38 (18)
Looked for and got professional help	21 (10)
Looked for, but did not get professional help	9 (4)

Reasons for not seeking help are presented in Table 5.5. Some women indicated a variety of reasons.

Table 5.5: Reasons for Not Seeking Help for Sexual Violence

	% (n)
Did not know where to look	20 (9)
Fear of retaliation	16 (8)
Did not understand what was happening at the time	8 (4)
Was afraid to cause trouble in the family	8 (4)
Too ashamed	4 (2)
Would not have been believed	4 (2)
Was too involved in drug abuse to do so	2 (1)

Women who availed of help were asked about type and effectiveness of the help received in a series of open questions. Counselling was the most common and the most valued form of help available to the women. Methods of referral and access varied widely. In total, 23 women availed of counselling through the agencies listed in Table 5.6.

Table 5.6: Health, Social and Law Enforcement Services Used by Homeless Women as a Consequence of Sexual Violence

	% (n)
Rape crisis centre	26 (6)
Psychiatric services	13 (3)
Social worker referral	9 (2)
Drug treatment centres	9 (2)
Legal/justice system	9 (2)
Other	35 (8)

Of those who expressed an opinion (n = 12), the majority (75 per cent) were satisfied or warmly appreciative of the counselling they had received, while three women were not pleased. The other 13 women were non-committal when asked. One woman, in a particularly distressed state following the abuse, was refused counselling because she was on a methadone maintenance programme.

Sexual Violence: Getting Justice and Protection

Recourse through the legal system was reported as causing more problems than it solved for the three (of 49) women who pursued that option. One woman reported the perpetrator to the police. He was taken in for questioning and then released — she was subsequently beaten severely as a result of "grassing him up". Another woman, now in her thirties, reported her abuse to the police as a fifteen-year-old girl and was turned away. A third case was of a woman who avoided her violent and sexually abusive partner. She eventually secured a barring order against him. This legal process allowed her abuser to find out her new address and she was subsequently raped and beaten by him, with great violence.

Open questions addressed the issue of how the abusive behaviours experienced by the women were brought to an end. Table 5.7 categorises and outlines the responses.

Table 5.7: How Sexual Abuse Was Ended or Avoided

	% (n)
Woman left the environment where abuse occurred	24 (12)
Disclosure led to cessation	16 (8)
Woman learned to avoid perpetrator	10 (5)
Perpetrator was removed (barring order n=1; imprisoned n=2)	6 (3)
Death of perpetrator	4 (2)

The most common way to end the exposure to sexual abuse was for the woman to move away from the setting of abuse. This was often the woman's home.

Sexual Violence: Case Histories

The quantitative information presented can be more vividly appreciated when details of the lives of some of the individual women are consolidated.[3]

Example 1

This woman in her thirties has had multiple episodes of hospitalisation for self-harm and suicide attempts. She described how, from early childhood, she was raped repeatedly by her father who also made her available to a paedophile ring. "I don't remember any of their faces, just the pain and feeling like I couldn't breathe and the flash of the camera when one of them would be on top of me . . ."

---

[3] The women interviewed gave consent for "pen pictures", without clearly identifying features, to be printed.

Example 2

> A woman in her twenties was regularly raped by her alcoholic father in childhood, and impregnated by her first "boyfriend" who beat her severely and mutilated her genitalia with a sharp knife. One of her own children was also abused by the child's grandfather (i.e. the same abusive relative). The woman also suspected sexual abuse of another of her children who had spent some time in care. This woman has been awaiting access to a counsellor for the past three months, with increasing desperation.

Example 3

> As a child, this woman was reared by her grandparents when abandoned by her own mother. She was sexually abused by her grandmother's partner — the grandmother was complicit in the abuse.

Example 4

> This woman, when she complained as a child to her mother of her grandfather's assault and rape of both herself and her sister, was told by her mother to "shut up about it . . . you must have deserved it anyway . . ."

Abuse of the Children of Homeless Women

Of the 100 women in the study, 82 had a total of 173 children under age 18 years. Eight of the 100 women knew and/or strongly suspected that their child(ren) had been sexually abused. Seven of these women had themselves been exposed to sexual violence. Six of these women (86 per cent) had become homeless as a consequence of removing their child(ren) from the abusive situation. One woman put her child into care because she felt the environment in the B&B was unsuitable for children. Now she strongly suspects that her child was sexually and physically abused while in care. Thus, in some instances homelessness may be a stark consequence of mothers trying to find a safer place for children than their own homes.

Sexual Violence and Homelessness

The profile of the homeless women who had been abused before becoming homeless was contrasted with that of those not reporting sexual violence in order to consider whether such experiences were associated with homelessness (e.g. did abused women become homeless at an earlier age) or factors increasing the risk of homelessness (e.g. illicit drug use) (Table 5.8).

Table 5.8: Demographic and Lifestyle Profile of Women not Reporting Sexual Violence in Comparison with those Abused before Becoming Homeless

	No Abuse Reported* mean (SD); median; range (n = 51)	Abused before Homeless mean (SD); median; range (n = 34)
Current age (years)	28 (10.7); 25; 17–65	23 (7.0); 25; 18–44
Age at first homelessness (years)	25 (10.9): 21; 12–64	23 (7.9); 21; 10–40
Number of children (n)	2.5 (1.9); 2; 1–7	2.4 (1.5); 2; 1–6

* Women abused since becoming homeless (n = 8) or women reporting abuse but unwilling to give further details (n = 7) were excluded from these analyses.

There were no differences in current age or age at first homelessness or in number of children. Another important comparison is between women grouped on the basis of reporting ever or never having experienced sexual violence (Table 5.9). Some differences did emerge. For women who had experienced abuse, this was less likely to be their first episode of homelessness. They were less likely to have social support in terms of supportive relatives; they were more likely to have experienced physical as well as sexual violence in their childhood and adulthood, and more likely to have used anti-depressant medication.

Table 5.9: Comparison of Experience of Sexual Violence by Social, Lifestyle and Health Factors in those who Had or Had Not Experienced Sexual Violence

	Ever Experienced Sexual Violence % (n = 49)	Never Experienced Sexual Violence % (n = 51)
First time homeless	47 (23)	75 (38)**
Ever taken anti-depressant medication	61 (30)	36 (18)***
Childhood experience of physical violence	67 (33)	31 (16)***
Adult experience of physical violence	88 (43)	41 (21)**
Have no supportive relatives	67 (33)	33 (17) ***
Ever used heroin	49 (24)	43 (22)
Problematic alcohol use	16 (8)	8 (4)
Reported chronic illness	90 (44)	75 (38) *
Ever had a smear test	59 (29)	50 (26)
Ever had any gynaecological exam	61 (30)	62 (32)
Ever had contraceptive consultation	80 (39)	75 (38)
Currently pregnant	8 (4)	14 (7)
SEIQoL score: Mean (SD); Range	36.1 (14.4); 8–55	40.4 (14.7); 11–70
GHQ score: Mean (SD); Range	6 (5); 0–12	6 (7); 0–12
GHQ "cases": Score ≥ 3 (%)	69	71

* $p < .05$; ** $p < .01$; *** $p < .001$.

There were few statistically significant differences across a wide range of variables. Differences between the groups in terms of al-

cohol and heroin use, reporting of chronic illness and gynaecological health and practices were not significant. Standardised
measures for psychological well-being (General Health Questionnaire (GHQ) scores) (Goldberg and Williams, 1988) and quality of
life indices (the Schedule for the Evaluation of Individual Quality
of Life (SEIQoL) scores) (O'Boyle et al., 1995), while indicating
that both groups fared poorly compared with the general population, were not significantly different from each other.

The data show that, beyond having few differences in mental
health, both these groups of women showed very high scores.
Over two-thirds of both groups (69 per cent who had experienced
abuse and 71 per cent who had not) had psychological scores in
the clinical or "case" range. This means they reported a profile of
symptoms which are seen as sufficiently serious to warrant professional attention. The similarities between groups illustrate the
point that sexual violence is only one of a number of life experiences which can have serious consequences for later well-being.
Recent work shows that child sexual abuse is among a set of adverse experiences linked in a strong graded manner to adult psychopathology and suicide (Dube et al., 2001).

Children of Homeless Women

Of the 49 abused women, 40 had a total of 86 children under the
age of 18 years. Sixteen women had all of their children living
with them; 22 had none of their children with them. This latter
figure constituted almost half of the sexually abused mothers (45
per cent) while only 19 per cent (p < .01) of those without a history
of abuse were separated form their children.

DISCUSSION AND CONCLUSIONS

Figures indicating that almost half of these women disclosed serious sexual violence suggest that this experience is virtually "normative" for Irish homeless women. This is a harrowing pattern,
similar to what has been suggested by the international literature.
These lifetime levels are significantly higher than those found in

the SAVI survey for Irish women in general (49 per cent for homeless women versus 32 per cent for SAVI survey participants concerning lifetime experience of contact and penetrative abuse). The figures for rape emphasise this discrepancy even more (31 per cent for homeless women versus 10 per cent for SAVI survey participants). The scale of the difference highlights how vulnerable homeless women in Irish society are *vis-à-vis* sexual violence. The service implications of these findings need to be addressed if outreach and other service approaches are to acknowledge the particular risks and challenges of this group. They face dealing with the many challenges which are the aftermath of abuse, including addressing these issues in therapy, in an already compromising and unsupported set of life circumstances. As the CHAR (Hendessi, 1992) report suggested, the needs of those recovering from sexual violence "sit uncomfortably with the pressure on resources for all homeless people". There is a concern that already stretched services are unable to provide the specialist care needed to address such specific and sensitive concerns regarding abuse. Consideration must be give to the best methods of ensuring that this group of particularly vulnerable women receive the services they need regarding sexual violence.

Proposals for Future Consideration

- Sexual violence, although a significant problem for these homeless women, must be viewed in the wider context of the extensive range of problems and challenges faced by them. Their most pressing need is, without doubt, for stable accommodation for themselves and their children.

- There needs to be a co-ordinated approach to the delivery of a range of therapeutic and drug-related services for these women. Given their difficult lifestyles, there needs to be consideration of how, where and by whom such services should be delivered.

- Services need to be easily and rapidly accessible with co-ordinated referral systems across different services.

- Health and social services professionals should avail of "windows of opportunity" to offer a wide set of relevant services to homeless women in a way that is supportive and de-stigmatising. The challenge of providing accessible services combines with the need to balance specialist and mainstream services for these women.

Recommendation

- That the management of consequences of sexual violence for women and their children be addressed in a manner which provides tailored, sensitive and co-ordinated services. The health boards, through their Homeless Persons Units, should ensure liaison among those agencies needed to provide such services.

Chapter 6

TRAVELLERS AS A MARGINALISED GROUP IN IRISH SOCIETY: CHALLENGES TO REPORTING AND ACCESSING SERVICES FOR SEXUAL VIOLENCE

INTRODUCTION

There are approximately 25,000 Travellers in the Republic of Ireland. They constitute a minority ethnic group in Irish society who may face particular challenges when dealing with sexual violence. Services that have been designed with the settled and majority community in mind may not allow for cultural and other barriers facing Travellers (and members of other ethnic minority groups). Services that do exist may therefore be considered with some suspicion by these groups. Travellers' nomadic lifestyle may hinder their ability to access services, in particular counselling services that by their very nature require an ongoing commitment. Travellers may have little opportunity to obtain knowledge of local or nearby services since many of them are regularly on the move. High levels of illiteracy, lack of telephones, finance and transport may also pose problems in accessing services.

METHOD

As many Travellers would not be contactable by a landline telephone and thus could not by definition be adequately represented in the SAVI national telephone study, it was decided to approach

Pavee Point[1] to set up a focus group to discuss the specific challenges facing Travellers with regard to sexual violence. A researcher met initially with three women workers at Pavee Point (two of whom were members of the Travelling community). A subsequent, two-hour focus group was conducted with a group of ten Traveller women aged approximately 25–60 years to represent a wide range of viewpoints. (Researchers were advised that a mixed sex group would be very difficult to constitute because of cultural norms dissuading Traveller men from discussing such topics in the presence of women.) Two researchers led the focus group, which was tape-recorded with the women's consent. The discussion followed an open and unstructured format with specific questions suggested at the outset. The open-ended questions which were used to generate discussion are listed below:

- What would you consider sexual violence to be?

- How likely do you think Travellers would be to tell someone if they had an experience of sexual violence?

- What, if any, services would you look for if you or someone close to you were a victim of sexual violence?

- Do you think the barriers to seeking help are different for the Travelling community than for the settled community?

- Within the Travelling community, what are the implications of disclosing sexual abuse and violence?

- Are the barriers to disclosure any different for males than for females?

- Do you think attitudes and views about sexual abuse and violence have changed in the Travelling community in recent years?

---

[1] Pavee Point is a non-governmental organisation comprised of Travellers and members of the majority population who work together to address the needs of Travellers as a minority group in Irish society.

Following the session, tapes were transcribed and analysed. The subsequent drafts of this report were reviewed by members of Pavee Point to confirm the authors' interpretations of the content.

RESULTS AND DISCUSSION

The challenges of sexual violence facing Travellers were seen as being divided into two broad categories: those that are associated with Travellers' marginalised position in Irish society, and those that are more specific to Traveller culture. Parallels to difficulties faced by members of other ethnic minority groups were noted. Therefore some of the findings and proposals outlined below may also be of relevance to such groups as refugees and asylum seekers.

The first broad challenge relates to the position of Travellers as a marginalised group. Not wishing to endorse negative portrayals of Travellers in society at large, ethnic solidarity can silence those who experience sexual violence. Travellers may find it difficult to speak out about problems faced within their own community. When disclosing violence or abuse of any kind, not only do they face the same difficulties (shame, fear of blame, a desire to protect others, etc.) as the settled community but also, they risk damaging the image of their own ethnic group and thereby adding to already existing prejudices. Some comments from the women illustrate this viewpoint:

> "Travellers suffer so much discrimination in this country every day of their lives that sexual abuse is something that they certainly wouldn't want to come out or tell about because then they'd really be looked down on altogether."

> "It would make it worse. . . . Settled people would think that all Travellers must be doing this, you know, must be abusing their children."

However, positive developments in the area of speaking out about so-called domestic violence[2] would indicate that this barrier is already being addressed within the Travelling community.

Travellers choose not to approach service providers for a variety of reasons other than shame or stigma. These included their belief that they would be unfairly treated or discriminated against. The general consensus about approaching the Gardaí was negative. One woman said:

> "I suppose there's good and bad everywhere but the experience that Travellers would have with guards would be very negative."

And another:

> "To be honest, Travellers would be wary about reporting things to the guards. I know I would if it concerned my kids or anybody else's kids, but Travellers don't get great treatment from the guards. They would be very wary."

This problem is compounded by a lack of faith in the response of the Gardaí. For example, one woman cited the Gardaí not intervening in cases of physical violence as being indicative of their lack of interest:

> "I don't know about the guards because the guards in this country as far as I'm concerned, if a Traveller woman goes to them and her husband is after giving her a bad hiding, they have no time for her whatsoever."

Some of the women attending said they would definitely report to the Gardaí if they suspected their own children were being abused by a family member. On the other hand, it was felt that a

---

[2] See *Pavee Beoirs Breaking the Silence: Traveller Women and Male Domestic Violence,* an initiative piloted by Pavee Point with the ERHA and Women's Aid in response to the issue of male domestic violence within the Travelling community and jointly funded through the EU New Opportunities for Women (NOW) Community Initiative and the ERHA (1998–1999).

Traveller mother would take her children and leave home if she discovered they were being abused by the father. They felt she might tell no one what had happened in order to avoid scandal. If a case of child sexual abuse did become known, the view was that Travellers would not go to the police but would deal with the matter in their own way, treating the abuser as an outcast and disowning "him". In this regard, it was outlined that Travellers might take revenge for sexual abuse against members outside of the law and judicial system. There was a general feeling that the legal system was too lenient in its treatment of abusers.

> "I've seen so many children abused and they [the perpetrators] are getting out. They are getting two or three years and a child's life is destroyed."

The women also expressed distrust of Social Services, fearing, for example, that children would be taken into care if cases of incest were to be disclosed.

> "Traveller women would be very afraid to speak to a social worker. They'd be put on the 'at risk' register, wouldn't they?"

> "They would be afraid to get social welfare involved in case they'd take the children off her."

The majority of the women said they would choose to confide in their mothers (or mothers-in-law) if they knew their own children were being abused and several women spontaneously said that they would feel comfortable talking to a priest about such matters. In that regard, GPs (among others) were viewed with some suspicion. In the words of one woman:

> "If you went into a doctor and you told him that you were raped and that you didn't want your husband or your family to know, he would agree there and then (to keep it confidential), but when you go out, that's a thing that he'd have to report to the guards."

Practical barriers were also identified. Access to services may be hindered by, for example, isolation, illiteracy and a lack of information, money and transport.

The second broad challenge to disclosing and seeking services for sexual violence is more culture-specific. At the broadest level of discussion, sexual matters, including telling children about reproduction, were described as topics that are not easily discussed by Travellers. A mother, rather than tell her own daughter about menstruation, for example, might approach another young female relative to have her do this task for her. Sexual matters would not be discussed in mixed groups. Attitudes towards sexuality in general were seen to be changing gradually, however. The group illustrated this by noting that a generation ago some Traveller women camouflaged their pregnancies even from their spouses. Some of the women present recollected being punished as children for mentioning that a woman was "expecting" (i.e. pregnant). Such incidents as these would not occur today.

The greatest barrier to disclosing sexual violence was seen to be the shame that disclosure would bring on the abused person themselves and their family. This was seen as compounded by the high value of virginity in the Traveller community. The cost of disclosure within the Travelling community is simply too high. One woman described a viewpoint reiterated several times during the discussion:

> "It [child sexual abuse and adult rape] is never talked about. If you went out about that child or that woman, their life is destroyed. Ten years down the line that would be talked about."

Given the importance of secrecy surrounding sexual violence, confidentiality and anonymity were seen to be of paramount importance. It was felt that a Traveller woman would not approach a Rape Crisis Centre for fear of being seen and having it known:

> "In the Travelling community, if you were going in [to a RCC] it would be: 'What is she going in there for?' . . . if she

came back from the Rape Crisis Centre, they'd destroy her with talk."

This concern was also seen to influence decisions to approach professionals.

This stance is not unique to the Irish Travelling community. A report concerning work with refugee women and asylum seekers who have suffered sexual violence expresses it as follows:

> In Kosovo, it was said to me that, traditionally, if a woman was raped it was better for her to die than admit that she was raped because she would be dishonouring her family. These are the deeply entrenched attitudes that are within families and communities which silence women. Loss of virginity or chastity, the fact that a woman has been touched or seen by another man brings shame upon the honour of the family and in disclosing it the woman thereby dishonours her family. (McCarthy, 1999, p. 34)

Marriage and family are held in high regard within the Travelling community. If a young girl was abused it would be considered too detrimental to her future prospects of marrying and setting up a family of her own to disclose this. She, her family and her extended family would be "dishonoured" by the violence committed against her. One woman said of those who experienced child sexual abuse:

> "They'd never be married. Nobody would want them because they'd already know what happened to that child."

Again this is reported to be a view held by other minority groups:

> There is also the attitude towards the raped single woman that she is no longer marriageable. Or, if she is married, there is a fear that if her husband discovers, he may think differently of her and that he may abandon her. (McCarthy, 1999, p. 34)

As outlined, this view is often adopted by the abused person:

> "For a girl, 16, 17, 18, she wouldn't even tell that herself [that she was raped] 'cause she would think of her future. She's dirty. No Travelling boy would ever marry her. He wouldn't think she was raped. He would say that she went with him."

In other words, the abused person is held accountable, not the perpetrator. This view is mirrored also in reports on sexual violence against refugee women:

> There may also be the attitude in her country of origin that the raped woman has contributed to the sexual attack and it is amazing how things get reversed. In some cultures, instead of saying that the woman has been raped it may be said that she "made love to" another man. Therefore, she is the culprit and it is she who must be punished (McCarthy, 1999, p. 35).

Fear of blame silences those who have experienced sexual violence in the Travelling community. One woman said:

> "You wouldn't come back and tell your husband or your family because you'd know you would be blamed for it. You know, you'd be looking for it."

It is not just the Travelling men who would blame the person who was abused:

> "It's even within the family itself, your mother, father, or brothers, sisters."

Several women in the group said that if they were raped, they would not tell their husbands or families. It was felt that the researchers as settled women would be in a position to speak out if they were raped — not so the Traveller women:

> "For you to get raped . . . you could go home and tell your husband. Well, he'd have all the sympathy in the world for you but if I went home and told my husband that I got raped I'd just have to pack my bags because he wouldn't live with me."

Another woman said:

> "You'd just have to get up and go. I'd never tell him. I'd never tell anybody."

Some particularly negative ramifications of disclosure, for instance, family break-up or suicide as a consequence of disclosure, have been experienced within the Travelling community. In such a small community, knowledge of these experiences was seen by the group as reducing further the likelihood that people would disclose sexual violence in the future. One woman said:

> "So I think if something like that ever happened to a Traveller again I don't think . . . I think it would just be let go and there'd be no talk about it."

Rape within marriage has been recognised as a crime in the Irish legal system since 1991. However, rape within marriage as a concept was seen to be foreign to many, although not all, Traveller women. It is not known how common this attitude is in the majority population. The Traveller women felt that rape within marriage was seen by many as something that women have to put up with:

> "We thought that it's a thing you have to put up with. You know, that it wasn't rape. . . . Well, a man wants his way. . . He'll have it and that's it and there's nothing you can do about it."

The question of abuse of males was raised by the researchers. It was not seen as an issue in the Travelling community although the women said this did not mean that it never happened. When talking about a case of past institutional abuse in an establishment run by a religious order, the women noted that settled men came forward to disclose their abuse as children there. However, the Traveller men did not:

> "There was no way they would [disclose] . . . because they're too embarrassed. They just wouldn't talk about it. It would be worse for a boy even than for a girl. Traveller

men are macho. . . . Other Traveller men would make a laugh of him."

The women said they were aware that most rapes and sexual assaults are committed by a person known to the abused person. Yet, there was some discrepancy in their own behaviour since when warning their children about the risk of sexual violence, they resorted to the "stranger rape" stereotype, warning their children to be careful of: "fellows following you in cars" or "kidnappers".

The general consensus from the group was that sexual violence was less prevalent in the Travelling community than in the majority population. Reasons cited for this were:

- Cultural differences relating to dating patterns and forming relationships which mean, for example, that virginity, monogamy and early marriage are highly valued.

- More segregation of the sexes in Traveller culture.

- Chaperoning of girls in Traveller groups; not allowing them go out alone; not allowing them go out after dark and not allowing them go to social events such as discos.

- Not allowing males (even older brothers or uncles) to babysit.

It is not possible to assess the veracity of this belief. The key question is whether sexual violence is less prevalent or more hidden in Traveller groups? It seems reasonable to suggest, however, whatever the prevalence, that the silencing of those who have experienced sexual violence because of the very grave consequences for them, their families and the Travelling community as a whole, provides a strong case for expecting even less disclosure than in the settled community.

PROPOSALS FOR FUTURE CONSIDERATION

A series of suggestions for improving prevention, disclosure, health and related service responses and police and legal responses were developed in consultation with Pavee Point members and are outlined next.

- There is a need to offer a more culturally appropriate service. The cultural impact of rape must be recognised and response by service providers must be sensitive to the cultural meaning of the experience. Choice of language to describe body parts and details of sexual violence needs to be dealt with sensitively by service providers.

- In order to achieve more culturally appropriate services, the provision of training to increase both awareness and skills amongst service providers is needed. This should include awareness-raising regarding racist attitudes.

- Advice regarding training initiatives and service development should be sought from Traveller women such as those involved in the Primary Health Care for Travellers Project. Since 1994, Pavee Point in partnership with the ERHA has trained Traveller women as health care workers in their own communities. This model should be considered. For example, specialist organisations such as the Rape Crisis Centres could train a small group of Traveller women to train other Traveller women (in awareness-raising regarding sexual violence, in listening skills, in skills which facilitate disclosure, in provision of information regarding available services, and so on). Dialogue with Traveller women should inform trainer input regarding specific challenges and cultural differences.

- Because of the nomadic lifestyle of many Travellers, outreach services should be provided. The Dublin Rape Crisis Centre already offers such a service in the Well Woman clinic in the Northside Shopping Centre, Coolock.

- Given that matters concerning sexuality would be discussed in women-only groups in the Traveller community, it may be advisable that female counsellors and doctors be available to deliver services, at least in the early traumatic stages following events and/or disclosure. (Parallel service plans may be

needed for men. In this regard a men-only focus group might
be consulted in future research.)

- It was not seen as feasible for Traveller women to train, for
  example, as volunteer telephone counsellors with organisations such as the Rape Crisis Centres since many cannot afford
  to work without payment. Some funding must be put in place
  if the Traveller-provided service model is to be developed.

- Travellers are generally not aware of services that are available
  to those who have been sexually abused. A proactive approach
  must be taken to rectify this gap. There is a need for sexuality
  education, including education regarding sexual violence, in the
  Traveller community. Given the emphasis on an oral culture,
  combined with literacy problems, this should be delivered in a
  way that achieves its aims of effective communication. Traveller
  education was stressed as an important issue, particularly with
  regard to the issue that "Travellers are ignorant of the fact that
  the [abused] girl is an innocent victim".

- Getting information to the Traveller community about available services for sexual violence would include the provision
  of leaflets and posters to sites and centres Travellers attend;
  and having information outlined orally to the community by
  trained Travellers and via family doctors and nurses.

Recommendation

Many of the necessary aspects of developing and delivering a service to promote prevention, detection and management of sexual
violence for members of the Travelling community are already
identified in the community. Resources are needed to enable
Travellers and others to work together to tackle the particular
challenges sexual violence poses for them.

Chapter 7

SEXUAL VIOLENCE IN THE PRISON POPULATION: PERCEPTIONS OF PRISON PERSONNEL

INTRODUCTION

The prevalence of sexual violence in prison is a combination of pre-prison and in-prison instances of abuse. Research addressing levels of sexual violence in this population almost entirely focuses on pre-prison episodes of abuse (Struckman-Johnson et al., 1996). Different methodologies and questions are addressed in such research. For instance, in a consecutive sample of 500 women admitted to a US prison in 1994, 26 per cent reported a history of sexual abuse "while growing up" (Mullings et al., 2000). In this study childhood abuse was associated with higher levels of HIV sexual risk-taking in adulthood. For men, 27 per cent of a random sample of "habitual offenders" in another US study reported childhood sexual abuse (Irwin and Austin, 1994). High rates of sexual abuse are also evident in sex offenders in prison, with those diagnosed as having a paraphilia having significantly higher levels of childhood sexual abuse in their past (McElroy, 1999). Sexual violence also occurs in prison with, it is perceived, little attempt to prevent what is seen as "a convenient form of inhumane justice" (Scarce, 1997). Reported rates of sexual violence vary widely and are almost all derived from US studies. The estimated average is 20 per cent (Kupers, 1996). One large recent study of both men and women in US prisons found a self-reported rate of unwanted sex-

ual experiences in prison of 20 per cent; 22 per cent for men and 7
per cent for women (Struckman-Johnston et al., 1996). Three-
quarters of these cases reported serious assaults or rape with 18
per cent of all cases identifying prison staff as perpetrators. Supporting the validity of the prisoners' reports, a sample of prison
staff estimated the assault rate to be 15 per cent. UK psychiatrist
Michael King, who studies male rape, estimates that there is significantly less sexual violence in the UK prison system than the
US (c.f. Scarce, 1997).

RECENT IRISH STUDIES OF THE PRISON POPULATION

Two major studies of the prison population in Ireland were completed in the year 2000. The first was a general study of health and
healthcare in the overall prison population undertaken by the
Centre for Health Promotion Studies of National University of
Ireland Galway (2000). They surveyed 777 prisoners in 13 of the
15 national prisons; 59 of these were women. This represented 26
per cent of the male and 75 per cent of the female prison population with 777 participants representing a study response rate of 88
per cent. Prisoners completed questionnaires alone or were as-
sisted and were also examined by a nurse or doctor. Almost half
(48 per cent) of men and 75 per cent of women scored as "cases"
on the General Health Questionnaire, a 12-item measure of psychological distress. (This means that they presented symptoms
which would warrant mental health intervention.) Forty-two per
cent had seen a prison doctor in the previous two weeks. Sexual
violence was not a specific focus of the study. However, relevant
information can be obtained from their work. Participants were
asked a range of questions regarding the adverse effects of alcohol
use. One question asked if they had experienced adverse events as
a result of someone else's alcohol use. Sixteen percent of women
and 3 per cent of men reported being sexually assaulted as a consequence of alcohol use by another person. The parallel figures for
physical abuse were 17 per cent (men) and 28 per cent (women).
When asked about the experience of violence in prison, 27 per

cent of men and 5 per cent of women reported physical abuse by prison officers while 13 per cent of men and 7 per cent of women reported such abuse by fellow prisoners. There is no way to evaluate if instances of sexual violence occurred in the prison from these figures and no way to know if sexual incidents were incorporated into definitions when reporting "being physically abused" in prison. One of the recommendations of the study concerning a health-promoting prison environment was that "the precise nature and extent of the verbal and physical abuse reported by prisoners must be investigated and, if indicated, anti-bullying and other strategies implemented" (p. 63).

The second Irish report was conducted by the Department of Community Health and General Practice in Trinity College Dublin (Allwright et al., 2000) and focused on infectious disease prevalence (hepatitis B and C and HIV) in the prison population. A total of 1,205 prisoners (57 were women) (88 per cent response rate) were surveyed in 9 of the 15 Irish prisons. A self-completed questionnaire and unlinked oral fluid specimen was collected. While questions on sexual practices were asked, no information on sexual violence was compiled.

An earlier study of the Mountjoy prisoner population (O'Mahony, 1997) focused on social, family and criminal background, health status, substance abuse problems and, to a limited extent, experiences of and views on prison life. A total of 108 prisoners were interviewed including being asked if they had ever been sexually assaulted in prison by another prisoner or staff member. Four claimed to have been sexually assaulted by another prisoner and four others by a prison officer (a prevalence of 7.4 per cent). None of the assaults involved rape.

Some insight into pre-prison and in-prison experiences of sexual violence may be obtained from health service provision in prison. A Clinical Psychology Service for the Department of Justice, Equality and Law Reform was established in 1980. It provides, among other services, a psychological service for individual offenders, and their 1999 annual report records consultations with 588 individual offenders, 20 per cent of whom were sex offenders.

Most offenders sought help for a number of concerns, which may include child sexual abuse and rape. In 1999, an average of 22 offenders addressed issues of CSA and rape each month.

METHOD

For the purposes of the SAVI study, individuals from the various professions who work directly with prisoners were selected by a process of recommendation of key informants and interviewed, either in person or by telephone, using an open-ended approach. A total of 12 professionals were interviewed including a prison governor, prison officers, a prison nurse, psychologists, chaplains, and a senior probation and welfare officer. Those interviewed worked in the following prisons: Mountjoy, the Curragh, Wheatfield, Cloverhill, Cork, Dochas Centre (female prison), Shelton Abbey and Shanganagh Castle. Participants were asked their views on pre-prison and in-prison prevalence of sexual violence; on disclosure patterns and challenges; on the provision of counselling services; and on their views of what is needed to best address the issue of sexual violence for prisoners. The assessment of either pre-prison or in-prison abuse presents major challenges for researchers. It was decided not to interview prisoners directly for this study. The reasons for this were twofold. Firstly, there are concerns regarding asking prisoners to disclose a history of sexual abuse in an environment where they spend many hours of the day alone and do not have the support of family and friends to deal with emotions raised in this way. The risks of damaging their well-being, including self-injury and suicide, are by no means insignificant. A second ethical concern is about conducting such sensitive research with a vulnerable and captive group without being in a position to provide services to deal with issues that might emerge from the interviews.

FINDINGS AND DISCUSSION

Given the varied sample, the views and opinions expressed were not always consistent. In the summary as presented, it is important to note that the observations are based on *perceptions* of those working in the prison service. Staff perceptions regarding past histories of sexual violence among prisoners, including child sexual abuse and adult sexual assault and rape, varied from those who could not give an opinion about whether this problem might be greater than in the general population, to those who felt the prevalence might be as high as 40 per cent in the male and 50 per cent in the female prison population. One participant said that he would go as far as to say that a history of child sexual abuse is almost a criminogenic factor (i.e. a factor leading to involvement in crime). The majority felt that, whatever the prevalence rates, a history of sexual violence is a feature in the lives of at least some offenders. The general consensus was that many female prisoners have suffered child sexual abuse. It was suggested that this would be the case for almost all of those convicted because of soliciting (i.e. prostitution). However, many felt that women speak out more readily about emotional and other issues and that it may be their greater ease with disclosure rather than higher prevalence that leads to this perception. One view was that those (including men) who self-harm often have a history of sexual abuse. Many of the long-term intravenous drug users in the 30–40 year age bracket (many of whom had been in institutional care) were also believed to have been abused. Another participant believed that a significant percentage of the younger prisoners in St. Patrick's Institution (a centre for 16–20-year-olds) have suffered past abuse, including incest. Regarding identification of abuse, there is no systematic screening of prisoners for past abuse of any kind. Currently, the only information prison personnel have regarding a prisoner is what is provided on the arrest warrant.

Professionals thought that ongoing sexual violence within the prison setting was quite rare but that it did happen. In any case, it was felt that this crime was rarely reported although there is a protocol in place for dealing with allegations.[1] It was also felt by

---

[1] However, if there is an allegation of sexual violence, it is more usual to move the person making the report rather than the alleged perpetrator.

some that an assault would have to be accompanied by some physical violence before it would be reported. There were seen to be many opportunities for sexual coercion in prison but that this may be viewed as consensual sexual activity. If there is no evidence of physical force having been used, there may well be a belief, held by staff and prisoners alike, that "he must have agreed to it". It was seen to be the most vulnerable prisoners who are at risk. One viewpoint was that overcrowding (having two or three prisoners to a cell) facilitated sexual violence in the prison setting. Yet others said that assaults have occurred in shower areas. It was felt by some that there is an unspoken "let's not open a can of worms" attitude towards ongoing sexual violence. Prison officers receive no training in this area (including no training on how to deal with disclosure). Most are believed not to be aware of what, if any, services are available for those reporting abuse.

All were in agreement that sexual violence was a very difficult topic for prisoners (and more particularly male prisoners) to discuss. Barriers to disclosure were seen as numerous and are summarised as follows:

- Prisoners do not confide easily in "officialdom". There was seen to be very much a "them and us" attitude towards prison personnel. Prison psychologists, for example, prepare court-ordered reports prior to sentencing an offender and, although this is a very small part of their work, this was seen as having the potential to affect levels of trust in them by prisoners. Chaplains seemed to be in an exceptional role in this regard by many staff as it was felt that prisoners know that what they say to chaplains is confidential (no notes are kept and no reports written). Also, there was not the same stigma attached as chaplains see prisoners on the landings and not in their own rooms. One chaplain said:

  "They could be talking to us about anything. We might just be arranging a phone call to a girlfriend. No one would know."

- There was seen to be a commonly held attitude amongst prisoners that if a person has been abused they too would abuse. If a prisoner were to disclose past abuse this could be used against him; for instance, he might be bullied. Another participant said, "Child sexual abuse is an absolute secret for prisoners."

- Shame was also a very big factor. Added to this, to disclose sexual abuse was seen as lessening the "macho" image that is so strong in the prison setting. This links to a certain stigma being attached to taking up services like counselling or talking to the Samaritans.

- There was seen to be a fear that, once a disclosure was made, the prisoner would have no control over where that information would go. There are also perceptions of fears and confusion about mandatory reporting. It was felt that people have some sense of control if they are living in the community. This is not the case when they are in prison.

- Sex offenders were seen to be so reviled that a prisoner would not wish to be connected with this crime in any way, not even as a victim of it. One participant described sex offenders as "the lepers of today".[2]

- Erroneous "rape myths" were believed to be held by many prisoners, particularly with regard to sexual violence committed against males. Lack of education was seen as a big factor in these misconceptions.

---

[2] Sex offenders constitute approximately 11.6 per cent (n = 350) of the Irish prison population. They are kept segregated in the main, primarily for their own safety. One problem in this regard is that those who have committed more minor offences are housed with the most serious sex offenders. As one participant said: "Young offenders are segregated and incarcerated with hardened offenders for the most formative years of their lives and are offered little or no help in dealing with their offending behaviour. They are the most marginalised group, often the victims themselves of sexual abuse."

- Another perceived barrier to disclosure was the perception that a prisoner who discloses abuse may be concerned that others may view him as sexually available or otherwise vulnerable to further abuse.

- Prisoners may not disclose incidents of sexual violence within the prison setting, it was felt, because of fear of reprisals. Rather, they may ask to be transferred to another cell or another prison and refuse to give a reason. To disclose sexual abuse constitutes a very real risk for a prisoner, particularly if he has a long sentence ahead of him. "If it got out he would be slagged" and "the bully will still bully".

- One challenge to disclosure of or treatment for past abuse was seen to be the large percentage of prisoners who are active drug users. These are not typically in a position to deal with challenging emotional issues of past abuse.

- Lack of resources and lack of personnel generally were seen to pose a problem in relation to prevention, disclosure and treatment. One source said that a previous partial solution where external therapists and counsellors had volunteered their services was met with opposition from within.

The question of how to deal with disclosure of sexual violence is a highly complex one. Historically, prison has been seen as a place of punishment. There has not been a culture of caring or rehabilitation although this may be changing now, not least, it was felt, because of the input of chaplains who are, and are seen to be, totally independent of the system. The chaplains were reported to have "tremendous credibility", primarily because they offer absolute confidentiality. This changing approach to prisoner as "victim", and not merely as perpetrator, may be viewed by some as innovative. The prison setting was seen as a very harsh and possibly unsuitable environment in which to tackle such painful issues as sexual abuse.

> "Many are not able to do deep therapy work while in prison because they may become distraught, and then they are left."

In any case, available services were reported as extremely stretched, particularly the Clinical Psychology Service. Some women and men attend the Dublin Rape Crisis Centre while serving their sentences.

Many felt that there was a need for a totally independent therapy or counselling service for those who wished to avail of it. This should be a separate service that has nothing to do with "good" reports, "bad" reports or a release date. It was felt that prisoners might not be honest if a report was to be made that would affect their release date. A two-dimensional therapeutic or counselling service was proposed: one representing the State (for example, to give a psychological opinion) and the other a totally confidential "no-strings-attached" service for the prisoner who says, "I have a problem and I want to deal with it." This viewpoint was not, however, unanimous. A strong word of caution was put forward with regard to sex offenders, murderers and others who have committed violent crimes. Offending behaviour was seen as needing to be addressed simultaneously with meeting prisoners' needs.

> "A balance must be worked between the prisoner as a victim and the prisoner as someone who has victimised another person."

The concern was that, if there was not a multi-disciplinary and coherent approach, prisoners might only want to look at issues concerning themselves as the focus of abuse, not also as offenders against others.

PROPOSALS FOR FUTURE CONSIDERATION

- To heighten awareness among prison personnel through the provision of education regarding child sexual abuse and sexual violence. Uptake would have to be voluntary. Training should be process-oriented in order to challenge attitudes and existing prejudices.

- To train prison officers regarding how to deal with a disclosure of sexual violence by a prisoner.

- To provide a similar type of education for prisoners, preferably in the wider context of personal development.

- To introduce proper sentence-planning to include an induction process consisting of a range of interviews to address the medical, psychological and training/employment needs of each prisoner alongside their offending behaviour. Sentence planning should address the question, "How best could this person benefit from the time spent serving their sentence?"

- Given that prison is a place of enormous distrust, prison management needs to be innovative and proactive in setting up structures that will maintain prisoners' confidentiality. Prisoners need reassurance and clarification about who has access to the information held on their files.

Further research is needed. The above proposals are starting points to guide such research but in themselves they represent the views of a non-random selection of prison personnel. A more extensive investigation needs to take into account a wider constituency including prisoners themselves. Furthermore, it is important to emphasise that the problems seen in prisons are primarily problems from elsewhere. Child sexual abuse and other forms of sexual violence cannot be seen as an aetiological factor in subsequent criminality without also considering other challenges to child and adolescent development such as neglect, poverty, lack of education and physical violence. In the longer term, greater investment should be put into prevention in its wider sense — into pre-school education, parenting skills training, and into offering tailored support to families who are vulnerable for whatever reasons.

Chapter 8

WOMEN IN PROSTITUTION: THE CHALLENGE OF SEXUAL VIOLENCE

INTRODUCTION

The number of women involved in prostitution in Ireland is un-known. However, the Ruhama[1] Women's Project has over 500 women on its database, the majority of whom are Irish and work-ing in street prostitution. Ruhama staff are aware that there are very many more women working in "indoor" prostitution, for example, in brothels and escort agencies, but they have no contact with this more hidden group. Other women working in prostitu-tion have become less visible in recent years due to the increased use of mobile phones. This effectively means that these women can work out of their homes and other places without needing to go out onto the streets.

Previous international research suggests that women working in prostitution have a higher incidence of child sexual abuse than women in general (Bagley and Young, 1987; Potter et al., 1999; McClanahan et al., 1999). Bagley and Young found that 73 per cent of former prostitutes had experienced child sexual abuse compared to 29 per cent of a control group obtained in a random population survey. Potter et al. interviewed a group of female "sex workers" and compared their findings with those from the

---

[1] Ruhama is a voluntary organisation working with, and for, women involved in prostitution. The name Ruhama comes from Hebrew and means, "She that was unloved is loved".

Otago Women's Child Sexual Abuse study. They found that those working in prostitution were significantly more likely to report histories of child sexual abuse. McClanahan et al.'s study of female prisoners in the US found that those who had engaged in prostitution were almost twice as likely to have experienced child sexual abuse than the other prisoners in the sample. However, this view is not unanimous with other authors claiming that this link is not clear-cut (Nadon et al., 1998; Widom and Ames, 1994). Other factors, such as running away from home, are also reported to be pathways to prostitution. Drug addiction is often implicated but it is unclear whether this is a causal factor or whether, in fact, women working in prostitution become addicts because of their lifestyle.

It may be more difficult for these women to access services, and for those who do access services their care may be fragmented. For example, a woman may receive treatment for drug addiction while the fact that she is working in prostitution may be neglected, or not even known by the service providers.

As the prevalence of sexual violence may be higher among women who work in prostitution, and the likelihood of their being adequately represented in the SAVI national telephone survey was small, it was decided to investigate the issue of sexual violence with this specific group separately.

METHOD

After an interview with the director of the Ruhama Women's Project it was concluded that there were inherent difficulties in approaching the women who worked in prostitution themselves to discuss the main issues of the survey. It would be extremely difficult to identify women to take part as there was no official "list" or register of those who work in prostitution, nor would any woman want her name on such a list, as these activities are illegal. Accessing this group of women is extremely difficult, even for those who seek to help them, such as Ruhama. This organisation patrols the areas where they believe they are most likely to find the women, and then it is up to the women themselves to approach the service. The chaotic lifestyle and difficult hours that these women work present major challenges to conducting any type of "traditional" survey or even a focus group. Many women involved in prostitution are drug addicts and this also poses a barrier to interviewing them directly.

As an alternative, it was decided to approach the volunteers and staff who have been working with this group of marginalised women and to ask them to speak on their behalf. While it is acknowledged that asking the women in prostitution themselves may yield different and more specific information, it is hoped that the information provided by these "spokespersons" may at the very least provide useful guidelines for service provision and outline avenues for further in-depth research.

Based on a review of the literature and the interview with the director of Ruhama, a questionnaire was developed to be filled out by staff and volunteers at Ruhama. Where possible, questions mirrored those that were asked in the SAVI national telephone survey of the general public in order to make comparisons.

Eight women and one man working either as volunteers or as full-time staff with Ruhama completed questionnaires. These participants had worked for Ruhama for one to eight years. The majority came into direct contact with women in prostitution in the course of their work, with participants at minimum having had contact with 14 women up to approximately 500.

RESULTS AND DISCUSSION

Prevalence of Sexual Abuse and Assault among Prostitutes

As the main aim of the national study was to estimate the prevalence of sexual violence among the general population, obtaining comparable figures for women who were involved in prostitution was of key interest. When asked to estimate the percentage of women in prostitution who were raped or sexually assaulted by a non-family member before they were aged 17, participant estimates ranged from 30–60 per cent. A question about that same group experiencing incest yielded much more variability, with estimates from 10–90 per cent. Although no figures were available for the average age at which women may begin prostitution, it appears that these participants believe a sizeable number of women may have already experienced sexual abuse while they were children and quite possibly before they took up prostitution. The estimates for women in prostitution who are sexually assaulted as adults were significantly higher, ranging from 60–95 per cent. Although these figures were estimates based on the perceptions of the staff and volunteers who work with the women in prostitution, it is striking that their estimates were much greater than those of the general population.

In order to get an indication of the possible contributory role of sexual violence in leading women into prostitution, we asked this group of participants to consider a number of factors that have been identified in the international research. Participants were asked to indicate which of the items they believed were contributory factors for women in prostitution in Ireland (based on their own work). The item identified most frequently as being contributory was experiencing child abuse or incest, with financial reasons as a close second. Homelessness and running away from home were also considered to be contributory factors by most participants. Drug addiction was the item most often spontaneously added by participants when asked if they thought there were other major factors. Other factors nominated by participants included such things as experiencing abuse of any kind (e.g., physical, emotional, neglect), being forced into prostitution by others (including their family), the trafficking of foreigners, and related activities such as lap dancing, strip shows and escort services.

While sexual abuse and assault were certainly viewed as factors which lead to a life of prostitution, once a woman engages in prostitution it appears she has an even greater risk of becoming abused again. When participants were asked what percentage of women are raped as a direct result of their involvement in prostitution, almost all of them estimated the proportion to be at 70 per cent or above. Further, the mean frequency of the sexual assaults or rapes that they experience was estimated at one every one to two months. If these figures have merit, then the level of sexual violence that these women experience far exceeds that of the general population.

As with the national survey of the general public, access to professional support services and perceptions of the quality of those services was of interest. The participants were asked to serve as the "spokespersons" for the women they worked with when answering the questions about services. The items regarding satisfaction with services were the same as those used with the general public and included: seeing the woman promptly; taking the woman's experience seriously; not making the woman feel responsible; encouraging the woman to make a report; keeping the woman's case confidential; being sensitive to the woman's feelings; providing explanations about their procedures; and providing explanations of other services available. These key indicators of a quality service were rated on a five-point scale ranging from "excellent" to "very poor". Participants were also given the option of indicating that they did not have enough experience with the services to judge a particular quality.

Experiences with Medical Professionals

When asked what percentage of women in prostitution (who are raped or sexually assaulted) seek help from medical professionals, the participants had widely differing views. Estimates ranged from two to 70 per cent as to the uptake of medical services. Participants were also asked to estimate the percentage who may go to a medical professional, but do not mention the rape or sexual assault. Again, estimates varied so widely as to lack any utility for assessing the true frequency of utilisation of medical services. It is noteworthy that these workers "on the frontlines" have difficulty with these estimates, but reinforces the fact that the best way to understand the position of women in prostitution about their use of medical services would be to ask the women themselves directly.

Responses were somewhat more consistent when participants were asked where women would typically go when seeking medical help, with most indicating that they would likely go to Accident and Emergency Departments. A sexual assault unit was also mentioned, and one participant indicated that if they went to the police first, they would be more likely to be sent on to the sexual assault unit. Other places mentioned for medical help were the Woman's Health Project and their own organisation (Ruhama).

Participants were also asked what they thought were the main reasons the women decided not to go to medical professionals when they really should given their level of injuries. The most frequently cited reason (by all but two) was that they were afraid they would be treated badly by those in the profession. The next most frequently cited reason for not seeking medical help was that they (the women in prostitution) were ashamed and blamed themselves for what happened. As one participant stated:

> "Women are ashamed to say how they incurred their injuries; they expect to encounter a 'you deserve what you get' attitude."

Several other reasons for not seeking medical care were spontaneously noted by the participants. One participant stated, "Women who are involved in prostitution want to keep that fact deeply hidden." The fear of meeting someone they know while waiting in casualty seemed to be a factor, while another participant said they won't go to a GP for fear that the GP would break their confidentiality and tell their family (which was especially true for young women in prostitution). One participant reflected on the whole experience of being in prostitution, saying, "Their own health is very low on their list of priorities in a very chaotic existence."

Key indicators of the quality of medical services were rated. Overall, most participants rated professional medical services for women in prostitution as "adequate to poor". Participant ratings indicated that participants felt that medical professionals did things like "keeping her case confidential" and "seeing the woman promptly" quite well. They were rated as much worse on items such as "being sensitive to the woman's feelings" and "taking the woman's experience seriously". Other indicators of quality were given mixed reviews, and no item was rated "very poor".

When asked in an open-ended question if there was anything medical professionals could do to help and support women who engage in prostitution, a variety of suggestions were given which mainly stressed the need for awareness and education amongst medical professionals. A few suggested in-service education for those working in Accident and Emergency and other staff more generally:

> "Awareness of this issue is needed for professionals in order to break any stigmas or prejudices. Women need a holistic approach to their healthcare."

Another added:

> "Medical professionals would provide a tremendous support simply by keeping in mind that in these circumstances they are dealing with a hugely traumatised woman. It may appear that the woman in prostitution deliberately places herself in a position of danger or is herself directly responsible for being medically compromised. However, the woman is very often in prostitution because of prior traumatic life-circumstances."

Another participant stressed the importance of their role as medical professionals, given their stature in society, stating:

> "I think that the women could have a high level of trust in medical staff, so the staff could effectively encourage the woman to a) make a report, b) inform them of other services available, and c) generally talk about the risks and dangers of the 'lifestyle' for the woman and her children if she has family."

Experiences with Gardaí and Legal System

The percentage of women in prostitution who are raped or sexually assaulted and who report their abuse experience to the Gardaí was estimated from 1–40 per cent, although half the participants did not guess at the estimate. Multiple reasons were cited as
to why women decide not to go to the Gardaí, including that they
are afraid they would be treated badly, they blame themselves for
what happened, and they don't think they would be believed. As
one participant stated:

> "A really deep-seated reason for women not going to Gar-
> daí is that the woman's sense of self-worth is so low, and
> sense of shame so great, on account of prostitution, that at
> some level she believes she deserves the assault/attack, and
> she expects Gardaí and others to share this belief."

Notably, most also feared repercussions because of their work in
prostitution, and that there was no point, as the abuser always
seems to get away with it. One participant made reference to the
fact that Gardaí may be in a double-bind situation:

> "From what I know of the women's attitude to the Gardaí
> and given that it is the Gardaí that 'hassle' and arrest them,
> the Gardaí are unlikely to be seen as supportive in such a
> situation."

Other reasons women do not report were cited as well. One participant said that a prostitute told her that she:

> ". . . could not report 'this man' as he had a wife and young
> children and she could not put them, especially the little
> kids, through this."

When asked to rate the quality of the services provided to the
women by Gardaí, items such as "keeping the woman's case confidential", "seeing the woman promptly", and "encouraging the
woman to make a report" were rated most highly. Gardaí received much lower ratings on items such as "being sensitive to the

woman's feelings" and "providing explanations about procedures". Overall, however, there did appear to be a wide range of quality in their services, where individual Gardaí may provide a high quality service while others do not. As one participant said:

> "It is hard to rate this, as I would say it depends on the individual Garda and it depends on what the woman is presenting. If it's a serious crime like assault and she goes to the Gardaí who are familiar with the prostitution and crime scene, the service is good overall. But if it's in an area where Gardaí are not familiar with the vulnerability of the women, there can be prejudices."

When asked in an open-ended question what else the police could do to help and support women who engage in prostitution when a crime has been committed against them, several areas for improvement were suggested. Training and education featured frequently among responses, stating that more training "could be built in" to help the women. References to the conflicting roles that police are faced with (viewing women as engaging in illegal activities, but who are also victim to heinous crimes) were frequently made. As one participant said, Gardaí should be better equipped to be able to:

> ". . . respond and be clear with regard to their own upholding of the law of the land without denying any woman her own innate rights for personal safety."

Another expressed the feeling that police training:

> ". . . suppresses their ability to put themselves in the women's 'shoes' and their job is to gather information which is necessary."

This participant suggested that an experienced post-traumatic stress counsellor could be made available as statements are taken and for follow-up work. Another suggested having more female Gardaí involved, again with more training. Others had suggestions for the legal system in general, such as monitoring the men who frequent the red light district — have them arrested and appear before court.

> "Start looking for men who commit such crimes and be really serious about it."

Another suggested that for the women who appear in court there should be "a support programme through collaboration with the court, probation service, etc. (not fines or prison)". It was suggested that a key element is collaboration of services:

> "connect the woman with all relevant services that are there to help her — health, drugs, HIV, welfare, probation, social services, community services."

The questionnaire also asked about the effect police "crackdowns on prostitution" have on the women involved. Several points were made by the participants:

- Increased police presence on the streets means that the women in prostitution do not have the time to screen or "weigh up" clients as carefully as they would otherwise. This puts them at greater risk of encountering dangerous men.

- If a police crackdown is meant to "clean up" a particular area, the women will move and work somewhere else. The demand for their services is so large and the network so well established (so they can survive), that this sort of police effort does not prevent prostitution from happening. In fact, the participants believed that "drawing it [prostitution] off the streets" makes the women more open to danger. Further, it makes it more difficult for support to reach the women (e.g., Ruhama).

- If a police crackdown is focused on making arrests and sending the women to court, again, the consequences for the women are severe. Women who are fined often turn around and work (in prostitution) even more to come up with the money to pay the fines. In addition, women face humiliation and can be "totally degraded" by the court appearance.

Only a few questions were asked of participants about the legal system. When asked to estimate the percentage of women in prostitution that go to court with a case of sexual violence, participant's estimates ranged from 0.5–20 per cent, with many not putting forward any estimate. Further, almost all the participants did not make an estimate of the percentage of cases that result in criminal prosecution. Although few ventured even a guess at the figures, these estimates appear to be significantly lower than the estimates yielded by the national survey for the general population.

Experiences with Counselling or Psychological Professionals

The percentage of women in prostitution who have been sexually assaulted and seek help from counselling or psychological professionals was estimated to be from one percent to 20 per cent. Given these estimates, psychological services do not seem to be a major source of support for most women in prostitution. The main reasons cited for not utilising these professionals were: they did not think the professionals could do anything to help; they felt ashamed and they blamed themselves for what happened; and they felt they couldn't discuss sexual matters with a stranger. Spontaneous reasons given for not utilising these services centred around difficulties in how the services have traditionally been structured. As one participant explained, "Women's lives are so chaotic . . . they can't commit to a series of appointments." Others emphasised the lack of awareness about what the service has to offer and the waiting lists often associated with these services.[2]

> "Some say they don't understand what counselling is or how it will help."

One participant summed the situation up, saying that the women:

---

[2] While service providers reported making special provision to see those experiencing sexual violence in the last year promptly, the view of those reporting on service access was of delays in accessing needed services.

> ". . . seem to think that counselling will not help — unless there are changes in the woman's own practical circumstances (e.g., a woman who is homeless, drug-dependent and assaulted), she is simply unable to access or see the value of psychological support/counselling services."

When asked to rate the services provided by counselling or psychological services, participants viewed the services overall as "adequate". Items rated highest were "taking the woman's experience seriously" and "being sensitive to the woman's feelings", followed by "not making the woman feel responsible". Psychological services were seen as performing least well on "seeing the woman promptly". It should be noted that the number of women judging these services was very small, with many stating that they could not rate the service at all for a few items (i.e., encouraging the woman to make a report, and providing explanation of other services).

Suggestions for what psychological and counselling services could do to improve their services for women in prostitution were put forward by the participants. As with other services, many re-iterated the need for additional training and education specifically focusing on issues for women in prostitution:

> "Most of the professionals lives are so far removed from the reality of the lives of women in prostitution that they do not have the skills to help even if well intentioned."

Another suggested that professionals:

> ". . . educate themselves on the issues for women . . . develop other therapeutic ways to help women besides one-to-one counselling (e.g. art or group counselling)."

Changes in how services are organised or structured were suggested by a number of participants. One participant felt that women need:

". . . brief periods of support on demand, independent of the woman's involvement with other agencies (e.g. drug clinics, sexual assault unit, etc.)."

Another participant expanded on these suggestions saying:

"I believe counselling and psychological professionals have great ability to help and support women, but the service needs to be regular and frequent. Very often, the service falls apart because the woman does not keep her appointment — but the women in prostitution need assistance in keeping such appointments. By definition, a service has regard for the circumstances of the user. Therefore, a 'psychological service' for women in prostitution must practically consider the implications of the psychological and emotional chaos in the life of the woman in prostitution, for her ability to access professional services."

Timeliness and access were underlined as major difficulties, as another participant stated:

"There are not enough counselling or psychological professionals available to the women when they need them — they have to wait for everything. Their self-esteem is so low they would not be able to access such services on their own."

Lastly, one participant also mentioned the need for "publicising the services available and demystifying them".

PROSTITUTION IN SOCIETY: WAYS FORWARD

Participants were asked if they think that Irish society today is more or less violent than in the past for or towards women in prostitution. Sadly, most participants indicated that it was either "somewhat more" or "a lot more" violent. When asked why they thought this, most indicated that they felt there was a greater level of violence in society in general with less respect for human life. Some participants mentioned the increased access to pornography on television and in videos as a key contributor to the violence, while a few others mentioned prostitution's links to the drug industry. Only one participant felt it was "somewhat less" violent towards women in prostitution, stating that "despite setbacks, society improves its attitude on these matters year on year".

As a final question, participants were asked about any specific changes that could be made with regard to supporting women who engage in prostitution. Two major approaches were suggested: public awareness and education aimed at increasing the understanding of the situation of women in prostitution and preventing more young women from taking up prostitution, and significant changes in the legal and social services for women who are already involved in prostitution to help them leave prostitution. The following points were made:

- The general public needs to view prostitution as "violence against women and as a human rights issue". Further, "it is not acceptable for any man to abuse any woman in this way".

- The general public needs to be made more aware of the reasons why women engage in prostitution, the number of women involved, their age-range and "the hardship, suffering and danger attendant on this lifestyle". In particular, young people need to be "made aware of the risks involved in prostitution and the routes into it". This needs to be coupled with knowledge about the "difficulties facing any woman who tries to extricate herself from this lifestyle".

- Ireland needs to "change the law so that women are not victimised". "Men (pimps and customers) should be prosecuted more vigorously." As one participant stated, we need to "acknowledge the reality that for every one woman, there are at least 10 men involved", which she felt was a "conservative estimate". Alongside these measures, one woman thought that society needed to "deal with issues relating to the perceived right of those who demand prostitution be available".

- Support services need to be linked, freely available and accessible. "A very radical approach needs to be taken by government on this issue. Women in prostitution need major support when they choose to exit the life." One suggested that "each large town in Ireland needs services similar to Ruhama". Others saw the need to "develop more collaboration" between the courts, probation, social services, and alcohol and drug treatment.

- "Real" alternatives to prostitution need to be developed. Young people need help finding alternative ways of earning a living, with educational opportunities and other supports "to meet her where she is at" and "empower [her] in [her] choice out of prostitution (e.g. childcare, increase in social welfare, low income housing)".

- Lastly, in order to prevent women from taking up prostitution, the poverty of women in society needs to be reduced and ultimately eliminated.

Recommendation

The complex challenges of sexual violence in the lives of women in prostitution needs further research. This should involve working directly with these women to consider how to promote good management of past abuse and protection against sexual violence in the future. A key aspect of achieving these goals will be to work with health and law enforcement agencies in the interests of those involved in prostitution.

Chapter 9

THE SEXUAL ABUSE OF PEOPLE WITH LEARNING DISABILITIES[1]

INTRODUCTION

Persons with learning disabilities (or "mental handicaps")[2] constitute a vulnerable group with regard to sexual violence. This overview considers the particular vulnerabilities of this group both in terms of being targets for sexual violence and subsequently in terms of disclosure and verification of that abuse. International evidence is considered and combined with available information from Ireland. Considering the data in the international literature and anecdotal reports, there is no reason to believe the problem in Ireland to be less prevalent than elsewhere. Contact with key Irish informants has facilitated identification of practices being developed or promoted in the Irish setting. The present Irish situation with regard to guidelines for the protection of persons with learning disabilities and the current related law is outlined. Legal and programmatic challenges for the future are considered.

---

[1] This Chapter was written in association with Dr James Kelly, SAVI team member.

[2] The term "learning disabled" is used throughout this chapter to cover populations variously categorised as "mentally handicapped", "mentally retarded", etc.

Prevalence, Vulnerability to Abuse, and Challenges to its Validation

Researchers agree that sexual abuse and assault among people with learning disabilities is a significant problem (Westcott and Jones, 1999; Dunne and Power, 1990; Brown and Craft, 1989; Schor 1987; Elkins et al., 1986; Chamberlain et al., 1984). International studies show that learning disabled people are at a greater risk for sexual violence than their non-disabled peers (Kelly, 1992; Westcott, 1991; Muccigrosso, 1991; Ammerman, Van Hasselt and Hersen, 1988). Published prevalence estimates vary enormously and range from 8 to 58 per cent (Brown and Turk, 1994). This variation is due to a number of confounding issues that make such research highly complicated. These are discussed later. No study to date has assessed the prevalence of sexual violence in this population in Ireland. There is considerable discussion of the factors that appear to increase the vulnerability of this population, including deficiencies of sexual knowledge, physical and emotional dependence on caregivers, multiple caregiving, limited communication skills, and behavioural difficulties. A focus on "compliance teaching", in which service users are trained to follow orders and directions of staff and caregivers without question or resistance, is also seen as a contributing factor by several researchers in the field (Brown and Turk, 1994). Kempton and Gochros (1986) have suggested that people with learning disabilities are more trusting of strangers than others, may be unable to discriminate between appropriate and inappropriate behaviour, readily comply with the requests of others, may be unable to defend themselves, and may not report incidents as sexual abuse or assault. Research in the US has shown that children with disabilities are twice as likely to be physically, emotionally, and sexually abused (Westcott and Cross, 1996).

A key factor that increases the vulnerability of this population is the perception on the part of some staff that allegations of sexual violence are not believable. Sometimes symptoms of sexual abuse and assault may be attributed to the person's disability and thus be overlooked (Sobsey and Mansell, 1990). Schor (1987) described a "crisis of disbelief" about sexual abuse for learning disabled as well as for non-learning disabled adolescents (Dunne and Power, 1990). Dunne and Power contend that the allegations of learning disabled adolescents are more easily discounted than those of other adolescents. A generally desexualised image of people with disabilities often results in a failure to recognise the possibility of their being sexually abused. Other factors that contribute to the vulnerability of learning disabled people include limitations of personal control, privacy and personal autonomy in some institutional settings, more extensive caretaker contact compared to other members of the community, and developmental limitations in assessing dangerous situations (CARI (Children at Risk in Ireland), 2001).

Another factor increasing challenges to the validation of abuse is the limitation of many research studies. Retrospective studies assessing childhood abuse and past abuse of adults can serve to identify problems of under-reporting. However, the target population's inherent problems, likely to be in part due to poor communication skills and reduced capacity to recall and articulate events, render this method somewhat unreliable. The validity of reported cases, where there is little or no corroborating evidence, is similarly problematic for researchers. Levels of learning disability vary greatly; thus methodologies to assess abuse need to be similarly varied. However, few studies focus specifically on any given level of intellectual capacity. Thus it is difficult to develop expertise on the measurement and meaning of abuse reporting levels by intellectual capacity. A focus on the general child literature may benefit research here since issues of comprehension and expression of feelings and experiences concerning sexual abuse in young children may inform understanding of intellectually challenged children and adults.

Most studies do not distinguish between various types of abuse: single events and ongoing abuse, contact (penetrative/non-penetrative but tactile) and non-contact abuse (perpetrator and/or abused person exposure, exposure to pornography), and not all studies clarify their definition of abuse in terms of consent. Consent and capacity to consent issues must be considered, both regarding the incidents themselves as well as for participation in surveys using direct interview methodologies. Murphy and Clare (1995) compared two different approaches for assessing capacity to consent: diagnostic and functional. The diagnostic approach is when an individual is identified as a member of a group which is considered to have a lack of capacity to consent, for example, being in a certain intellectual range. The functional approach focuses on particular skills or knowledge in a given context, as is the case in Irish law. These issues have confounded the establishment of consistent working definitions of sexual violence amongst this population.

Further issues complicating research methodologies in learning disability are co-morbid conditions such as psychological/ behavioural difficulties, epilepsy, and medical/physical limitations, as each of these imply vulnerability factors that are difficult to differentiate from the learning disability itself.

IMPACT OF SEXUAL VIOLENCE ON PEOPLE WITH LEARNING DISABILITIES

Short-term effects of the sexual violence on learning disabled people have been reported to include generalised anxiety, distress, and fearfulness. Three main areas emerge in terms of long-term effect, and are summarised in Dunne and Power (1990) thus:

> **Effects on the quality of life** — Sexual abuse increases the vulnerability of the abused person with learning disabilities to other abuse, and results in the imposition of additional restrictions on their freedom of movement in the community.

> **Emotional problems** — Abused persons with learning disabilities have a higher risk of emotional problems, including depression and anxiety, often of a long-standing nature.

> **Sexuality** — Many people with learning disabilities who are abused become inappropriately sexualised, while the sexual orientation of others can be affected, leading to an increased likelihood of further sexual abuse. Some of those who are abused go on to become abusers themselves.

PROFESSIONAL AND INSTITUTIONAL RESPONSES
TO ALLEGATIONS OF ABUSE

Internationally, disclosures of sexual abuse and assault among learning disabled populations have prompted various responses from academics, social services agencies, advocacy groups and governmental agencies. The sexual abuse of all children and young people in institutional care in the US has been underestimated (National Association for Young People in Care, 1989; c.f. Kelly, 1992). Several studies discuss a wide variation in response to abuse allegations as well as in the development of intervention and prevention strategies (Brown and Turk, 1994; Carmody, 1991; Stromsness, 1993; Sobsey and Mansell, 1990). The reported variety in agency response to sexual abuse and assault in Carmody's (1991) Australian study included:

1. Ignoring allegations

2. Requiring alleged perpetrator to leave or terminate employment with no formal investigation

3. Requiring the abused person to leave a facility, or harassment of the abused person

4. Notifying police, arranging for crisis care for the abused person

5. Conducting internal agency investigation

6. Interrogating the abused person in front of other staff and/or alleged perpetrator

7. Failing to ascertain the wishes of the abused person regarding the assault and to provide assistance

8. Notifying the licensing body, i.e. social welfare, and requesting a formal investigation.

In Stromsness's (1993) US study of characteristics and experiences of sexual violence among learning disabled women, institutional obstacles were cited as largely contributing to the low reported response rate. Staff in one regional centre refused to co-operate with researchers unless it was agreed that the researchers:

- Eliminate questions about reporting abuse to case managers, about case managers' levels of compliance with mandates to report suspected cases of client sexual abuse and assault, and about case managers' investigation and follow-up on reports of sexual violence; and

- Have learning disabled clients of the centre waive any financial obligation by the regional centre should they admit to being sexually abused and be in need of psychotherapy.

The director of another regional centre would only participate with the approval of the state agency responsible for regional centres. The assistant director of that agency, while claiming to support the intent of the study, refused to endorse it because:

- The study might re-traumatise the participants by awakening dormant memories of past abuse;

- Participation might provoke additional abuse; and

- No resources were available to mitigate the trauma or end the abuse.

It has been suggested that bureaucratic structures similar to those encountered by the researchers are those which impede efforts to intervene at the time when learning disabled women are being sexually abused (Stromsness, 1993).

Many service providers fail to report abuse for fear of direct retaliation by the abuser or administrative retaliation from authorities that are embarrassed by the reports of abuse within the service delivery system for which they have responsibility (Sobsey and Mansell, 1990). In their examination of prevention programmes in Canada, Sobsey and Mansell suggested that institutions have failed to recognise their legal obligation to maintain a level of personal safety similar to that of the general community. Several court decisions in Canada and the US point to a diminishing tolerance for this irresponsibility, holding staff legally responsible because they knew of the vulnerability of the learning disabled client and failed to take action to ensure their safety.

Enquiries into allegations of neglect and abuse have not shown them to be isolated incidents committed by individual members of staff as much as "a subculture within which the (organisational) hierarchy who at least passively acknowledged or condoned what was going on" (Brown, 1996). This subculture can, in turn, maintain the position of people with learning difficulties as "potential victims on whose behalf neither the risks nor the consequences of sexual exploitation are taken seriously" (Brown and Craft, 1996).

THE CONTEXT OF INFORMATION GATHERING ON SEXUAL VIOLENCE IN LEARNING DISABLED POPULATIONS: AN OVERVIEW OF METHODOLOGIES AND FINDINGS

A variety of methods and purposes provide information relevant to sexual violence in learning disabled populations. These are outlined here. The research studies are not comparable in terms of how the information was gathered, working definitions of abuse, or population demographic profiles such as age and level of disability. They are, however, indicative of the vulnerability of this population to sexual violence and demonstrate the need to develop appropriate interventions.

A number of studies adopt the approach of checking for abuse in specialist health clinic attendees or searching case notes of learning disabled persons. For instance, Chamberlain et al. (1984) assessed sexual activity, abuse, and contraception use among young females with developmental delays in an adolescent clinic in the US. This study was carried out by retrospective chart review, so the population prevalence of sexual violence was probably over-represented by the specialist nature of the clinic, while clinic sample prevalence was underestimated by use of case notes rather than interviews. Of 87 charts reviewed, 22 cases of sexual assault were indicated (a 25 per cent prevalence rate). Elkins et al. (1986) studied the reproductive health and sexuality concerns of women with learning disabilities in a new clinic and found that 10 of the 37 women seen (27 per cent) reported having been sexually abused; in eight cases, this resulted in unwanted pregnancies. It was not clear if interview or case review methodologies were used. Hard and Plumb's unpublished 1987 report (c.f. Turk and Brown, 1993) described interviews with a large group of people with learning disabilities in England. Sixty-five of the 95 people attending a day centre were asked if they had been sexually abused or assaulted and 38 (58 per cent) reported sexual violence. The interviewers were well known to those interviewed, possibly increasing the likelihood of reporting. This study gives one of the few estimates of prevalence of sexual violence as disclosed by a relatively unselected sample (c.f. Turk and Brown, 1993).

Other research has focused on service providers. Sobsey and Varnhagen's (1989) large-scale survey of children and adults with disabilities in Canada used survey forms that were sent to a sample of national agencies that provide services to disabled adults. No prevalence or incidence statistics were computed, but other detailed aspects of the sexual violence were provided. This study included children and adults without a learning disability, however, so results are somewhat unclear. Sobsey and Mansell (1990), in a review of Canadian institutions and available research, maintain that risk of sexual violence was 2–4 times higher for those housed in institutional settings. Learning disabled service users who were regularly restrained (chemically or physically) were also found to be at higher risk.

Buchanan and Wilkins (1991) developed a form that was completed by residential and field workers in Berkshire, England. Fifty professionals who were attending in-service courses at a college of adult education, and who were working full-time with the adult learning disabled, were asked to complete the form. Thirty-seven participants from 24 establishments catering for 847 people returned completed forms. Results were extrapolated to populations covered to indicate an overall prevalence rate of 8 per cent. The authors proposed that this figure was "the tip of a very large iceberg". A 1992 survey of staff views on sexual assault of adults with learning disabilities gave no overall prevalence figures, but asked health service and local authority staff in day and residential facilities in Nottingham, England such questions as whether they knew of people who they *thought* had been sexually assaulted (Allington, 1992). Of 300 questionnaires circulated, one-third were returned and revealed 109 counts of potential cases of sexual assault, and a further 51 confirmed cases of sexual assault (Brown and Hunt, 1994; Turk and Brown, 1993). Turk and Brown (1993) developed a survey of the incidence of new cases of sexual assault of adults with learning disabilities, which occurred within a two-year period. In a large regional health authority in the UK, main statutory providers of services for learning disabled adults were targeted. Definitions and parameters for the qualifying incidents were provided, as well as a checklist for classification into varying levels of certainty or proof. A total of 138 completed questionnaires were returned, twelve of which did not meet the project criteria (e.g. those abused were under 18 years of age, or had experienced sexual assault outside the specified time frame). Eighty-four of the cases (70 per cent) were either proven or deemed to have sufficient evidence to suggest that sexual assault was likely to have occurred.

Carmody (1991) found that most disability services in Australia did not collect data on this issue. Frequently, learning disabled people who had experienced sexual violence did not receive counselling and medical services at the time of the disclosure and were not referred to services until many weeks after the crisis. This was seen to result in the abused persons requiring longer treatment as well as causing difficulties for police in obtaining evidence and statements from witnesses.

In 1995, Beail and Warden examined case notes for 88 American adults with a learning disability and found sexual violence in 22 cases. Of these, 13 reported that the sexual assault had occurred in the year prior to disclosure. The authors proposed that there was a link between sexual violence and sexualised and inappropriate behaviour amongst men with learning disabilities. In a study of learning disabled young women (12–25 years old) in Germany, Klein, Wawrok and Fegert (1999) found that nearly one-third of the 147 examined from 26 residential institutions had experienced sexual violence. Authors in this study relate the high rate of sexualised violence in these institutions to a lack of psychosocial support.

O'Sullivan, Carr, MacIntyre et al. (2001) evaluated the effectiveness of aspects of a comprehensive child abuse prevention programme designed to address the needs of various types of disabled children in Ireland. Matched school classes were randomly assigned to treatment and waiting list control groups. Knowledge was assessed before and after the programme, and again at a 10-week follow-up. Significant gains were reported for the 124 children from seven randomly chosen schools in Dublin, Wicklow, Mayo, Meath, Kilkenny and Cork.

There has been one study in Ireland addressing the issue of sexual violence of learning disabled adults. This did not specifically address incidence or prevalence. Dunne and Power (1990) documented the findings of a three-year study of learning disabled people who were sexually abused. Incidence information based on case review was given on 13 cases of the sexual assault or abuse of adults and children. These were reported to a community-based service with responsibility for 1,500 people with learning disabilities over a three-year period from January 1986 to December 1988. A semi-structured interview was conducted with all clinicians (psychologists, psychiatrists, and social workers) that had been involved in the various cases, using the Sexual Abuse Survey Questionnaire[3] (Dunne and Power, 1990). The survey contained detailed questions on the background of the abused person and the abuser, the type of sexual abuse, how disclosure occurred, the investigations that were carried out by the team, case management, and treatment of the abused person and the abuser. It also attempted to investigate the short-term and long-term effects of the abuse on the offender, all of whom, in this study, were

---

[3] A revised version of this instrument, adaptable for use by any service providing agency, is available, with permission from the author, from the Health Services Research Centre, Department of Psychology, Royal College of Surgeons in Ireland, Mercer Street, Dublin 2.

known to the abused person. In 5 of the 13 cases, the abuse was intra-familial. Eight of the 13 cases described were of ongoing abuse, with 4 continuing over a period of months and 4 continuing over a period of years. The authors considered the most important finding in this study to be the possibility that behaviour problems and "acting out" are significant indicators of sexual violence having taken place, particularly among those who do not have the verbal skills to say what has happened to them. It is not possible to ascertain what proportion of sexual violence these 13 cases represent. The low number of reported cases may be due to the study being retrospective and to a lack of recognition or unreported abuse. However, the study provides a profile of the number of new cases that might be disclosed over a given time period, and thus could be of value to service providers, management and staff.

Other studies evaluated the status of the perpetrator. The sexual assault of adults with learning disabilities perpetrated by other adults with learning disabilities was examined in Connecticut, USA, by Furey and Niesen (1994). Over a five-year period, all alleged cases of sexual assault were investigated with 72 cases being substantiated. There were a total of 49 perpetrators. The perpetrator was found to be responsible in 31 cases, both abuse and neglect were confirmed in 6 cases and facility neglect accounted for the remaining 35 cases. Those involved represented all levels of learning disability and very few had physical or other disabilities. Men were as much at risk as women. Most (94 per cent) of the perpetrators were men and 81 per cent had lived or still lived (at time of publication) in large institutional settings. In a related study (Furey et al., 1994), sexual violence committed against learning disabled individuals by others with learning disabilities was compared to cases where the perpetrator was a paid staff or family member or other person. Of 171 substantiated cases, 42 per cent involved learning disabled perpetrators. Perhaps the most striking difference between the two groups was that men comprised 44 per cent of those who had been abused by learning disabled perpetrators and only 15 per cent of those abused by staff, family and others. The majority of perpetrators in both groups were male.

Other studies serve as descriptors of the abuse. Stromsness's (1993) US study described sexual abuse in 14 mildly learning disabled adult women and focused on the associated characteristics and experiences of the abuse. Eleven women reported 59 separate instances of sexual abuse, with almost 82 per cent having occurred before their eighteenth birthday. Sex education did not appear to prevent sexual abuse, but did increase the likelihood of its being reported. Their results describe the difficulties women with learning difficulties face in gaining access to medical, psychological, and legal help when sexually abused. McCabe, Cummins, and Reid (1994) compared levels of sexual knowledge and experience of sexual violence among 30 people with learning disabilities (aged 16–40) and 50 undergraduates without learning disabilities. Results demonstrated a lower level of sexual knowledge amongst those with a learning disability but no differences in the level of incest and other unwanted sexual activities. A high percentage of learning disabled people believed that someone else decides about the level of their sexual experience, and they expressed less negativity about sexual abuse.

Representing the findings elsewhere in the international literature Turk and Brown (1993) have found that the reporting source is most likely to be the abused person themselves, that a high percentage of cases are contact abuse, that a high percentage of cases involve male perpetrators generally known to the abused person (which is consistent with child sexual abuse findings in the general population) and that the largest group therein are also service users (as distinct from service providers or the general public).

GOOD PRACTICE GUIDELINES

Researchers have recommended that research evidence on the level and nature of sexual abuse or assault of learning disabled clients be used for the development of good practice guidelines to facilitate staff training, to increase the recognition of and response to sexual violence in this population, and to promote the early implementation of sexual abuse avoidance curricula. Good practice guidelines can be used to document the need for expanded resources and services, to develop reporting and investigation protocols and to advocate for effective legislation regarding the sexual abuse of such vulnerable populations.

The questions as outlined below (Table 9.1), developed by Brown and Craft (1996), may provide a starting framework for the development of policy within service-providing agencies.

Table 9.1: Framework for the Development of Policy within Service-providing Agencies

- Are there guidelines about sexuality in operation which clearly set out the boundaries within which staff should relate to service users?

- Is sexuality raised routinely within the context of individual planning meetings and, if so, how is the individual's confidentiality respected?

- Is there a clear, well-publicised complaints procedure for service users and for staff?

- Is a list of possible signs and symptoms of sexual abuse circulated to all staff and included in operational policies or staff guidelines about sexuality?

- Have staff been instructed to view sexual "acting out" as a possible indicator of abuse?

- Are there close links between learning disability services and the child sexual abuse team, and who is responsible for maintaining these?

- Are appropriate "sex education" groups available to children and adults with learning difficulties? Do these groups include self-protection and assertiveness training in their curricula?

- Are some key members of staff trained in sexual counselling and education, including techniques for facilitating disclosure of abuse?

- Does the organisation support key individuals in acquiring such expertise/qualifications?

- How are sexual problems dealt with and responded to in the service?

Brown and Craft (1996) pointed out that good practice needs to take into account individual differences in sexual activity and orientation and concern needs to extend to the way intimate care is given. They offer guidelines for agency staff and commissioners (Table 9.2).

Table 9.2: Guidelines for Agency Staff and Commissioners

- Front-line staff will talk respectfully about sexual matters and relationships; service users' feelings will not be trivialised nor have their appearance made fun of.

- Intimate care will usually be offered by staff of the same sex.

- A balance between privacy and openness will be sought in the way care is offered; for example, bathroom doors will be closed, but other staff will be around and aware of who is with a particular service user.

- Staff will be able to acknowledge and manage a certain amount of "difficult" sexual behaviour, such as masturbation in public areas, without taking a blaming or "smutty" attitude.

- Some staff — under supervision from senior staff and/or after further training — will be able to run sex education sessions with small groups or individuals. Appropriate educational materials will be available.

- The rights of service users to have consenting sexual relationships will be respected and actively supported, whether these are heterosexual or homosexual. Sometimes this will necessitate sensitive consultation with parents, especially where people with learning disabilities continue to live at home into adulthood.

- Written guidance for all staff will be available reflecting these principles; individual records and care plans will show that sexual behaviour is being addressed properly.

- All service users will have access to adequate health care, including attention to sexual health issues. This should include screening and access to the same range of treatments and interventions as other people of their age and gender.

- Staff will know that service users with severe learning disabilities are deemed, in law, not to be able to give consent to sexual acts and will interpret this sensitively. Where uncertainties arise, there should be consultation among the provider, care manager, relatives or advocates, and relevant professionals in order to arrive at a shared decision.

- Individual rather than "blanket" decisions will be made about such issues as oral contraception and sex education.

- Staff will intervene to prevent abusive, non-consenting, exploitative or violent relationships between service users. They will recognise that sex in the context of a family, care-taking or other markedly unequal relationship, is an abuse of power.

- Staff and volunteers will be clear that they should not themselves have sex with service users because of their authority/power.

- Staff meetings will demonstrate that the staff team can discuss sexual issues in a professional way.

- Relationships within the staff team itself will provide a good model for service users. There will be no sexual harassment or teasing between staff, or lack of respect between women and men workers.

Professionals dealing with learning disabled populations continue to call for the inclusion of training in the areas of assertiveness, empowerment, recognising the difference between appropriate and inappropriate requests from others and improvements in sex education within the educational curriculum for learning disabled children (Westcott, 1991). Some agencies have focused on specific issues such as necessary educational and legal changes. For instance, a group of three voluntary agencies representing those with learning disabilities in the UK have jointly developed a set of proposals to change UK law on sex offences to protect people with learning disabilities from sexual abuse (VOICE, Respond, Mencap, 2001). Recommendations range from criminalising any sexual relations between staff and clients in care settings through training for police and the judiciary to abuse prevention work with learning disabled people themselves.

THE IRISH SITUATION

Some service providers may argue that guidelines that are developed outside Ireland are not all entirely adaptable to service providers here. Philosophical barriers to some of the guidelines above may arise particularly when agencies are jointly administered, e.g. by a religious and a state organisation. However, research on staff attitudes to sexuality and people with intellectual disabilities in

Northern Ireland has been conducted with largely positive attitudes being expressed (Ryan et al., 2000). A lack of sexual knowledge amongst learning disabled people is widely considered a major contributor to their abuse (Turk and Brown, 1993; Furey and Niesen, 1994; Stromsness, 1993). Delays in the development of prevention, assessment, intervention and treatment techniques and policies can compound this issue. Some service providers in Ireland have already developed guidelines for staff for dealing with sexual violence and sexual activity more generally amongst service users. For example, the Brothers of Charity Service in Galway have developed a set of guidelines for staff of centre-based and residential services entitled *Personal Development, Relationships and Sexuality* (Brothers of Charity, 2000).[4] Education and training guidelines for service users are included. They aim to reflect a balanced approach to such issues as exploitation and abuse, positive and pro-social sexual development, and practical aspects of sexuality, such as sexual education and consent issues. This document draws extensively on a range of previous reports from various Irish settings: *Relationships and Sexual Development* (Hospitaller Order of Saint John of God, 1995), *The Bawnmore Personal Development Programme* (Toomey, Kilgarriff and Ryan, 1988), and *Brothers of Charity: Guidelines on Relationships and Sexuality* (Brothers of Charity, 1999). The report provides a constructive set of guidelines for dealing with these highly charged issues in the Irish setting.

In the Brothers of Charity Services document *Reporting Abuse Guidelines for All Staff* (McGinley, 2000a), a recommendation is made for staff to become familiar with the Department of Health and Children and the Western Health Board Child Abuse Guidelines on reporting suspected or alleged physical or sexual violence. Included are names and contact information for designated persons within the organisation. Also included is the following simple, five-

---

[4] Copies of these documents are available from Brothers of Charity, Woodlands Centre, Renmore, Galway.

stage checklist for designated persons who receive a report alleging abuse. It provides a standardised procedural protocol (Table 9.3).

Table 9.3: Checklist for Designated Person on Receiving Report Alleging Abuse (Brothers of Charity, 1999)

- Stage 1: Consult medical opinion (parents' permission to be sought as appropriate) and call together appropriate people to assist initial assessment of situation and obtain written reports.

- Stage 2: Inform Director of Services where allegations of abuse involve an employee or where an offence is suspected.

- Stage 3: Inform Manager of Child and Family Services (Community Care) when alleged victim is under 18 years and ensure that the family is informed.

- Stage 4: Designated Person informs Gardaí if an offence is suspected.

- Stage 5: Plan for client's immediate and long-term well-being.

Assessment tools for prevention are particularly valuable for developing a child protection policy in settings serving learning disabled people. *The Dangerous Places Risk Assessment Scale* (McGinley, 2000b) was developed in Ireland to assist in strategic planning for a safe environment for service users. Based on previously identified factors that contribute to dangerous institutional situations, it is an example of a short, easily administered checklist covering several broad areas of institutional administration and policy.

A number of recent training initiatives in Ireland are relevant to the prevention and disclosure of the sexual abuse of people with a learning disability. Two examples illustrate the types of activity that have been undertaken. Firstly, the Stay Safe Programme Learning Disabilities Pack, part of a comprehensive programme for all children, *The Stay Safe Programme* (MacIntyre and Lawlor, 1991) provided accessibility to children with various disabilities, including children with learning disabilities (O'Sullivan et al., unpublished). A second example also exemplifies consideration of sexual abuse in a wider relationships and sexuality setting and starts by consulting young people with a learning disability.

It is a project conducted by the Galway Association for Mentally Handicapped Children (GAMHC) in association with the Western Health Board's Department of Public Health (Walsh and Evans, 2001). They ran six focus groups with learning disabled individuals to inform the organisation's management of relationships and sexuality issues. They are using information from these in developing a general policy on relationships and sexuality for GAMHC. Some evaluative research on training needs and outcomes has been conducted in Ireland. Regarding service providers, Ryan and McConkey (2000) sought to identify staff experiences as well as attitudes to inform the planning of staff training initiatives. Regarding service users, a study focused on training for children has been conducted (O'Sullivan et al., unpublished).

LEGISLATION AS IT RELATES TO SEXUAL OFFENCES AGAINST PEOPLE WITH A LEARNING DISABILITY

In order to fully utilise any existing law, there needs to be an individual who is willing and able to undertake reporting any offence to the Gardaí. As is true of most criminal cases, the issue of proof of allegations of sexual offences is crucial to successful prosecution. Sexual offences can be particularly problematic when the abused person has a learning disability. It may be relatively easy to establish that a sexual act took place, particularly when there is corroborating evidence such as samples of semen or bodily tissue or where over time there is evidence of sexually transmitted diseases or pregnancy. It can be somewhat more difficult to establish that it was the accused who perpetrated the event, or that the act was not understood to be consensual by the allegedly abused person in cases of adult assault where a third party makes an allegation. Further, the person who is alleged to have been abused must be able/capable of taking an oath and be competent to give evidence in court.

In Ireland, the Law Reform Commission has pointed out several problems with Irish law in its 1990 *Report on Sexual Offences Against the Mentally Handicapped* (LRC 33-1990). Section 5 of the Criminal Law (Sexual Offences) Act 1993 implemented most, but not all, of the Commission's recommendations (O'Malley, 1996). The offences created by this section and their maximum sentences following conviction on indictment are as follows:

- Sexual intercourse or attempted sexual intercourse with a mentally impaired person (ten years' imprisonment for the completed offence, three years for attempt in the case of a first conviction, five years for attempt in the case of a second or subsequent conviction)

- Buggery or attempted buggery of a mentally impaired person (same maximum sentences as for sexual intercourse and attempted intercourse)

- The commission or attempted commission of an act of gross indecency by a male with another male who is mentally impaired (two years imprisonment).

The Law Reform Commission had recommended that if both parties were mentally impaired, it should not be considered an offence. However, this recommendation was not taken up, and instead of providing a guideline based on the perpetrator's level of functioning or some similar criterion, it appears to be left up to prosecutorial discretion should this issue arise. The Law Reform Commission had also recommended that Section 254 of the Mental Treatment Act of 1945 be retained and the maximum sentence be increased to ten years. This would have provided for a separate, more serious offence for institutional abuse. O'Malley (1996) speculated that the Commission's recommendations regarding institutional abuse were not followed because of the establishment of a general ten-year sentence for *any* offence involving a completed act of penetration. O'Malley synopsised the changes that were made in Irish law regarding sexual offences against mentally impaired persons in *Sexual Offences: Law, Policy and Punishment* (1996):

> The reforms enacted in s. 5 of the Act of 1993 are less than satisfactory as they fail to reflect a holistic appreciation of the rights and needs of mentally disabled persons. This is largely due to modern law reform policy in Ireland which

almost invariably concentrates on "lawyers' law" rather than widen the scope of the enquiry to include historical, sociological and, where necessary, medical perspectives. While there are many aspects of the section to be welcomed, notably the range of offences covered and their gender-neutral application, it reflects certain ancient biases against mentally disabled persons as being incompetent to make personal decisions and the more insidious prejudice against mentally disabled women who were traditionally deemed "uncontrollable" so long as they were fertile.

There are yet to be addressed aspects of related law that may be worthy of consideration. As in child protection, there is the unresolved issue of mandatory reporting of suspected abuse in Ireland. Jurisdictions elsewhere have adopted various versions of this provision, coupled with protection for reporters. Furey and Haber (1989) described a model statute for protecting adults with learning disabilities. Regarding mandatory reporting, the following personnel are specified in this model statute: physicians, nurses, dentists, dental hygienists, occupational and physical therapists, psychologists, social workers, teachers, speech pathologists, police officers, and "any person paid for caring for persons in any facility". However, such laws can be by design sufficiently wide in scope to include most of the people who work daily with the learning disabled, and thus increase the likelihood that suspected abuse would be reported. Should a mandated reporter fail to report suspected abuse, and it was subsequently discovered that the abuse was known to them, violators might be subject to a fine according to the proposed statute. It would provide for a five-calendar day period in which the mandated party must report, or ensure that a report is made, even if they did not personally make the report themselves. Protection would be provided in law for the person who submits a good faith report of suspected abuse, and they would be immune from civil or criminal liability. Conversely though, if it could be demonstrated that a report was malicious, the person could be subject to a fine. Anyone who "hinders or endangers" a person reporting abuse would be subject to this fine as well. Furthermore, protection would be provided in the law for reporters of abuse from reprisal or being discharged from employment as a result of making a good faith report of abuse or neglect. The service providers themselves would also be mandated by law to co-operate with any subsequent investigations, including giving access to client records (unless the client disagrees). In the scheme of the model statute, such a law would contribute to the reduction of under-reporting and the "say nothing" cultures that perpetuate the abuse of such vulnerable populations (Connecticut General Statutes, 19a-458 (1985) c.f. Furey and Haber, 1989). Some of the proposals outlined in the model statute, for example the protection of those reporting abuse in good faith, are already in place in Ireland through policy documents such as *Children First* (Department of Health and Children, 1999).

CONCLUSION

While no study in Ireland has specifically focused on the prevalence of the sexual abuse of our learning disabled population, the sexual abuse of people with learning disabilities is acknowledged as a problem in many countries. Good practice in relation to the well-being and safety of those with a learning disability does not depend on documentary numbers and proof. As elsewhere, recommendations and guidelines have been developed and adapted in response to the challenges in Ireland. Good practice guidelines should be adopted by all service-providing agencies.

Recommendations to address sexual abuse for people with learning disabilities in Ireland can be summarised as follows:

- Written guidance, training, support, and supervision on issues of sexuality, sexual abuse and other related issues such as intimate care should be developed in all services and made available to service staff. Staff should be trained to recognise the signs and symptoms of sexual abuse.

- Staff should be trained to discriminate between mutual and abusive sexual relationships, and service users should be given similar, developmentally appropriate training and education to develop these skills.

- Complaint procedures and protocols should be included in training for both staff *and* service users. Relatives should be made aware of these as well.

- Directors of service-providing agencies have an inherent responsibility to develop strategic planning that ensures the provision of services which are safe and accountable. Policies that govern them should foster an ethos that is supportive of adults with learning disabilities as sexual beings yet provide for their protection from exploitation and abuse, and articulate positive response protocols to be applied when these rights are breached. Systems designed to audit and ensure these tenets should be an integral part of this strategy.

Concise guidelines that address all areas of abuse serve to raise awareness in the staff, client group, and general public and are crucial to responsible care and management. Without clear policies, training or guidance, there is not likely to be a meaningful positive response to the sexual abuse of people with learning disabilities, nor any progress toward its prevention. With them, people with learning disabilities are afforded a better opportunity to learn to live relatively normal and fulfilling lives, including the rich and rewarding sexual and social experiences most people take for granted.

Chapter 10

THE CHALLENGES OF ADDRESSING SEXUAL VIOLENCE IN PSYCHIATRIC SETTINGS

INTRODUCTION

Psychiatric patients are an important group to consider when addressing sexual violence. On the one hand, there are concerns that sexual abuse may be a causal factor in subsequent psychiatric conditions while, on the other hand, there may be concern about the risk to personal (including sexual) safety of vulnerable psychiatric patients in a variety of care settings. Evidence on these issues is briefly overviewed.

In general population studies, past history of abuse has been linked to higher levels of psychological disorder for those concerned (Hill et al., 2000; Mullen et al., 1998). There is also a significant body of evidence demonstrating that psychiatric patients are more likely to have experienced sexual abuse in their past than others (Read and Argyle, 1999; Figueroa et al., 1997; Wurr and Partridge, 1996; Sykes Wylie, 1993). Sykes Wylie estimated that 50–60 per cent of psychiatric patients had experienced physical or sexual abuse or both in their past and that this may be an unrecognised aetiological factor in the subsequent development of some psychiatric disorders. Figueroa suggested that a correlation exists between childhood sexual abuse and diagnosed borderline personality disorder. It is unclear how often sexual violence is either disclosed or enquired about in psychiatric settings. In a US study, 51 per cent of a group of 105 female state hospital patients were found to have been sexually abused in childhood or adolescence. Only half of these 105 women had been identified during their treatment as having experienced sexual abuse and of these, only 20 per cent believed they had been adequately treated for their abuse (Craine et al., 1988).

Another concern in the domain of sexual violence for psychiatric patients is their vulnerability to abuse as a consequence of their psychiatric status, i.e. while in the care of the health services (Thomas, Bartlett and Mezey, 1995; Wood and Copperman, 1996). For instance, in Thomas et al.'s UK study in an inner-city psychiatric hospital, 75 per cent of inpatients reported unwanted physical or sexual experiences. A third of women (32 per cent) reported sexual molestation and 4 per cent sexual assault (equivalent figures for men were 7 per cent sexual molestation and no sexual assault). Wood and Copperman summarise their view of the UK health system as it relates to sexual risks for women:

> Women are being sexually harassed, assaulted and raped across the full spectrum of mental health service provision: in special hospitals and secure units, in psychiatric hospitals, in residential homes, in day centres and in counselling and psychotherapy. (p. 128)

In the UK, practices such as housing patients on mixed sex wards have been objected to because of such concerns. We did not find research evidence on the issue of ongoing sexual violence in psychiatric settings in Ireland.

Only one Irish study, to our knowledge, has examined the prevalence of sexual violence in a group with psychological problems (Cheasty, Clare and Collins, 1998). A total of 237 women, 132 of whom were diagnosed as depressed, were interviewed in three general practices (one middle-class suburban, one inner city and one rural). Thirty-seven per cent of the depressed interviewees (versus 23 per cent of non-depressed interviewees) reported histories of child sexual abuse under age 16. A significant correlation was found between the more severe forms of abuse and depression. All of the women who had experienced penetration and 86 per cent of the women who had experienced attempted penetration were depressed. In another Irish study, 26 women who had been sexually abused in childhood were assessed by means of structured interview (O'Neill and Gupta, 1991). Nineteen (73.1 per cent) were found to be suffering from PTSD. Comparing PTSD to non-PTSD groups, PTSD was found to be associated with penetrative and more frequent abuse. No studies were identified which addressed the location of abuse, including any likelihood of abuse in psychiatric settings.

It is clear that information regarding the prevalence of sexual violence in the Irish psychiatric population is lacking. This substudy focused on ways to address this gap. However, it must be noted that this is a small attempt to explore what is a complex issue.

METHOD

A number of proposals were made as to how to access information regarding histories of sexual violence in the Irish psychiatric patient population. The first was to conduct a review of hospital charts. The second was to interview patients directly, and the third was to speak with professionals working in the area.

Initial discussions with health professionals suggested that a chart review was likely to seriously under-represent the problem. The view was that histories of sexual violence are neither routinely asked about nor noted. This opinion is supported in the international literature. For example, a chart review of 100 inpatients in the US who had previously been interviewed by professionals and asked directly about past assault experiences (physical and sexual) showed that only 9 per cent of their reported assault histories were recorded (Jacobson, Koehler and Jones-Brown, 1987). Some people told researchers about abuse experiences they had not disclosed to hospital staff. In total, 21 per cent of patients had reported sexual assault as an adult but this was evident in only 1 per cent of the patients' charts. A recent US review regarding the sexual abuse of boys in North America reported a chart review of psychiatric inpatients with a prevalence rate of 6 per cent, while face-to-face interviews with the same population showed a prevalence rate of 26 per cent (Holmes and Slap, 1998). One reason given to explain why Irish health professionals might not ask about histories of child sexual abuse is the fact that in some organisations they are mandated to report cases of abuse to the Director of Community Care. This may pose a dilemma for health professionals if they view this obligation as a breach of therapeutic confidentiality and as damaging to the therapeutic relationship.[1]

Calculating the prevalence of sexual violence in the general psychiatric population by direct interviews was seen as a formidable challenge logistically but also in terms of the ethical challenge of conducting such research in a supportive way and with adequate supports in place for those who disclosed abuse. Such a project was beyond the capabilities of the SAVI study. It was decided in this setting to identify issues relevant to the experience, disclosure and recording of sexual violence through a series of semi-structured interviews with a group of relevant professional informants. Five professionals were selected (four psychiatrists and one clinical psychologist) through previous contacts and interviewed concerning their perspectives on the various challenges in disclosing and managing abuse in psychiatric settings.

RESULTS AND DISCUSSION

Participants considered that past experiences of sexual violence were significantly higher in this population than in the population at large. However, it was felt that there was a resistance among

---

[1] This argument is refuted however by the ISPCC report *Another Brick from the Wall: The Case for the Introduction of Mandatory Reporting of Child Abuse and Neglect in Ireland* (1996) which states: "The suggestion that mandatory reporting could damage the trust inherent in many professional relationships, such as the doctor/patient relationship, heretofore seen as inviolable simply ignores the reality that no principle of confidentiality is absolute" (p. 14). It also reports that international experience has shown that mandatory reporting increases rather than decreases the number of both children and adults who do seek and receive help.

many health professionals to discuss this problem and that patients were not routinely asked about histories of sexual violence. While there is no concrete evidence to support this view, it is supported by the results of the main SAVI survey, which found that those who had experienced attempted or actual penetrative abuse were eight times more likely to have been an inpatient in a psychiatric hospital than participants who disclosed less serious abuse or no abuse. A clear association was also seen between higher levels of lifetime use of medication for anxiety and depression and having experienced sexual violence. Added to this, 25 per cent of women and 16 per cent of men who disclosed histories of sexual violence in SAVI also reported symptoms of PTSD at some time in their lives.

Barriers to disclosure and to accessing services to deal with past experiences of sexual violence were seen to include a range of points:

- **Lack of resources and personnel**: It was felt there was a general shortage of staff to spend quality time interacting with psychiatric patients. Given lengthy waiting lists, it was felt that many psychiatrists would not have time to deal with issues of sexual violence during consultations which may be expected to be of a 5–10 minute duration. If patients were to disclose a history of child sexual abuse they might be referred to a social worker or psychologist for a consultation.

- **Lack of training**: It was felt that many psychiatrists may not have adequate specialist training to deal with sexual violence, particularly those who are longer qualified. One informant described the management of sexual violence as "an Achilles heel of psychiatry".

- **Lack of psychotherapeutic skills**: Dealing with sexual violence was seen to require specific counselling and psychotherapeutic skills. However, psychiatry as practised in Ireland is separate from psychotherapy. For example, there are few funded positions in the country for child psychotherapists. It was felt that the potential contribution of the more holistic approach of psy-

chotherapy was not being reflected in the health boards' recruitment and staff profiles.

- **Professional discomfort with the topic of sexual violence**:
  There may be professional discomfort in discussing this topic.
  According to one informant, "Sexual violence is not asked
  about and, if people try to talk about it, nobody listens." It was
  also felt that, because of the stigma attached to sexual violence, those who do disclose may do so in a "roundabout"
  way and this partial disclosure may not be pursued further by
  the professional involved. Furthermore, there may be an attitude among some that it is in fact damaging to have people
  talk about experiences of sexual violence. A "let sleeping dogs
  lie" attitude may prevail in some settings.

- **A clash of perspectives?** It was felt that some psychiatrists
  may not ask about experiences of sexual violence because this
  problem does not fit into the traditional medical model. One
  participant said, "there is no pill to cure this problem". Those
  working within a biomedical perspective may not feel comfortable working with patients or conditions which require
  psychotherapy or psychological support services.

Other points made by informants included the fact that sexual
violence is but one of a series of adverse life events often experienced by the same individuals. Timing was seen as important
where service provision and management of sexual violence was
concerned. It was acknowledged that many people firstly need
support with more "proximal" problems such as poverty, homelessness or drug and alcohol addictions before they are ready to
deal with sexual violence. Different approaches across services,
e.g., requirements for mandatory reporting in some health board
but not voluntary agency services, may prove a barrier to service
uptake.

A number of suggestions for improvement in the management
of sexual violence in psychiatric settings were made by the key
informants. More training for general health personnel in dealing

with the disclosure and treatment of sexual violence was advocated. It was felt that adding one simple question regarding a history of sexual abuse in initial assessment interviews in psychiatric settings would indicate the acceptability of discussing these matters in such settings. It was also felt that one person with psychotherapeutic training should be included in every multidisciplinary health professional team to assist with sexual violence issues. From the public's perspective, it was felt that the health boards should strive to make necessary psychologically based services available to all within a reasonable timeframe. Those in more deprived areas were seen as having limited and delayed access to psychological services and psychotherapy in comparison to those in more affluent areas who can afford private care.

As stated at the outset, the aim of this small sub-study was to identify some of the issues for further consideration rather than definitively answer questions.

PROPOSALS FOR FUTURE CONSIDERATION

A coherent programme of research and professional development is needed to address the challenge of sexual violence in psychiatric patients. The programme is best developed through an extensive consultation process with the wide variety of interested parties. Such a programme needs to incorporate the following very diverse elements:

- The need to consider the role of past sexual violence in the current difficulties presented in psychiatric settings — how to promote disclosure; how to identify such experiences; how to manage them; and the role of mandatory reporting.

- The need for professional training — protocols to identify and manage sexual violence; protocols to protect psychiatric patients from sexual violence. These protocols will have to address the challenges of inter-disciplinary practice and differing professional perspectives if the various constituencies are to work together in the best interests of patients.

- The need for adequate staffing and resources to provide protection and management of sexual violence in psychiatric settings.

- The need to establish audit and information systems to document the extent of the problem and to monitor change over time and in relation to changing practice. As in other pertinent areas of medical practice, it may be more important to provide consistent enquiry and documentation of psychiatric patient responses concerning sexual violence than to estimate prevalence through once-off research projects.

In summary, the complex and layered problems which constitute sexual violence in the Irish psychiatric population require an equally complex and layered programme of action if real and sustained progress is to be achieved.

THE EXPERIENCE OF SEXUAL VIOLENCE BY MARGINALISED GROUPS IN IRISH SOCIETY

The experience of sexual violence in Irish society is even more challenging for groups marginalised for a variety of reasons including culture, intellectual capacity, psychological well-being, location (being homeless or a prostitute). Risks of sexual violence are believed to be higher for many, although not all, marginalised groups and barriers to disclosure are more complex. Thus the challenges for law enforcement and health-related professionals are multiplied and differ across marginalised groups. The challenges for researchers in documenting risks of abuse are also compounded and require considerable attention and resources to do so in a manner that is safe, valid and respectful for all concerned.

Section IV

DISCUSSIONS, CONCLUSIONS AND RECOMMENDATIONS

Chapter 11

DISCUSSION AND CONCLUSIONS

This study aimed to provide an in-depth analysis of the prevalence and nature of sexual violence in contemporary Irish society. Building on the experience of international research teams and having a detailed training and support system helped to achieve a high survey response rate on such a sensitive issue. Notwithstanding this, there was also a strong sense from participants at the follow-up interview stage that most were pleased to have taken part in the study. Many people spontaneously and strongly expressed the view that the time is now right in Ireland to consider the problem of sexual violence in a public, calm and open manner. Thus, both the response to the study, in terms of interview participation rate, and the response about the study, in terms of the welcoming comments of many participants, augur well for the purposes of the overall study.

PREVALENCE OF SEXUAL VIOLENCE

Because sexual violence exists along a continuum and because it makes conceptual sense to consider child and adult and male and female rates separately, there are a myriad of figures which can be considered in discussions on prevalence. For this reason, it may be useful to focus on two categories of abuse when considering priorities for understanding abuse and in planning action from this study. These are penetrative abuse (oral, vaginal or anal sexual acts) and other forms of abuse involving physical contact. Focusing on these two types of abuse in subsequent discussion of the study requires an important caveat. Doing this does not assume that the level of physical contact involved in an abusive situation will have a direct relationship with the meaning and impact of the event on the abused person. Many individuals reported cases involving minimal or no physical contact which were psychologically devastating, for example, in terms of a lengthy duration over which abuse occurred or in terms of the potential for unknown acts of abuse into the future which posed an ongoing threat to the person's sense of safety. Focusing attention on contact abuse and promoting public unacceptability of non-consensual sexual actions *per se* should reap benefits across the spectrum of sexual violence, from harassment through to penetrative abuse.

A first impression of levels of penetrative sexual abuse may be that percentages are indeed relatively low; 5.6 per cent for girls, 2.7 per cent for boys, 6.1 per cent for women and 0.9 per cent for men. Given that some individuals experience abuse as adults and children, the overall rate is 10.2 per cent for women and 3.2 per cent for men. Considering levels in childhood, the percentage figures offer cold comfort when worked through to estimate just how many Irish adults this involves. Using 2001 population figures, a 5.6 per cent rate of penetrative sexual abuse experience as a child means that over 81,000 adult Irish women have been exposed to serious sexual crime as a child. The figures for men are over 37,000. To make this more concrete, consider that in the average line-up of players on the field in a men's football match, one player will have been subjected to penetrative sexual abuse as a child. In a women's football game, the number of players on average will be three. Just how many perpetrators there are among the spectators is impossible to know. What is virtually certain is that there are some, since abusers are most often related to, or known by, those who have been abused as children.

Whatever the percentages, they are but the first element of the wider story of sexual violence. To paraphrase Salter (1992), the answers to the question concerning the "why" and "how" of sexual violence will not be found in the numbers. A later discussion focuses on abuse in three distinct subgroups — children, women and men — in order to make conceptual sense of the information obtained and to consider the different nature of sexual violence in these subgroups.

Comparisons with other studies and over time suggest that the levels of sexual violence outlined in the SAVI study are similar to international data collected in a similar way (i.e. personal contact by telephone or interview versus questionnaire methods). This includes the similarity in patterns of higher female than male abuse and with these discrepancies being greater in adulthood (Finkelhor, 1994). The pattern of abuse across cohorts of individuals has been examined most clearly and completely within the area of childhood abuse. The pattern of abuse in Ireland, moving from those study participants who were children in the earlier part of the 1900s and then through the twentieth century, showed a profile of increasing rates over time to 1970 and then a decrease from the 1970s. This profile of lowering levels of abuse finds support from research evaluations in the US (Finkelhor, 1998). Finkelhor describes the scale of reductions in *reported* child sexual abuse in the US as unprecedented in the last decade and outlines possible explanations for this, including more conservative or cautious decisions on making formal reports by health and social service professionals because of issues such as false memory syndrome and litigation. He also considers the option of a real reduction in levels due to more public awareness of the crime and its consequences and to increased vigilance by public and professionals. The results in the SAVI survey seem consistent with a pattern of reduction in all forms of sexual abuse against children alongside possible increases in the levels of sexual assault against adults. Further investigations of patterns across time are essential to understand if and how these changes are occurring. From the most conservative but nonetheless extremely important perspective, what the SAVI child sexual abuse data show is that there is definitely no evidence of an increase in child sexual abuse in recent decades.

DISCLOSURE OF SEXUAL VIOLENCE

One of the most striking findings of the SAVI study is the extent to which sexual violence is still a completely private and hidden matter for almost half of those affected. With increased media and professional attention and increasing numbers reporting, it has been easy to consider that there had been a thorough airing of the subject into the public domain with no "surprises" remaining. This clearly is not the case. Evidence from other countries illustrates that the challenges of disclosure are universal. In almost every situation, only a minority of those who acknowledged abuse in population survey settings had revealed their abuse to others. This is particularly so in relation to disclosure to professionals. A "health promotion" perspective on disclosure would recommend that role models for successful disclosure are necessary, both at the level of telling family or friends and at the level of telling professionals. By that it is meant that people need to see others going public about their experiences and being treated in a fair and reasonable manner as a consequence. A recent Irish example of such a role model is Sorcha McKenna who, in November 2000, waived her right to anonymity in a court case which found her father guilty of 31 counts of sexual abuse through her childhood. Following the court case, she publicly campaigned for longer prison sentences for convicted sex offenders (her father had received a three-year sentence). She collected over 200,000 signatures and successfully petitioned the Minister of Justice for reform of sentencing in this area. She was awarded one of the ESB/Rehab People of the Year awards in 2001 for her bravery in publicly addressing such a difficult personal tragedy.

Some of the very real challenges to disclosure are likely to relate to the level of control there is perceived to be following disclosure. Concerns about the involvement of law enforcement agencies, or the ability of the person disclosing to then keep the disclosure within particular boundaries acceptable to them, are issues that need to be addressed in a strategy which aims to increase disclosure. It is not known what effect mandatory reporting, or discussion of same, have on either public or professional willingness to disclose or encourage disclosure.

Disclosure is, of course, also a significant methodological challenge. Most prevalence studies rely on memory, very often of events many years ago in childhood. Evidence suggests that the likely effect of this is to find reported prevalence rates to be lower than actual rates. A notable illustration of this is a recent analysis by Widom and Morris (1997). They reported on a series of US court-substantiated cases of child sexual abuse who were revisited 20 years later — they comprised 75 women and 19 men. Just over half of the women (64 per cent) and less than one-fifth of the men (16 per cent) considered their early experience to have been sexual abuse. Thus there was substantial underreporting of sexual abuse among those confirmed as having been abused and this underreporting was particularly notable in men. Such findings remind us that caution is needed when recording and interpreting findings. They do not distract from the important need to document, in so far as is possible, the prevalence of sexual violence in society.

STUDY IMPLICATIONS

Information on abuse in three distinct groups is considered next to focus attention on strategies for prevention and management of abuse.

SAVI — Study Implications for Children

Abuse in childhood in the SAVI study typically occurred in children's own homes or familiar environments and it typically involved people known to them. There appeared to be two clusters of abuse — that perpetrated against young children and that perpetrated against children as "mini-adults". Black et al. (2001), reviewing risk factors for child sexual abuse, also highlighted the late child/early adolescent period as a particularly vulnerable time. Regarding prevention, the Stay Safe Programme (MacIntyre and Lawlor, 1991) is now used in the vast majority of Irish schools and has been extended for use with learning disabled children

(MacIntyre, Lawlor and Cullen, 1996). More broadly, the topics of relationships and sexuality are addressed in the Social, Personal and Health Education (SPHE) programme of the Department of Education which is currently being developed in schools nationally. These services are to be commended. The necessary balance of specific sexual abuse prevention strategies aimed at children and at adults is discussed later in the section on public awareness. It must be remembered in a broad system of child protection and welfare, that child sexual abuse affects a minority of children at risk. Ferguson and O'Reilly (2001) summarised the child service workload of the Mid-Western Health Board and found that 13 per cent of children at risk were at risk because of sexual abuse, 8 per cent for physical abuse, 4 per cent for emotional abuse and 21 per cent for neglect.

Regarding management of child sexual abuse, there are ongoing concerns about system demands for assessment but a relative neglect of professional services for children once abuse is ascertained. Ferguson and O'Reilly (2001) showed that the situation was not so bleak as is often estimated: 63 per cent of children confirmed as having been abused were in long-term treatment programmes. They highlighted lack of parental co-operation as a major barrier to treatment. More broadly, they described the services as being too narrow, with a forensic approach which militates against the needs of children and non-abusing parents. The challenge for services in this regard are to meet the philosophy espoused in the report *Children First: National Guidelines for the Protection and Welfare of Children* (1999) — to encourage, support and protect children.

Finally, special consideration should be given to the special needs of children with a learning disability or other disability which may increase vulnerability and/or increase difficulties of communication.

SAVI — Study Implications for Women

The SAVI results demonstrated that women remained just as vulnerable to the experience of serious penetrative abuse in adulthood as they had been as children. Many women were abused by those close to them — men with whom they were involved in intimate relationships. These finding pose a profoundly disturbing challenge in a country which sees itself on the one hand as friendly, welcoming, fair and concerned about the welfare of "unfortunate" others, and on the other as educated, progressive and open-minded.

SAVI — Study Implications for Men

Adult men typically experienced abuse in the context of interactions with friends and acquaintances. Alcohol was involved in about half of the cases. Levels of disclosure of abuse were lower than for women. Awareness of where to seek professional help was also low. Among the sample of men, willingness to disclose abuse if an event was to happen to them was also low. Young men appeared to be particularly reluctant to disclose and also to be less knowledgeable about possible sources of professional support. Higher levels of endorsement of rationalisations and victim-blaming beliefs about sexual violence by men means that the micro-culture in which they live makes disclosure and management of sexual violence even more challenging than for women. Greater appreciation of the reality of sexual violence against men, while still acknowledging that the majority of those abused are women and children, may help to bring together the sexes in a common voice expressing the unacceptability of this behaviour for individuals and society more generally.

Regarding the first challenge — to make the abuse of men more visible — a review of 149 studies of adult male recollection of child sexual abuse summarised possible reasons for underreporting of sexual violence by men in general (Holmes and Slap, 1998). Firstly, men may believe that they have failed to meet a social expectation of self-protection by failing to prevent the abuse. This can be expressed as shame or unwillingness to disclose but may also result in cognitive attempts to redefine the events as minimally abusive or acceptable. Experiencing physical pleasure or having erectile responses during the abuse can also result in reduced willingness to acknowledge or report abuse. Connotations of homosexuality are another challenge to reporting abuse. Finally, abuse by women, particularly where more passive coercion is used, may be defined by the men themselves, as well as by others, as normative or difficult to challenge. In this study, the finding that no men reported completed anal rape as adults contrasts with data seen in therapeutic settings. For instance, the Dublin Rape Crisis Centre reported 49 cases of rape (defined as Section 4 rape — either oral or anal sexual abuse) among its 99 male counselling clients in 2000. Regarding prevalence rates in other population studies, a large UK study of men completing an anonymous computer survey in a general practice setting reported a prevalence rate of 0.3 per cent (7 of 2,474 men reporting adult anal rape)[1] (Coxell et al., 2000). Thus the prevalence was also very low in the UK study. The combination of low population prevalence figures with a relatively high proportion of cases of male rape in clinical settings suggests a filtering system where those relatively small proportion of men who have experienced very serious levels of sexual violence choose to only disclose and to only seek help in confidential professional settings. The SAVI study evidence suggests that this is indeed the case.

These three groups can be further extended to consider the implications for children, women and men in marginalised groups in Irish society.

SAVI — Study Implications for Service Providers

One clear message from the SAVI study, and supported by previous studies, is that much sexual violence remains unknown but

---

[1] Statistical method for estimating the true range within which a population score lies given a particular prevalence rate in a sample of that population is called the confidence interval. The confidence interval for the UK study is a prevalence ranging from 0.11–0.58 per cent. For the SAVI study, finding no cases in 1,515 reports indicates a confidence interval of 0.0–0.25 per cent, i.e. the highest estimate of likelihood is one quarter of a percent. If one case had been reported in SAVI, the confidence interval would be 0.0002–0.37 per cent, i.e. very little difference in the estimated range of possible prevalence in the population.

that people may be willing to disclose abuse if asked. A recent Australian study of 402 women attending a family planning clinic reported that 78.4 per cent of women had previously been sexually abused with 66 per cent revealing this information for the first time. Addressing the issue of sexual violence in a more routine way in medical settings may help to identify and manage more cases of sexual violence. Two recent studies in Ireland and the UK, involving almost 3,000 women, found that almost 80 per cent would find a question about "domestic" violence to be acceptable from their general practitioner (Bradley et al., 2002; Richardson et al., 2002). The value of questions in hospital accident and emergency settings has also been demonstrated, with a minimum number of questions (3) found to be just as effective as lengthier investigations (Feldhaus et al., 1997). However, even when those who have been abused attend specialist clinics, follow-up rates are quite low (e.g., 31 per cent, Holmes, Resnick and Frampton, 1998). Thus the challenges of medical service provision are multiple. They certainly include a requirement for more training and protocols to support health workers in making such enquiries more routine and acceptable to them and the public. Routine questions concerning sexual or other forms of violence have an important function in making disclosure acceptable. As Bradley et al. (2002) noted in the context of domestic violence:

> [questioning] should be thought of as a way of uncovering and reframing a hidden stigma. From this perspective, the purpose of questioning is to de-stigmatise the issue by naming and accepting it . . .

A second clear message for service providers and planners is that the demand for medical, counselling and law enforcement resources is almost inevitably going to rise. Only a small minority of those abused currently seek professional help, but the trends for help-seeking in this study were of a clear pattern of increase in recent decades. Plans need to be made to cope with this likely increase. While recent Department of Health and Children projections address the shortfall in the disciplines of physiotherapy, occupational therapy and speech and language therapy, a similar exercise may be necessary to identify the staffing needs for counselling and psychotherapeutic staff for this, alongside other demands.

Alongside service shortages, there needs to be attention to those services already in existence. It was notable that many people, particularly younger people, felt that they would not know where to go to receive assistance if they were sexually abused. A very useful *Directory of Services for Women Experiencing Violence or the Threat of Violence* was compiled nationally in 2001 and distributed widely (copy available on the website of the Department of Justice, Equality and Law Reform).

This type of activity needs to be combined with public awareness strategies if available services are to be made visible and accessible. The shortfall in information provision across services (Gardaí and medical) in this study highlights the value of a common and comprehensive set of information. As Leane et al. (2001), in their review of law enforcement contacts with those who have been raped, recommended:

> The development of an information pack for victims which would address such issues as myths about rape, sexual assault; the feelings and emotions associated with being a victim of sexual crime; the stages involved in giving a formal report and giving a statement; the nature and purpose of the FME (forensic medical examination); the possibility of pregnancy and STDs (sexually transmitted diseases) and the services available in this regard; and details of the legal and court system (p. 5).

MEDIA ROLE IN CHALLENGING SEXUAL VIOLENCE

The media are pivotal in the challenge to reduce sexual violence. They cannot be neutral — media activity can either assist or hinder efforts to increase awareness and understanding of sexual violence and to increase its unacceptability in society. Even lack of coverage of the topic is a powerful weapon of the media. As McDevitt (1998) paraphrases, the media may not tell us what to think but they tell us what to think about. Many cautions are necessary when considering how best to represent sexual violence in the media. Sexual violence is a serious category of criminal behaviour and a significant contributor to psychological and social problems *per se* but also because of its hidden and stigmatising characteristics. It is, however, only one of a number of adverse life circumstances (such as neglect and physical abuse) which have important effects on the lives of individuals and families. A special focus on sexual violence is necessary more because of its hidden nature than because it constitutes an experience outside the realm of other types of adversity. Public representations of sexual violence, e.g. rape, as being a terrible, an unnatural and bizarre act, as a fate worse than death, as committed by monsters, and as an experience that should be resisted whatever the consequences to physical safety, all contribute to a culture of non-disclosure and are obstacles to calm reflection on how to prevent or manage the problem (Burt and Estep, 1981).

These caricatures of experiences such as rape are not the way in which most people experience rape. Unwillingness to identify with a victim role or to label one's very different set of experiences in a way that conjures up such caricatures is likely to contribute to an unwillingness to report episodes of abuse or accept labels such as "raped" or "abused". There is a difficult balance to achieve among those interested in sexual violence: how to make reporting of the crime more acceptable so that it is more likely to be detected, while also keeping society at large interested and perturbed enough about it that it continues to support prevention, therapeutic and rehabilitation activities.

One of the developments in recent years has been the introduction of sexual violence into television popular drama. Many "soaps" have featured a "rape" story and programme producers have in many instances consulted with service and prevention agencies in making their stories relevant and reflective of the complexities concerned. An example was a rape story in ITV's *Coronation Street* on Easter Sunday night 2001. This was widely announced in advance and was seen as likely to guarantee a large television audience. Counselling services worked in conjunction with the TV schedule to ensure that those with concerns following the episode could call free-phone numbers for support or advice. The evolving nature of sexual violence, including "date" rape, drug-assisted rape and sexual violence linked to the internet, are all made more real to the public through media coverage. As already recommended in previous reports such as in the *Task Force on Violence Against Women* (Department of Health, 1997), there needs to be a good working relationship between the media and those charged with increasing the profile of sexual violence.

IRISH GOVERNMENT POLICIES AND SEXUAL VIOLENCE

A systemic approach to tackling sexual violence has to start with Government policy. Irish policy pertinent to sexual violence is considered here. The Irish Government's most recent and relevant policy statement is the Department of Health and Children's strategy launched in late 2001. Entitled *Quality and Fairness: A Health System for You*, it sets a large number of targets within focused objectives for health services into the next decade. Objective 4 focuses on 11 specific quality of life themes. These are mental health, ageing, family support services, a crisis pregnancy strategy, chronic disease management protocols, rehabilitation services, palliative care services, hepatitis C strategies, an AIDS strategy, measures to prevent domestic violence and support victims, and sheltered work for people with disabilities. Specific resources are indicated for alcohol services, the Social Personal and Health Education programme for school-based prevention and funds for refuges, rape crisis centres and other agencies to support victims of domestic violence (p. 73).

In a related document, the *National Health Promotion Strategy (2000–2005)*, a topic approach was adopted as one of the aspects of the Strategy. Nine topics were identified: positive mental health, being smoke-free, eating well, good oral health, sensible drinking, avoiding drug misuse, being more active, safety and injury prevention and sexual health. Under the topic of sexual health the focus is on sexually transmitted diseases (in particular HIV), and contraceptive use and pregnancy. The strategic aim of this topic is "to promote sexual health and safer sexual practices in the population". Objectives are to support school-based personal development programmes, to foster a working partnership regarding teenage pregnancies and to decrease crisis pregnancies, to reduce sexually transmitted infections, to implement the AIDS strategy and "to initiate research into the need for a national sexual health strategy that would encompass the prevention of STIs [sexually transmitted infections] and crisis pregnancies".

The problem is that the topic of sexual violence "falls between stools"; it is a multi-factorial problem involving at minimum education, health and law enforcement concerns. The terms "safety and injury prevention" in Government documents is typically limited to addressing accidents in public places and in the home, to reducing sporting, work-related and home-based injuries and to managing health challenges such as falls by older people. Sexual violence is also subsumed under actions concerning "domestic" violence. Here the actual focus of activities may be on adult women, for political, philosophical or simply pragmatic concerns in dealing with such large challenges. It was recognised some years ago that children in Irish society were served by a myriad of Government agencies but lacked a consolidating forum to ensure their interests were best served by the various sectors of government. A special section of the Department of Health (now the Department of Health and Children) was established to achieve this co-ordinating function. This may be a useful blueprint for sexual violence. Some accountable agency or group needs to have responsibility to co-ordinate the multi-sectoral task of reducing sexual violence.

One of the challenges of such a group is to develop a public awareness campaign to start the process of making sexual violence everybody's business. A number of authors have critiqued many developments which effectively give children the primary role as preventers of child sexual abuse. For instance, Daro (1994) makes the point that adults are typically the focus of prevention efforts for physical abuse of children, yet with sexual abuse, the main focus is on children as prevention agents. This, he proposed, reflects the generally inadequate way of addressing sexuality in society generally; the categorical way in which sex offenders are seen (i.e., there is no point in appealing to them to try prevent their behaviour); and a general haste to protect children in the context of sustained media attention. He cautions that we should put more of the responsibility on the general adult public for child protection in this regard. This is one of the issues for discussion in planning a national public awareness strategy.

An example of a community-level child sexual abuse prevention programme (which targets the general population and potential abusers as well as children in its prevention efforts) has recently been developed in the state of Vermont in the US (Morbidity and Mortality Weekly Report, 2001). Among its early achievements has been increased community knowledge about details of child sexual abuse (44.5 per cent in 1995 compared to 84.8 per cent in 1999 could properly describe child sexual abuse). Furthermore, in four years, 118 people (20 adults and 98 adolescents) presented themselves to authorities as child abusers because of a programme emphasis on taking responsibility for one's own abusive behaviour. Such programmes can usefully be evaluated for development in the Irish context although the programme authors caution that well-developed services, including offender rehabilitation services, need to be in place to make such a system work.

A research project such as this should be the first step in a programme of activity. This was certainly the feeling of many people who agreed to give of their time and experience to the researchers. The information collected is only of value if it enables the next step — informed planning of a strategy to address the problem of sexual violence. The next chapter presents recommendations for progress from here on the issue.

Chapter 12

SAVI STUDY RECOMMENDATIONS

PROVISION OF INFORMATION

Public Awareness

A public awareness campaign is needed to highlight the challenge of sexual violence in Irish society. This campaign needs to address complex issues in a clear and sustained manner over an extended period of time. The campaign should firstly increase public awareness of the nature and size of the problem of sexual violence. It should adopt a public health approach, in the same manner as recent campaigns to prevent drinking and driving, and emphasise the responsibility of the public in preventing, rendering unacceptable and reporting abuse. Information then needs to be available at multiple levels to address the varying demands arising from such a public focus on sexual violence. A widely-advertised national telephone helpline to address questions concerning abuse is an essential part of an interactive campaign. This helpline should be seen to be available to those who have experienced abuse, to those concerned about others in vulnerable situations and to those who are concerned about their own potential for abuse. Ongoing evaluation of the campaign is necessary to ensure that the desired outcomes are being achieved since sexual violence is a particularly complex issue to address through the relatively simple medium of social marketing strategies for the public.

The need for a public awareness campaign has been high-lighted in the Government report on the Task Force on Violence against Women (1997). Developing such a campaign needs expert input from health, childcare, education and justice perspectives and from statutory and voluntary agencies in partnership. This needs to be combined with input from the perspectives of those who have experienced abuse to ensure that messages are clear and supportive of vulnerable individuals in situations of abuse. The role of the media is crucial in developing an accurate and comprehensive understanding of sexual violence among the gen-eral public. Strategies to support the media in its representation of sexual violence should be considered as part of the public aware-ness campaign. It is appropriate to reiterate the well-argued views of previous Irish commentators in this regard. Leane et al. (2001), from their study of attrition in sexual assault offence cases, rec-ommended:

> . . . the development of an educational programme targeted at the public at large, which seeks to debunk myths regard-ing rape and to clarify that sexual activity without the full and conscious consent of all parties is a crime. Such a pro-gramme should also address those who encounter victims, to affirm the victim's lack of blame and to alert them to po-tential sources of help such as Rape Crisis Centres and the Gardaí (p. 5).

The development, delivery and evaluation of a public health campaign on sexual violence should be the responsibility of the Health Promotion Unit at the Department of Health and Children and should involve relevant statutory, voluntary and advocacy agencies. A Consultative Committee, to be discussed further in Recommendation 8 concerning implementation, should be estab-lished to support this and other recommendations.

RECOMMENDATION 1 — *That a comprehensive public awareness campaign on sexual violence be developed, delivered and evaluated in Ireland.*

Responsibility and timeframe: The Health Promotion Unit at the Department of Health and Children. Campaign to be developed in 2002/2003 with public launch of first phase in 2003. Consultation with the voluntary sector is essential in developing, delivering and evaluating this campaign. Report of progress to a Consultative Committee in 2004.

INFORMATION ON SERVICES

Information on services needs to be widely disseminated. Alongside a national telephone helpline, a plan for wide dissemination of information in health settings such as general practices, in social service settings, in Garda stations, schools and universities and in other public places is needed. Posters and leaflets can provide information about service access. More detailed material will also be needed for those who have been abused or those who are acting on their behalf. Information explaining responses to abuse, the services offered (counselling, medical/forensic and legal) and referral routes is needed in booklet and other forms such as video and internet. These need to integrate information on the various services and agencies the person may encounter and need to be available at the first point of contact. Special challenges to information provision for marginalised or vulnerable groups need to be addressed. Similarly, specific settings such as third-level colleges may provide a useful focus for delivering both awareness and service information messages to targeted audiences. The development of information materials requires a multi-agency approach. The co-ordination of this work should be the responsibility of the Health Promotion Unit at the Department of Health and Children.

RECOMMENDATION 2 — *That a range of information materials on services for sexual violence be developed and made available in appropriate settings and formats to assist those in need of such services.*

Responsibility and timeframe: *The Health Promotion Unit at the Department of Health and Children. Information to be developed in 2002/2003 with distribution to coincide with launch of public awareness campaign in 2003. Report of progress to be provided to a Consultative Committee on Sexual Violence in 2004.*

DISCLOSURE

Promoting and Managing Disclosure

Sexual violence is a crime. Efforts should be made at multiple levels to encourage disclosure of this particularly hidden crime. Each disclosure can provide the opportunity for the individual concerned to avail of services where needed but can also serve a wider community preventive purpose of creating a culture of willingness to disclose abuse which may dissuade potential abusers in the future. A range of frontline professionals from teachers to doctors are in positions where disclosure may occur more readily. Professionals need to indicate their willingness collectively and individually to hear disclosures of sexual violence. This will range from the provision of written materials such as notices in general practices or waiting rooms in Garda stations to the willingness to ask specific questions about sexual violence in high-risk situations such as A&E departments. Specific training will be needed to ensure that this is done sensitively and routinely. The public also has a responsibility to be willing to hear about cases of sexual violence from those known to them and a responsibility to encourage those who confide in them to consider disclosure to law enforcement and other professionals as appropriate. The responsibilities concerning disclosure also relate to consideration of the implications of future abuse by the alleged perpetrator. Disclosure should be seen as prevention in action.

Barriers to disclosure include personal distress and concern for the reactions of family and others in the person's life. They also include concerns about the responses of professionals and the capacity of authorities to protect and support the abused person and to punish the abuser. A range of inadequacies in the present system, both as perceived by the public and as experienced by those disclosing abuse, needs to be addressed to make disclosure a feasible option for more than the present minority who report. Similarly, the public awareness campaign needs to address the issue of disclosure to families and friends; how this might be encouraged and supported and how recipients of such information can best respond to hearing disclosures. Responsibility for educating the public broadly about disclosure should be with those developing the public awareness campaign. The challenges of removing barriers to disclosure in professional settings need to be addressed by a multi-agency group with input from service planners and providers and from service users and their representatives. The Consultative Committee should have responsibility to convene a multi-agency group to identify and propose methods of reducing barriers to disclosure. Much work has already been achieved through existing reports in identifying the barriers. These reports include reports with a general focus such as the *Report of the Working Party on the Legal and Judicial Process for Victims of Sexual and Other Crimes of Violence Against Women and Children* (1996) and the *Report of the Task Force on Violence against Women* (1997), and reports such as that of the Law Department, Trinity College, Dublin and the DRCC (Bacik et al., 1998) and that of Leane et al. (2001) from University College, Cork, both focusing on barriers in the law enforcement and legal system. A plan of action is now necessary to tackle the barriers.

RECOMMENDATION 3 — *That barriers to the disclosure of sexual violence be addressed at the level of the general public and the level of professionals and systems.*

Responsibility and timeframe: *Barriers in the general population to be addressed as part of the public awareness campaign on sexual violence being developed by the Health Promotion Unit at the Department of Health and Children. Campaign to be developed in 2002/2003 with public launch of first phase in 2003. Report of progress to the Consultative Committee in 2004. Barriers to reporting to professionals and institutions to be addressed by a multi-agency group convened by the Consultative Committee. Training of professionals to handle disclosure should be a priority of this group. Work to commence in 2003 with a report on progress in 2004.*

SPECIFIC PREVENTION STRATEGIES

Abuse of Children

Most child sexual abuse prevention programmes now focus on teaching children strategies to lower their risk of abuse. These are commendable and should continue. Alongside this, greater consideration should be given to strategies to focus responsibility on all adults, not just professionals, to protect children. Adults who may abuse, or adults who can intervene with potential abusers, or abusers themselves should be supported to act in ways to protect children. The vulnerability of children to sexual abuse by those known to them, coupled with the relatively high level of sexual abuse of children by adolescents, makes the responsibility of adults all the more notable.

Abuse of Adults — Women

Women are as likely to be sexually abused as adults as they are when children. Risks are significantly lower for men as children and reduce further in adulthood. This highlights the gendered nature of sexual violence. Intimate partners or ex-partners account for a significant proportion of abusers. The role of violence against women, including sexual violence, in interpersonal adult relationships, needs to be addressed at the level of public attitudes and in psychosocial and law enforcement settings. Alcohol was involved in a significant number of cases of sexual assault on women. The role of alcohol in sexual violence needs to be addressed.

Abuse of Adults — Men

While levels of sexual violence against men were lower than against women, cases represent a significant proportion of men. There is evidence of lesser likelihood of previous disclosure of abuse by men which can have consequences for personal well-being for the men concerned as well as consequences for prevention of abuse of men in general. Sexual violence often occurred in the context of alcohol use. As with women, the role of alcohol in sexual violence needs to be addressed.

Men as Abusers

The overwhelming majority of abusers were men. Some of these were adolescents at the time they abused another adolescent or child. A range of support and rehabilitation services, alongside appropriate law enforcement actions, is needed to address the continuum from recognition of a personal propensity to abuse through rehabilitation of convicted sex offenders.

Specific Contexts

While sexual violence is challenging for Irish society in general, there are a range of settings and groups who experience even greater challenges in addressing the issue. They include those who live in institutional settings such as institutions for those with a learning disability or a psychiatric condition, and prisoners. Those who are marginalised because of culture, for example Travellers, asylum seekers and refugees from other cultures, and those whose identity is linked with risky settings such as homeless people and prostitutes, also face additional challenges in addressing sexual violence. Public awareness campaigns need to address the challenges of communicating *per se* and of communicating effectively with these groups. Service providers need to consider how to offer health-related and law enforcement services in a supportive and accessible manner to these diverse groups.

RECOMMENDATION 4 — *That all of those responsible for promoting public awareness or providing educational, health-related or law enforcement-related service delivery on the issue of sexual violence incorporate information on the particular issues concerning vulnerability for specific groups in their activities. These groups include those abused as children, adult women and adult men; perpetrators of abuse; and marginalised groups.*

Responsibility and timeframe*: Those who can deliver on this recommendation include the Department of Health and Children; the Department of Justice, Equality and Law Reform, the Garda Síochána; health board and voluntary agency staff dealing with those who have been abused and abusers or those at high-risk of abusing; and professional bodies and academic institutions charged with training and updating professionals in their practices concerning sexual violence. Responsibility for raising these issues and identifying relevant information to all who can address prevention in this way should be with the Consultative Committee. Agencies to be contacted and invited to consider implications for particular groups in their practice in 2003. A report of progress to Consultative Committee in 2005.*

PROVISION OF SERVICES

Service Availability

A public awareness campaign will inevitably increase demand for a variety of services pertaining to sexual violence. Since many of the existing medical and counselling services are already overstretched, such a campaign needs to be planned in conjunction with increases in the capacity for service provision. Service development needs to be considered on a national level and also in relation to specific sub-groups of vulnerable or marginalised individuals who may not be able to avail of mainstream services because of cultural, intellectual or institutional challenges. Service development should be planned on the basis of a comprehensive evaluation of evidence for service demand. A service needs assessment for those who have experienced or otherwise been affected by sexual violence, to include all statutory and voluntary agencies and to address both medical and counselling services, should be completed by the Department of Health and Children. This assessment should form the basis for a five-year plan for service development.

Increased public awareness will also increase demands for prevention and services for abusers and those with the potential to abuse. A similar needs assessment of services addressing abusers, in custodial and other settings, is needed. This assessment should be the responsibility of the Department of Justice, Equality and Law Reform with input as appropriate from others on preventive strategies. The assessment should be followed by a five-year service plan. Adequate funding of agencies, including voluntary agencies with expertise in the area, needs to be available to implement such a plan.

Law enforcement services will also be expected to experience increased demand from sexual violence cases following a public awareness campaign. The Gardaí need to have adequate resources to meet such an increase. A similar review of service and training needs is necessary, as is a follow-up service plan over a five-year period. This assessment should be the responsibility of the Department of Justice, Equality and Law Reform.

RECOMMENDATION 5: *That the need for service developments be anticipated and planned on the basis of a comprehensive needs evaluation of evidence for medical, counselling and law enforcement services. This should take into account the potential increases in service demand as a consequence of public awareness campaigns. Co-ordination of service development and public awareness strategies is essential. A service needs assessment for those who have experienced or otherwise been affected by sexual violence, to include all statutory and voluntary agencies and to address both medical and counselling services, should be completed by the Department of Health and Children.*

Responsibility and timeframe: *The medical and counselling needs assessment should be the responsibility of the Department of Health and Children while the needs assessment for law enforcement and legal services is the responsibility of the Department of Justice, Equality and Law Reform. These assessments should be conducted in 2003 and form the basis of a five-year plan for service development. Interim reports should be provided to the Consultative Committee in 2005.*

Service Quality

Service quality can be maximised by providing appropriate and timely training for relevant staff and by incorporating feedback from service users into the planning and ongoing evaluation of services. Problems with professional services as outlined by those who used them, but also perceived problems which discouraged others from using services, should be examined in more detail as part of a concerted effort to improve service access and delivery. A number of recent Irish studies provide information on this issue.

RECOMMENDATION 6 — *That a range of educational materials on sexual violence in Irish society be developed for relevant professionals to complement a national public awareness campaign. In addition, that regular assessment of the user perspective be incorporated into service evaluation and planning for improvement.*

Responsibility and timeframe: The relevant professional bodies and training institutions should adapt training materials to incorporate recent Irish findings and the strategic approach of the public awareness campaign. The Consultative Committee should take responsibility to contact the relevant groups in 2003 and to facilitate information flow concerning the public awareness campaign. Report of progress to Consultative Committee in 2005.

RESEARCH

Research

A programme of research is needed to inform, support and evaluate developments in addressing sexual violence in the coming years. Some important areas for research are highlighted in other recommendations. Systematic evaluation of public attitudes to and experiences of sexual violence through surveys like the SAVI study should be undertaken on a regular (five-yearly) basis to monitor changes over time and in relation to changes in public awareness and public policy. A Consultative Committee (discussed further in Recommendation 8) should have responsibility for determining research priorities for this regular public survey and other research priorities. This group should consult widely so as to ensure its work complements other research developments such as national crime surveys.

RECOMMENDATION 7 — *That a systematic programme of Irish research is needed to inform, support and evaluate developments in addressing sexual violence in the coming years. This should include a regular national survey assessing public attitudes and experiences.*

Responsibility and timeframe: *A Consultative Committee should have responsibility for determining research priorities for a regular public survey and other research priorities. Annual priorities should be agreed by consultation with a plan to conduct a national survey similar to SAVI in 2006.*

IMPLEMENTATION OF RECOMMENDATIONS

Co-ordination of Implementation

The topic of sexual violence is already addressed by Government agencies in a variety of forums such as those on violence against women and on childcare protection. It is not, however, currently addressed in a comprehensive manner in a single forum. This means that progress on the issue cannot be co-ordinated or monitored. Sexual violence is acknowledged as part of a wider continuum of abuse and neglect in Irish society. However, its particularly stigmatising and secretive nature requires some specific focus, alongside attention in more integrated contexts, if real progress is to be made in highlighting, managing and preventing the problem. The establishment of a Consultative Committee on Sexual Violence is recommended to ensure that a uniform, concerted and strategic approach is taken to the management of sexual violence across agencies. This Consultative Committee would have the responsibility to ensure that recommendations arising from the SAVI study and similar reports are acted on by the relevant agencies. Committee membership should reflect the relevant Government and voluntary sector agencies and should be appointed jointly by the Minister for Health and Children and the Minister for Justice, Equality and Law Reform. The Consultative Committee should be constituted for five years in the first instance with an interim report after three years and with recommendations on the future of the Committee at the final five-year report stage.

Recommendations cannot be implemented without dedicated funding. A funding plan is needed to enable the relevant Government departments and service agencies to act on the recommendations. While some action on recommendations will be feasible in 2002, the first phased source of ongoing funding needs to be requested by the relevant Government departments in the 2003 budget estimates.

RECOMMENDATION 8 — *That a Consultative Committee on Sexual Violence be established with the responsibility and authority to ensure that recommendations arising from the SAVI Study and similar reports are acted on by the relevant agencies. This Committee should represent the broad constituency of interests which can contribute to effective management of the societal challenge of sexual violence.*

Responsibility and timeframe: The Consultative Committee should be appointed jointly by the Minister for Health and Children and the Minister for Justice, Equality and Law Reform. The Committee should be invited to serve a five-year term from 2002 to 2007. An interim report of progress to be provided jointly to the two relevant Government Departments in 2005 with a final report in 2007.

In summary, the findings of this study highlight sexual violence as a profoundly disturbing and pervasive dimension of contemporary Irish society which is under-acknowledged, under-reported and under-managed. The solutions to the problem are as complex as its aetiology. They challenge us to avoid procrastination and instead to plan and act now. In the words of an African proverb:

The best time to plant a tree is twenty years ago.
The second best time is now.

References

Abbey, A., Zawacki, T., Buck, P., Clinton, A.M. and McAuslan, P. (2001). Alcohol and sexual assault. *Alcohol Health and Research World, 25,* 43–51.

Allington, C.L.J. (1992). Sexual abuse within services for people with learning disabilities: staff perceptions, understandings of and contact with the problems of sexual abuse. *Mental Handicap, 20,* 59–63.

Allwright, S., Bradley, F., Long, J., Barry, J., Thornton, L. and Parry, J. (2000). Prevalence of antibodies to Hepatitis B, Hepatitis C and HIV risk factors in Irish prisoners: Results of a cross-sectional study. *British Medical Journal, 321,* 78–82.

American Medical Association Council on Scientific Affairs (1992). Violence against women: Relevance to medical practitioners. *Journal of the American Medical Association, 267,* 3184–3189.

Ammerman, R., Van Hasselt, V. and Hersen, M. (1988). Maltreatment of handicapped children: A critical review. *Journal of Family Violence, 3,* 53–72.

Andrykowski, M.A., Cordova, M.J., Studts, J.L. and Miller, T.W. (1998). Posttraumatic stress disorder after treatment for breast cancer: Prevalence of diagnosis and use of the PTSD Checklist — Civilian Version (PCL-C) as a screening instrument. *Journal of Consulting & Clinical Psychology, 66,* 586–590.

Bacik, I., Maunsell, C. and Gogan, S. (1998). *The Legal Process and Victims of Rape: A comparative analysis of the laws and legal procedures relating to rape, and their impact upon victims of rape, in fifteen member states of the European Union,* Dublin: The Dublin Rape Crisis Centre.

Bagley, C. and Young, L. (1987). Juvenile prostitution and child sexual abuse: A controlled study. *Canadian Journal of Community Mental Health, 6*, 5–26.

Beail, N. and Warden, S. (1995). Sexual abuse of adults with learning disabilities. *Journal of Intellectual Disability Research, 39*, 382–387.

Black, D.A., Heyman, R.E., Slep, A. and Smith, M. (2001). Risk Factors for Child Sexual Abuse. *Aggression and Violent Behaviour, 6*, 203–229.

Bradley, F., Smith, M., Long, J. and O'Dowd, T. (2002). Reported frequency of domestic violence: Cross-sectional survey of women attending general practice. *British Medical Journal, 324*, 271–274.

Breakey, W., Fischer, P., Kramer, M., Nesadt, G., Romanoski, A. and Ross, A. (1989). Health and mental health problems of homeless men and women in Baltimore. *Journal of the American Medical Association, 262*, 1352–7.

Brecklin, L.R. and Ullman, S. (2001). The role of offender alcohol use in rape attacks: An analysis of National Crime Victimization survey data. *Journal of Interpersonal Violence, 16*, 3–21.

Breen, M. (2000). The good, the bad and the ugly: The media and scandals. *Studies, 89*, 332–339.

Breen, R. and Rottman, D.B. (1985) *Crime Victimisation in the Republic of Ireland*, Dublin: The Economic and Social Research Institute.

Brookoff, D., O'Brien, K.K., Cook, C.S., Thompson, T.D. and Williams, C. (1997). Characteristics of participants in domestic violence: Assessment at the scene of domestic assault. *Journal of the American Medical Association, 277*, 1369–1373.

Brothers of Charity (1999). *Guidelines on Relationships and Sexuality: Interim Working Report*. Galway: Brothers of Charity.

Brown, H. (1996). Ordinary women: Issues for women with learning disabilities. *British Journal of Learning Disabilities, 24*, 47–51.

Brown, H. and Craft, A. (1989). *Thinking the Unthinkable: Papers on Sexual Abuse and People with Learning Difficulties*. London: Family Planning Association.

Brown, H. and Craft, A. (1996). *Towards Safer Commissioning: A Handbook for Purchasers and Commissioners on the Sexual Abuse of Adults with Learning Disabilities*, Brighton: NAPSAC/Pavilion.

Brown, H. and Hunt, N. and S.J. (1994). "Alarming but very necessary": Working with staff groups around the sexual abuse of adults with learning disabilities. *Journal of Intellectual Disability Research, 38,* 393–412.

Brown, H. and Turk, V. (1994). Sexual abuse in adulthood: Ongoing risks for people with learning disabilities. *Child Abuse Review, 3,* 26–35.

Buchanan, A.H. and Wilkins, R. (1991). Sexual abuse of the mentally handicapped: Difficulties in establishing prevalence. *Psychiatric Bulletin, 15,* 601–5.

Burt, M.R. (1980). Cultural myths and supports for rape. *Journal of Personality & Social Psychology, 38,* 217–230.

Burt, M.R. and Estep, R.E. (1981). Who is a victim? Definitional problems in sexual victimization. *Victimology: An International Journal, 6,* 15–28.

Campbell, R., Sefl, T., Barnes, H.E., Ahrens, C.E., Wasco, S.M. and Zaragoza-Diesfeld, Y. (1999). Community services for rape survivors: Enhancing psychological well-being or increasing trauma? *Journal of Consulting and Clinical Psychology, 67* (6):847–858.

CARI (Children at Risk in Ireland) (2001). *Annual Report 2000,* Dublin: CARI.

Carmody, M. (1991). Invisible victims: Sexual assault of people with an intellectual disability. *Australia and New Zealand Journal of Developmental Disabilities, 17,* 229–236.

Central Statistics Office (2001). *Quarterly National Household Survey: Population and Emigration Estimates.* Dublin: Stationery Office.

Chamberlain, A., Rauh, J., Passer, A., McGrath, M. and Burket, O. (1984). Issues in fertility control for mentally retarded female adolescents: I. Sexual activity, sexual abuse, and contraception. *Pediatrics, 73,* 445–450.

Cheasty, M., Clare, A.W. and Collins, C. (1998). Relation between sexual abuse in childhood and adult depression: Case control study. *British Medical Journal, 316,* 198–201.

Coid, J., Petruckevitch, A., Feder, G., Chung, W.-S., Richardson, J. and Moorey, S. (2001). Relation between childhood sexual abuse and physical abuse and risk of revictimisation in women: a cross-sectional survey. *Lancet, 358,* 450–54.

Committee on Professional Practice and Standards (1999). Guidelines for psychological evaluations in child protection matters. *American Psychologist, 54,* 586–593.

Condon, M. (2001). *The Health and Dental Needs of Homeless People in Dublin,* Dublin: Eastern Regional Health Authority.

Coxell, A., King, M., Mezey, G. and Kell, P. (2000). Sexual molestation of men: Interviews with 224 men attending a genitourinary medicine service. *International Journal of STD & AIDS, 11,* 574–578.

Craine, L., Henson, C., Colliver, J. and MacLean, D. (1988). Prevalence of a history of sexual abuse among female psychiatric patients in a state hospital system. *Hospital and Community Psychiatry, 39,* 300–304.

Crowder, A. (1995). *Opening the Door: A Treatment Model for Therapy with Male Survivors of Sexual Abuse.* New York: Brunner/Mazel.

Daro, D.A. (1994). Prevention of Child Sexual Abuse. *Future of Children, 4,* 198–223.

Department of Health (1996). *Putting Children First.* Dublin: Department of Health.

Department of Health (1997). *Report of the Task Force on Violence Against Women.* Dublin: Government Publications.

Department of Health and Children (1999). *Children First: National Guidelines for the Protection and Welfare of Children.* Dublin: The Department of Health and Children.

Doyle, P. (1988). *The God Squad.* Dublin: Corgi.

Dube, S., Anda, R., Felitti, V., Chapman, D., Williamson, D. and Giles, W. (2001). Childhood abuse, household dysfunction and the risk of attempted suicide throughout the lifespan. *Journal of the American Medical Association, 286,* 3089–3096.

Dublin Rape Crisis Centre (2000). *Annual Report 1998/99.* Dublin: Dublin Rape Crisis Centre.

Dublin Rape Crisis Centre (2001). *Annual Report 2000.* Dublin: Dublin Rape Crisis Centre.

Dunne, T.P. and Power, A. (1990). Sexual abuse and mental handicap: Preliminary findings of a community-based study. *Mental Handicap Research, 3,* 111–25.

Elkins, T.E., Gafford, L.S., Wilks, C.S., Muram, D. and Golden, G. (1986). A model clinic approach to the reproductive health concerns of the mentally handicapped. *Obstetrics and Gynecology, 68*, 185–8.

Ellsberg, M., Heise, L., Pena, R., Agurto, S. and Winkvist, A. (2001). Researching domestic violence against women: Methodological and ethical considerations. *Studies in Family Planning, 32*, 1–17.

Ernst, C., Angst, J. and Földényi, M. (1993). The Zurich Study: XVII. Sexual abuse in childhood: Frequency and relevance for adult morbidity data of a longitudinal epidemiological study. *European Archives of Psychiatry and Clinical Neuroscience, 242*, 293–300.

European Commission (1997). *The State of Women's Health in the European Community*. Luxembourg: Office for Official Publications of the European Communities.

Feldhaus, C.M., Koziol-McLain, J., Amsbury, H.L., Norton, I.M., Lowenstein, S.R. and Abbott, J.T. (1997). Accuracy of 3 brief screening questions for detecting partner violence in the emergency department. *Journal of the American Medical Association, 2277*, 1357–1361.

Ferguson, H. and O'Reilly, M. (2001). *Keeping Children Safe*. Dublin: A&A Farmar.

Figueroa, E., Silk, K., Huth, A. and Lohr, N. (1997). History of childhood sexual abuse and general psychopathology. *Comprehensive Psychiatry, 38*, 23–30.

Finkelhor, D. (1984). Child sexual abuse in a sample of Boston families. In Finkelhor, D., (ed.) *Child Sexual Abuse: New Theory and Research*, pp. 69–86. New York: The Free Press.

Finkelhor, D. (1992). What do we know about Child Sexual Abuse?. Presentation to the "Surviving Childhood Adversity" Conference: Trinity College Dublin.

Finkelhor, D. (1994). The international epidemiology of child sexual abuse. *Child Abuse & Neglect, 18*, 409–417.

Finkelhor, D. (1998). Improving research, policy and practice to understand child sexual abuse. *Journal of the American Medical Association, 280*, 1864–1865.

Finkelhor, D. and Dziuba-Leatherman, J. (1994). Children as victims of violence: A national survey. *Pediatrics, 94*, 413–420.

Finkelhor, D., Wolak, J. and Berliner (2001). Police reporting and professional help seeking for child crime victims: A review. *Child Maltreatment*, 6, 17–30.

Fitzgerald, L.F., Magley, V.J., Drasgow, F. and Waldo, C.R. (1999). Measuring sexual harassment in the military: The Sexual Experiences Questionnaire (SEQ-DoD). *Military Psychology, 11*(3):243–263.

Frazier, P., Conlon, A. and Glaser, T. (2001). Positive and negative life changes following sexual assault. *Journal of Consulting and Clinical Psychology, 69*, 1048–1055.

Friel, S., Nic Gabhainn, S. and Kelleher, C. (1999). *The National Health and Lifestyle Survey. SLAN.* Dublin: Health Promotion Unit, Department of Health and Children.

Furey, E.M., Granfield, J.M. and Karan, O.C. (1994). Sexual abuse and neglect of adults with mental retardation: A comparison of victim characteristics. *Behavioral Interventions, 9*, 75–86.

Furey, E.M. and Haber, M. (1989). Protecting adults with mental retardation: A model statute. *Mental Retardation, 27*, 135–140.

Furey, E.M. and Niesen, J.J. (1994). Sexual abuse of adults with mental retardation by other consumers. *Sexuality and Disability, 12*, 285–295.

Garda Síochána (2000). *Annual Report of the Garda Síochána: 2000.* Dublin: Government Publications.

Goddard, C. and Saunders, B. (2001). Child abuse and the media. *Child Abuse Prevention, 14*, 1–22.

Goldberg, D. and Williams, P. (1988). *A User's Guide to the General Health Questionnaire.* Windsor, England: NFER-NELSON.

Goldman, J.D.G. and Padayachi, U.K. (2000). Some methodological problems in estimating incidence and prevalence in child sexual abuse research. *Journal of Sex Research, 37*, 305–314.

Goodman, L., Saxe, L. and Harvey, M. (1991). Homelessness as psychological trauma: Broadening perspectives. *American Psychologist, 46*, 1219–25.

Goodman, L.A., Koss, M.P. and Russo, N.F. (1993). Violence against women: Mental health effects. Part 2. Conceptualisation of posttraumatic stress. *Applied & Preventative Psychology, 2*, 123–130.

Greenfeld, L.A. (1998). *Alcohol and Crime: An analysis of national data on the prevalence of alcohol involvement in crime.* Washington, DC: US Dept of Justice.

Hanson, R.F., Resnick, H.S., Saunders, B.E., Kilpatrick, D.G. and Best, C.L. (1999). Factors related to the reporting of childhood rape. *Child Abuse & Neglect, 23*, 559–569.

Hendessi, M. (1992). *Four in Ten. Report on Young Women Who Become Homeless as a Result of Sexual Abuse.* Surrey: CHAR (the Housing Campaign for Single People).

Hill, J., Davis, R., Byatt, M., Burnside, E., Rollinson, L. and Fear, S. (2000). Childhood sexual abuse and affective symptoms in women: a general population study. *Psychological Medicine, 30*, 1283–1291.

Holmes, M.M., Resnick, H.S. and Frampton, D. (1998). Follow-up of sexual assault victims. *American Journal of Obstetrics and Gynecology, 179*, 336–342.

Holmes, W.C. and Slap, G.B. (1998). Sexual abuse of boys: Definition, prevalence, correlates, sequelae, and management. *Journal of the American Medical Association, 280*, 1855–1862.

Hospitaller Order of St. John of God (1995). *Relationships and Sexual Development.* Dublin: Hospitaller Order.

Irish Marketing Surveys (1993). *Childhood experiences and attitudes.* Dublin: Irish Market Surveys.

Irish Society for the Prevention of Cruelty to Children (ISPCC) (1996). *Another Brick from the Wall: The Case for the Introduction of Mandatory Reporting of Child Sexual Abuse and Neglect in Ireland.* Dublin: ISPCC.

Irwin, J. and Austin, J. (1994). *Its About Time: America's Imprisonment Binge.* Belmont, CA: Wadsworth.

Jacobson, A., Koehler, J.E. and Jones-Brown, C. (1987). The failure of routine assessment to detect histories of assault experienced by psychiatric patients. *Hospital & Community Psychiatry, 38*, 386–389.

Johnson, H. and Sacco, V. (1995). Researching violence against women: Statistics Canada's national survey. *Canadian Journal of Criminology, July*, 281–304.

Kelly, L. (1992). The connections between disability and child abuse: a review of research evidence. *Child Abuse Review, 1*, 157–167.

Kelly, L., Regan, L. and Burton, S. (1991). *An Exploratory Study of the Prevalence of Sexual Abuse in a Sample of 16–21 Year Olds*. London, UK: The Polytechnic of North London.

Kemp, A. (1998). *Abuse in the Family: An Introduction*. USA: Brooks/Cole Publishing Co.

Kempton, W. and Gochros, J.S. (1986). The developmentally disabled. In: Gochros, H.L., Gochros, J.L. and Fischer, J., (eds.) *Helping the Sexually Oppressed*. Englewood Cliffs, NJ: Prentice Hall.

Kilpatrick, D., Acierno, Saunders, Resnick, Best and Schnurr (2000). Risk factors for adolescent substance abuse and dependence: Data from a national sample. *Journal of Consulting & Clinical Psychology, 68*, 19–28.

Kilpatrick, D. and Saunders, B. (1997). *The Prevalence and Consequences of Child Victimisation*. Rockville, MD: National Institute of Justice.

Kinard, E.M. (1996). Conducting research on child maltreatment: Effects on researchers. *Violence and Victims, 11*, 65–69.

Kitzinger, J. (1996). Media representations of sexual abuse risks. *Child Abuse Review, 5*, 318–333.

Klein, S., Wawrok, S. and Fegert, J.M. (1999). Sexuell Gewalt in der lebenswirklichkeit von Maedchen und Frauen mit geistiger Behinderung — Ergebnisse eines Forschungsprojeckts. *Praxis der Kinderpsychologie und Kinderpsychiatrie, 48*, 497–513.

Koss, M.P. (1993). Detecting the scope of rape: A review of prevalence research methods. *Journal of Interpersonal Violence, 8*, 198–222.

Kupers, T. (1996). Trauma and its sequelae in male prisoners: Effects of confinement, overcrowding, and diminished services. *American Journal of Orthopsychiatry, 66*, 189–196.

Lalor, K. (1999). A survey of sexually abusive experiences in childhood amongst a sample of third level students. *Irish Journal of Psychology, 20*, 15–27.

Leane, M., Ryan, S., Fennell, C. and Egan, E. (2001). *Attrition in Sexual Assault Offence Cases in Ireland: A Qualitative Analysis*. Dublin: Government Publications.

Leon, C. (2000). Sexual Offences in Ireland 1994–1997. The British Criminology Conference: Selected Proceedings. Liverpool: The British Society of Criminology; http://www.lboro.ac.uk/departments/ss/bsc/bccsp/vol03/leon.html.

Lottes, I. (1988). Rape Supportive Attitude Scale. In Davis, C., Yarber, W. and Davis, S., (eds.) *Sexuality-Related Measures: A Compendium*, pp. 235–237. Lake Mills, Iowa: Graphic Publishing.

MacIntyre, D. and Lawlor, M. (1991). *The Stay Safe Programme*. Dublin: Department of Health, Child Abuse Prevention Programme.

MacIntyre, D., Lawlor, M. and Cullen, R. (1996). *Personal Safety Skills for Children with Learning Difficulties based on The Stay Safe Programme*. Dublin: Department of Health and Children, Child Abuse Prevention Programme.

Malamuth, N.M., Sockloskie, R.J., Koss, M.P. and Tanaka, J.S. (1991). Characteristics of aggressors against women: Testing a model using a national sample of college students. *Journal of Consulting and Clinical Psychology, 59*(5):670–681.

Marolla, J.A. and Scully, D. (1986). Attitudes towards women, violence, and rape: A comparison of convicted rapists and other felons. *Deviant Behavior, 7*, 337–355.

McCabe, M.P., Cummins, R.A. and Reid, S.B. (1994). An empirical study of the sexual abuse of people with intellectual disability. *Sexuality & Disability, 12*, 297–306.

McCarthy, A. (1999). Sexual Violence against Refugee Women. In United Nations High Commissioner for Refugees (ed.), *UNHCR conference: Refugee Women — Victims or Survivors?* pp. 34–47.

McClanahan, S.F., McClelland, G.M., Abram, K.M. and Teplin, L.A. (1999). Pathways into prostitution among female jail detainees and their implications for mental health services. *Psychiatric Services, 50*(12), 1606–1613.

McDevitt, S. (1998). Media trends in child abuse reporting: the United States and the Republic of Ireland. *Journal of Child Centred Practice, 5*, 11–28.

McElroy, S.L. (1999). Psychiatric features of 36 men convicted of sexual offences. *Journal of Clinical Psychiatry, 60*, 414–420.

McGinley, P. (2000a). *Reporting Abuse Guidelines for All Staff.* Galway: Brothers of Charity.

McGinley, P. (2000b). Assessing Dangerous Places. *Journal of Intellectual Disability Research, 44,* 388.

McKay, S. (1998). *Sophia's Story.* Dublin: Gill & MacMillan, Ltd.

Moggach, D. (1998). *Porky.* London: Arrow Books.

Morbidity and Mortality Weekly Report (2001). Child sexual abuse prevention program targets abusers. *Morbidity and Mortality Weekly Report (Center for Disease Control), 50,* 77–78.

Morton-Williams, J. (1993). *Interviewer Approaches.* Dartmouth: Dartmouth Publishing Co.

Muccigrosso, L. (1991). Sexual abuse prevention strategies and programs for persons with developmental difficulties. *Sexuality and Disability, 9,* 261–271.

Mullen, P.E., Romans-Clarkson, S.E., Walton, V.A. and Herbison, G.P. (1988). Impact of sexual and physical abuse on women's health. *The Lancet, 1,* 841–845.

Mullings, J., Marquart, J. and Brewer, V. (2000). Assessing the relationship between sexual abuse and marginal living conditions on HIV/AIDS-related risk behaviour among women prisoners. *Child Abuse & Neglect, 24,* 677–88.

Murphy, G. and Clare, I.C.H. (1995). Adults' capacity to make decisions affecting the person: Psychologists' contribution. In R. Bull and D. Carson (ed.) *Handbook of Psychology in Legal Contexts.* Chichester: Wiley & Sons.

Murphy, W.D., Haynes, M.R. and Page, I.J. (1992). Adolescent Sex Offenders. In O'Donohue, W. and Geer, J.H. (eds.) *The Sexual Abuse of Children: Theory and Research, Volume 1,* pp. 394–429. New Jersey: Lawrence Erlbaum Associates, Publishers.

Nadon, S.M., Koverola, C. and Schludermann, E.H. (1998). Antecedents to prostitution: Childhood victimization. *Journal of Interpersonal Violence, 13*(2):206–221.

National Steering Committee on Violence Against Women (1999). *First Report of the National Steering Committee on Violence Against Women.* Dublin: The Stationery Office.

O'Boyle, C.A., Brown, J., Hickey, A., McGee, H.M. and Joyce, C.R.B. (1995). *Schedule for the Evaluation of Individual Quality of life (SEIQoL): a direct weighting procedure for quality of life domains (SEIQoL-DW) Administration Manual.* Dublin, Ireland: Department of Psychology, RCSI.

O'Mahony, P. (1997). *Mountjoy Prisoners.* Dublin: Government Publications.

O'Malley, T. (1996). *Sexual Offences: Law, Policy and Punishment.* Dublin: Round Hall Sweet & Maxwell.

O'Neill, K. and Gupta, K. (1991). Post-traumatic stress disorder in women who were victims of childhood sexual abuse. *Irish Journal of Psychological Medicine, 8,* 124–127.

O'Reilly, G. and Carr, A. (1999). Child sexual abuse in Ireland: A synthesis of two surveys. *The Irish Journal of Psychology, 20,* 1–14.

O'Sullivan, A., Carr, A., MacIntyre, D., Flattery, M., Shanahan, P. and Hefferon, M. Evaluation of the effectiveness of the Stay Safe Child Abuse Prevention Programme for children with intellectual disability. (Paper submitted for publication).

Ong, A.S.J. and Ward, C.A. (1999). The effects of sex and power schemas, attitudes toward women, and victim resistance on rape attributions. *Journal of Applied Social Psychology, 29*(2), 362–376.

Potter, K., Martin, J. and Romans, S. (1999). Early developmental experiences of female sex workers: a comparative study. *Australian & New Zealand Journal of Psychiatry, 33*(6), 935–940.

Read, J. and Argyle, N. (1999). Hallucinations, delusions and thought disorder among adult psychiatric inpatients with a history of child abuse. *Psychiatric Services, 50,* 1467–1472.

Resnick, H., Holmes, M., Kilpatrick, D., Clum, G., Acierno, R., Best, C. and Saunders, B. (2000). Predictors of post-rape medical care in a national sample of women. *American Journal of Preventive Medicine, 19,* 214–219.

Richardson, J., Coid, J., Pelrukevitch, A., Chung, W., Moorey, S. and Feder, G. (2002). Identifying Domestic Violence: Cross-Sectional Study in Primary Care. *British Medical Journal, 324,* 274–277.

Righthand, S. and Welch, C. (2001). *Juveniles Who Have Sexually Offended: A Review of the Professional Literature*. Washington, DC: US Department of Justice, Office of Juvenile Justice and Delinquency Prevention.

Russell, D.E.H. (1983). The incidence and prevalence of intrafamilial and extrafamilial sexual abuse of female children. *Child Abuse & Neglect, 7*, 133–146.

Ryan, D. and McConkey, R. (2000). Staff attitudes to sexuality and people with intellectual disabilities. *The Irish Journal of Psychology, 21*, 88–97.

Salter, A.C. (1992). Epidemiology of child sexual abuse. In O'Donohue, W. and Geer, J.H. (eds.), *The Sexual Abuse of Children: Theory and Research Volume 1*, pp. 108–138. Hillsdale, NJ: Lawrence Erlbaum Associates.

Saunders, B.E., Kilpatrick, D.G., Hanson, R.F., Resnick, H.S. and Walker, M.E. (1999). Prevalence, case characteristics, and long-term psychological correlates of child rape among women: A national survey. *Child Maltreatment, 4*, 187–200.

Scarce, M. (1997). *Male on Male Rape: The Hidden Toll of Stigma and Shame*. New York: Plenum.

Schei, B. (1990). Prevalence of sexual abuse history in a random sample of Norwegian women. *Scandinavian Journal of Social Medicine, 18*, 63–68.

Schor, D. (1987). Sex and sexual abuse in developmentally disabled adolescents. *Seminars in Adolescent Medicine, 3*, 1–7.

Sobsey, D. and Mansell, S. (1990). The prevention of sexual abuse of people with developmental disabilities. *Developmental Disabilities Bulletin, 18*, 51–66.

Sobsey, D. and Varnhagen, C. (1989). Sexual abuse and exploitation of people with disabilities: Toward prevention and treatment. In Sapo, M.C. and Gourgen, L. (eds.), *Special Education Across Canada*, Vancouver: Centre for Human Development Research.

Stromsness, M.M. (1993). Sexually abused women with mental retardation: Hidden victims, absent resources. *Women & Therapy, 14*, 139–152.

Struckman-Johnson, C., Struckman-Johnson, D., Rucker, L., Bumby, K. and Donaldson, S. (1996). Sexual coercion reported by men and women in prison. *Journal of Sex Research, 33*, 67–76.

Sykes Wylie, M. (1993). The shadow of a doubt. *Family Therapy Networker, 17*, 18–29.

Task Force on the Prevention of Workplace Bullying (2001). *Dignity at Work: The Challenge of Workplace Bullying*. Dublin, Ireland: The Stationary Office.

Thomas, C., Bartlett, A. and Mezey, G. (1995). The extent and effects of violence among psychiatric inpatients. *Psychiatric Bulletin, 19*, 600–604.

Tjaden, P. and Boyle, J. (1998). *National Violence Against Women Survey: Methodology Report*. Denver: Centre for Policy Research.

Tjaden, P. and Thoennes, N. (2000). *Extent, Nature, and Consequences of Intimate Partner Violence: Findings from the National Violence Against Women Survey*. Washington, DC: US Department of Justice, Office of Justice Programs, National Institute of Justice.

Tjaden, P., Thoennes, N. and Allison, C. (2000). *Effects of interviewer gender on men's responses to a telephone survey on violent victimisation*. Denver: Centre for Policy Research.

Travers, O. (1998). Treatment versus punishment: A case for treating sex offenders in the community. *Irish Journal of Psychology, 19*, 208–215.

Turk, V. and Brown, H. (1993). The sexual abuse of adults with learning disabilities: Results of a two-year incidence study. *Mental Handicap Research, 6*, 193–216.

Twoomey, S., Kilgarriff, J. and Ryan, T. (1988). *The Bawnmore Personal Development Programme*. Limerick, Bawnmore: Brothers of Charity Services.

Ullman, S.E., Karabatsos, G. and Koss, M.P. (1999). Alcohol and sexual assault in a national sample of college women. *Journal of Interpersonal Violence, 14*(6):603–625.

VOICE, Respond, Mencap (2001). *Behind Closed Doors: Preventing Sexual Abuse against Adults with a Learning Disability*. London: Mencap.

Walby, S. and Myhill, A. (2001). New survey methodologies in researching violence against women. *British Journal of Criminology, 41*(3), 502–522.

Walsh, C., and Evans, D. (2001). Relationships and Sexuality Policy for People with Learning Disabilities. Presented at the Health Services Research 2nd Conference, Ireland, 2001.

Ward, C.A. (1988). The Attitudes Toward Rape Victims Scale. *Psychology of Women Quarterly, 12*, 127–146.

Ware, J.E. and Sherbourne, D.C. (1992). The MOS 36-Item Short-Form Health Survey (SF-36). *Medical Care, 30,* 473–81.

Waterman, C.K. and Foss-Goodman, D. (1984). Child molesting: Variables relating to attributing of fault to victims, offenders and non-participating parents. *Journal of Sex Research, 20,* 329–349.

Watson, D. (2000). *Victims of Recorded Crime in Ireland: Results from the 1996 Survey.* Dublin: Oak Tree Press.

Westcott, H. (1991). The abuse of disabled children: A review of the literature. *Child Care, Health and Development, 17,* 243–258.

Westcott, H. and Cross, M. (1996). *This Far and No Further.* Birmingham: Venture Press.

Westcott, H. and Jones, D.P. (1999). Annotation: The abuse of disabled children. *Journal of Child Psychology, Psychiatry and Allied Professions, 40,* 497–506.

Widom, C.S. and Ames, M.A. (1994). Criminal consequences of childhood sexual victimization. *Child Abuse & Neglect, 18*(4):303–18.

Widom, C.S. and Morris, S. (1997). Accuracy of adult recollections of childhood victimisation: Part 2. Childhood sexual abuse. *Psychological Assessment, 9,* 34–46.

Wilcyzynski, A. and Sinclair, K. (1999). A moral panic? Representations of child abuse in the quality and tabloid media. *Australian and New Zealand Journal of Criminology, 32,* 262–284.

Wiley, M. and Merriman, B. (1996). *Women and Health Care in Ireland.* Dublin: Oak Tree Press.

Williams, J. and O'Connor, M. (1999). *Counted In: Report of the 1999 Assessment of Homelessness in Dublin, Kildare and Wicklow.* Dublin: ESRI/Homeless Initiative.

Williams, L., Forster, G. and Petrak, J. (1999). Rape attitudes amongst British medical students. *Medical Education, 33*(1):24–7.

Wood, D. and Copperman, J. (1996). Sexual Harassment and Assault in Psychiatric Services. In Perkins, R., Nadirshaw, Z., Copperman, J. and Andrews, C. (eds.), *Women's Mental Health in Context: Good Practice in Mental Health Services for Women.* London: Good Practices in Mental Health.

Working Party on the Legal and Judicial Process for Victims of Sexual and Other Crimes of Violence Against Women and Children (1996). *Report of the Working Party*. Dublin: Government Publications.

World Health Organisation (1999). *Putting women first: Ethical and safety recommendations for research on domestic violence against women*. Geneva, Switzerland: Global Programme on Evidence for Health Policy.

Wurr, C. and Partridge, I. (1996). The prevalence of a history of childhood sexual abuse in an acute adult inpatient population. *Child Abuse & Neglect, 20*, 867–872.

Wyatt, G.E. and Doyle Peters, S. (1986). "Issues in the definition of child sexual abuse in prevalence research". *Child Abuse & Neglect, 10*, 231–240.

Young, P., O'Donnell, I. and Clare, E. (2001). *Crime in Ireland: Trends and Patterns 1950–1998*. Dublin: The National Crime Council.

Young, M., Read, J., Barker-Collo, S, and Harrison, R. (2001). "Evaluating and overcoming barriers to taking abuse histories". *Professional Psychology: Research and Practice, 32*(4): 407–414.

Appendix I: Summary of Response Rates and Reporting of Sexual Violence Experiences in Sexual Violence Survey by Survey Methodology Adopted

Author(s)	Date	Methodology	Response Rate	Sample	Focus	Findings/Rates
Kercher, McShane*	1984	Mail survey	53%	Males and females; adults holding valid driver's licenses in Texas, USA; n = 1,054	Sexual abuse	Sexual abuse: F = 11%; M = 3%; No response = 7%
Koss et al.	1991	Mail survey	45%	Females only; adults aged 19-69 yrs; medical patients in US; n = 2,291	Criminal victimisation	Rape: 20%; incidence 15x higher than NCS estimates
Heiskanen, Piispa	1992?	Mail survey; reminders and new surveys sent out to those who did not reply 2x	70%	Females only; adults aged 18-74; random sample from population register in Finland; n = 4,955	Violence against women (broadly defined)	(No information – sexual assault not listed separately)
O'Connell, Whelan	1994	Mail survey	64.8%	Males and females? Adults aged 18+; random sample from electoral register in Ireland; n =1,000	Criminal victimisation	

Author(s)	Date	Methodology	Response Rate	Sample	Focus	Findings/Rates
Finkelhor*	1979	Questionnaire administered in classroom	92%	Males and females; college students in social science classes, US; n = 796	Childhood sexual abuse	Childhood sexual abuse: F = 19.2%; M = 8.6%
Sorrenti-Little, Bagley, Robertson*	1984	Questionnaire administered in classroom	Not stated	Males and females; college students, Univ of Calgary, Canada; n = 570	Sexual assault	Childhood sexual abuse prior to age 17: F = 19.6%; M = 8.5%
Canada*	1984	Questionnaires delivered personally; interviewers not allowed to discuss contents, but waited while filled out	88%	Males and females; adults; national representative sample of Canadians; n = 1,833	Sexual abuse?	Childhood sexual abuse prior to age 17: F = 17.6%; M = 8.2%
Smikle, Satin, Dellinger, Hankins	1995	Questionnaire (unclear where administered)	Not stated	Females only; patients in OB/GYN clinic; n = 531	Physical and sexual abuse	Lifetime sexual abuse = 14.7%

Author(s)	Date	Methodology	Response Rate	Sample	Focus	Findings/Rates
Mazza, Dennerstein, Ryan	1996	Questionnaire (completed in GP's waiting room or at home)	72%	Females only; adults aged 18+; patients in GP surgeries, Australia; n = 3,026	Physical, sexual and emotional violence against women	Childhood sexual abuse prior to age 16 = 40%; sexual abuse after 16 = 30%
Resnick, Kilpatrick, Danksy, Saunders, Best	1993	Telephone interviews (female interviewers)	85.2%	Females only; adults aged 18+; national sample, with oversample of women aged 18-34, US; n = 4,008	Criminal victimisation, traumatic events, PTSD	Lifetime: complete rape = 12.6%; other sexual assault = 14.3%
Finkelhor, Dzuiba-Letherman	1994	Telephone interviews: parental consent first obtained, then children asked to participate	88% = parental consent; 82% = eligible children	Males and females; children aged 10-16; US; n = 2,000	Childhood victimisation (broadly defined)	Attempted and completed sexual abuse: F = 15.3%; M = 5.9%; rape completed: F = 1.3%; M = 0.0%
Ageton*	1983	Direct interviews	73%	Females only; adolescent girls (age not stated); national sample; n = 1,716	Delinquency	Forced sexual behaviour: 5% – 11% per year

Author(s)	Date	Methodology	Response Rate	Sample	Focus	Findings/Rates
Russell	1984	Direct interviews	64%	Females only; adults; San Francisco, US; randomly selected; n = 930	Sexual abuse	Unwanted sexual experiences: prior to 18 yrs = 38%; prior to 14 yrs = 29%
Finkelhor*	1984	Direct interviews	74%	Males and females; parents of children between 6-14 yrs; Boston, US; n = 521	Childhood sexual abuse: public attitudes, knowledge of other's children abuse, own sexual abuse	Sexually abused in childhood: F = 15%; M = 6%
Baker, Duncan	1985	Direct interviews in the home (one item printed on card shown to interviewee)	87%	Males and females; adults aged 15+; random sample in Britain; n = 2,019	General attitude survey (one item on CSA embedded in it)	Childhood sexual assault prior to age 16: F = 12%; M = 8%; declined to answer = 13%

Author(s)	Date	Methodology	Response Rate	Sample	Focus	Findings/Rates
Wyatt*	1985	Direct interviews (interviews matched by ethnicity)	73%	Females only; adults aged 18-36; random sample from telephone directory until equal no. of Afro-American and white women matched for demographics, Los Angeles, US; n = 248	Childhood sexual abuse	CSA (broadly defined) prior to age 18 = 62%
Siegel, Sorenson, Golding, Burnam	1987	Direct interviews in the home (male and female interviewers)	68%	Same as above	Mental disorders and health service utilisation (paper focused on CSA only)	CSA (< 16 yrs old): F = 6.8%; M = 3.8%; overall = 5.3%
Burnam, Stein, Gold-ing, Siegel, Sorenson, For-syth, Telles	1988	Used same data as above	68%	Same as above	Lifetime sexual assault	Lifetime sexual assault: F = 16.7%; M = 9.4%
Golding	1994	Used same data as above	68%	Same as above	Physical health	

Author(s)	Date	Methodology	Response Rate	Sample	Focus	Findings/Rates
Golding	1999	Used same data as above	68%	Same as above	Psychiatric disorders	
ISPCC	1990	Direct interviews	Not stated	Males and females; adults aged 18-54; national sample in Ireland; n = 1,001	Childhood experiences of physical punishment, sexual abuse and relationships with parents	Contact sexual abuse: F = 15%; M = 9%; Full sexual intercourse: F = 1%; M = 1%
Schei	1990	Direct interviews	90%	Females only; aged 20-49; patients at OB/GYN clinic; n = 118	Lifetime sexual abuse	CSA involving contact: 8.5%; incest = 7%; SA by violent spouse = 10%; SA by non-violent spouse = 7%; SA by someone other than spouse = 5%
Davidson, Hughes, George, Blazer	1996	Direct interviews (sexual assault questions asked only in follow-up)	79% in Wave 1 of which 79% participated in follow-up	Males and females; adults, North Carolina, US; n = 2,918	Association of sexual assault and attempted suicide	Lifetime sexual assault: 2.9% (M and F combined)

Author(s)	Date	Methodology	Response Rate	Sample	Focus	Findings/Rates
McGrath, Hogan, Peipert	1998	Direct interviews administered as part of screening in hospital urgent care-triage unit (informed consent not obtained)	94%	Females only; convenience sample of patients in urgent care unit; n = 397	Prevalence of physical and sexual abuse	Physical and sexual abuse not separated in analyses
Kennedy, Maxwell	1992	Interviews with professionals	N/A	Professionals dealing with care/protection of children in Northern Ireland; n = 870 (completed incident questionnaires)	Incidence of CSA (notification of new cases of CSA)	CSA incidence rate = 0.9 – 1.85 per 1,000/year
Anderson, Martin, Mullen, Romans, Herbison	1993	2-stage design: a) questionnaire; b) direct interviews (those who disclosed CSA and control group)	a) = 73%; b) = 80%	Females only; adults aged ? – 65; n (a) = 3,000; n (b) = 298 (CSA) and 320 (controls)	Childhood sexual assault before age 16	Contact abuse: under 12 yrs = 16%; under 16 yrs = 25%

Appendix II

WORLD HEALTH ORGANISATION GUIDELINES, 1999

Putting Women's Safety First: Ethical and Safety Recommendations for Research on Domestic Violence Against Women

1. The safety of respondents and the research team is paramount and should infuse all project decisions.
2. Prevalence studies need to build upon current research experience about how to minimise the underreporting of abuse.
3. Protecting confidentiality is essential to ensure both women's safety and data quality.
4. All research team members should be carefully selected and receive specialised training and ongoing support.
5. The study design must include a number of actions aimed at reducing any possible distress caused to the participation by the research.
6. Field-workers should be trained to refer women requesting assistance to available sources of support.
7. Researchers and donors have an ethical obligation to help ensure that their findings are properly interpreted and used to advance policy and intervention development.
8. Violence questions should be incorporated into surveys designed for other purposes only when ethical and methodological requirements can be met.

Appendix III

SAVI TRAINING TOPIC OUTLINE

Training took place over twelve working days. Each day consisted of two modules, each lasting an hour and three-quarters. A half-hour break was held between the two modules each day. In session 11, interviewers began making study calls; on the morning of session 12, the previous day's calls and procedures were reviewed.

March 1 Thursday	1A	Objectives	To get to know members of the research team	
			To understand the purpose and history of the research study	
		Activities	Introductions	
			Presentation on the purpose and history of the study	
		Break		
	1B	Objectives	To provide an overview of the topics covered in the questionnaire	
			To understand the methodological decisions made in the feasibility study	
			To consider the implications of the definition of sexual abuse which is being used in the research (and legal definitions of rape, statutory rape, etc.)	
			To understand the importance of confidentiality and the safety of the respondent	
		Activities	Presentation on the topics, methodology, and issues around confidentiality	
			Discussion on confidentiality and safety	

March 2 Friday	2A	Objectives	To learn how to manage the telephone call sheets; how to record the outcome codes; how to check non-responding phone numbers for invalid/out-of-order, etc. To learn only the introduction section of the survey
		Activities	Practise the introduction only of the survey through a role-play
			Break
	2B	Objectives	To understand the importance of maximising response rates To learn how to encourage the public to take part in the survey
		Activities	Presentation on response rates Brainstorm with group on possible "refusal" scenarios Practise conducting interviews with series of "reluctant" respondents

** Interviewers were asked to take home the entire questionnaire and read it over the weekend, noting any questions that they had re: wording, skip patterns, etc.

March 5 Monday	5A	Objectives	To become familiar with the entire survey questionnaire: structure, wording, skip patterns
		Activities	Discuss any questions they have about the skip patterns, wording, etc.
			Break
	5B	Objectives	To learn how to fill out the form for "refusals" To learn how to conduct conversion calls
		Activities	Practise filling out refusals forms Practise making conversion calls using role-plays of "refusals"

March 6 Tuesday	3A	Objectives	To consider and explore the myths and attitudes prevalent in Irish Society towards Child Sexual Abuse and Adult Sexual Violence
			To understand the impact of these as they are internalised and externalised by the victim of abuse
			To consider the extent to which the interviewers have themselves internalised these attitudes, and how this may affect them in their work
		Activities	DRCC Trainer input
			Small group work
			Guided discussion
		Break	
	3B	Objectives	To consider the range of ways in which children are abused, and how it will be to hear about these; the impact, the difficulty of believing disclosures
			To gain information about the prevalence of abuse and the situations in which it occurs in Ireland
			To gain an understanding of the impact and effects of **child** sexual abuse on the individual: long-term effects, posttraumatic stress
		Activities	DRCC Trainer input
			Video
			Discussion
March 7 Wednesday	4A	Objectives	To learn listening skills: the qualities of the listener, basic listening skills, active listening, listening on the telephone
			To gain an understanding of the boundaries of their role (and the values of it)
		Activities	DRCC Trainer input
			Listening exercises
			Role plays and feedback
		Break	
	4B	Objectives	To learn about sexual harassment: definition, impact, etc.
		Activities	DRCC Trainer input
			Discussion

March 8 Thursday	6A	Objectives	To learn the attitudes and sexual harassment sections of the survey
		Activities	Practise conducting interviews on the introduction, attitudes, and sexual harassment sections (Sect. A-D) of the survey
		Break	
	6B	Objectives	To learn the sexual experiences section of the survey; become comfortable with using the sexually explicit terms
			To learn how to fill out the sexual experiences section of the survey, and respond appropriately for a respondent who has had an **adult experience** of sexual abuse
		Activities	Role plays to practise conducting the sexual experiences section of the survey using a simple (**no abuse**) scenario
			Role plays to using an **adult abuse** scenario
March 9 Friday	7A	Objectives	To understand the impact of adult sexual assault or rape on the individual; long-term effects, posttraumatic stress
			To explore the potential impact of the survey on the respondent: being aware of the potential impact, listening to distress
			To learn referral information and procedures; services of the Rape Crisis Centres and other services
		Activities	DRCC Trainer input
			Role plays using an abuse scenario in which the respondent is distressed by the interview — focus on how it feels to be in each role: the respondent and the interviewer, empathising with the issues which may arise for the respondent
			Feedback
		Break	

	7B	Objectives	To explore the potential impact of the work on the researcher
			To emphasise the importance of maintaining researcher well-being through self care, support and supervision
			To explore and learn alternative coping strategies
		Activities	DRCC Trainer input
			Small group work; Discussion
March 12 Monday	8A	Objectives	To learn how to fill out survey and respond appropriately for a respondent who has had a **childhood experience** of sexual abuse
			To learn the last sections of the interview
		Activities	Role plays to practise conducting survey using a **child sexual abuse** scenario
			Role plays to practise last section of interview (using a scenario of a respondent with **minor abuse** reported and no services utilised)
		Break	
	8B	Objectives	To learn how to fill out survey and respond appropriately for a respondent who has had **both an adult and childhood experience** of sexual abuse
			To gain practice in going through the whole interview from start to finish
		Activities	Role plays to practise conducting the sexual experience and disclosure sections of the survey using an **adult and child sexual abuse** scenario.
			Role plays to practise conducting the entire interview from start to finish

March 13 Tuesday	9A	Objectives	To consider personal issues re: talking about sexual subjects To explore the degree of researcher comfort with these issues
		Activities	DRCC Trainer input Small group work; Guided discussions; Role-plays and feedback
			Break
	9B	Objectives	Open session: To discuss any issues/concerns/ difficulties that the interviewers feel may impact their work on the project
		Activities	DRCC Trainer facilitate Open discussion
March 14 Wednesday	10A	Objectives	To get individualised feedback on conducting an entire interview To practise sections of the interview that are most difficult
		Activities	Interviewers will conduct one full practice interview with a staff member; feedback will be provided immediately following the interview Interviewers waiting for individual feedback will pair up and practise sections of the interview they find most difficult
			Break
	10B	Objectives	To learn about the purpose and procedure for call-back interviews
		Activities	Discussion on the form used for call-back interviews Practise call-back interviews using form Trial-run a mock-up call session; discuss any last minute details

March 15 Thursday	11 A	Objectives	To review the set-up and procedures for the study: how the forms will be stored, where to find them, what steps need to be done to start/finish a calling session, etc. To have each interviewer complete one short call session to gain additional experience in conducting the study
		Activities	Interviewers will work one call session (specific times to be arranged the previous day)
March 16 Friday	12A	Objectives	To review the procedures and outcomes of the previous full call session and allow time to reflect on any potential difficulties or concerns before continuing with the main study
		Activities	Discuss any problems or concerns with the previous day's call session Brainstorm and problem-solve any difficulties that have arisen

Appendix IVa

SURVEY TELEPHONE CALL CODING SYSTEM AND STUDY RESPONSE (PARTICIPATION) RATES

TELEPHONE OUTCOME CODES

Invalid Numbers

CM   Commercial/non-residential number — ineligible

Fx   Fax Machine

Disc   Disconnected/Number non-existent/Out of order (as checked with Directory Enquiries)

NA   No answer (after ten rings per call and ten separate calls)

AM   Answering machine (Did not leave a message; number tried ten separate times)

TP   Telephone problems (e.g., respondent identified, but faulty line)

Ineligible Respondents

NER   No respondent meets quota requirement

Kn   Respondent known to interviewer; inappropriate to conduct interview

O   Unable to contact adults in household

P   Eligible respondent in household but away for duration of survey period

IR   Impaired respondent (e.g. hearing difficulties, illness); unable to conduct interview

LB   Language barrier (unable to speak English)

Refusals

HR   Household refusal (no opportunity to ask for eligible respondent: study topic not explained)

RR   Respondent refusal

SR   Respondent initially agreed to interview but did not make themselves available: interviewer attempted a minimum of ten calls

HU   Hung up phone without comment as soon as introduction made

CVR   Conversion call — Person refused following second invitation by different interviewer

Completed Interviews

PI   Partial interview. Only interviews where experience of sexual abuse sections were completed were counted here. Other less complete interviews were counted as technical refusals

CI   Completed interview

CVC   Conversion call — Completed interview following second interview by different interviewer

Appendix IVb: Profile of Unique Telephone Numbers Called and Outcome Classifications for Survey

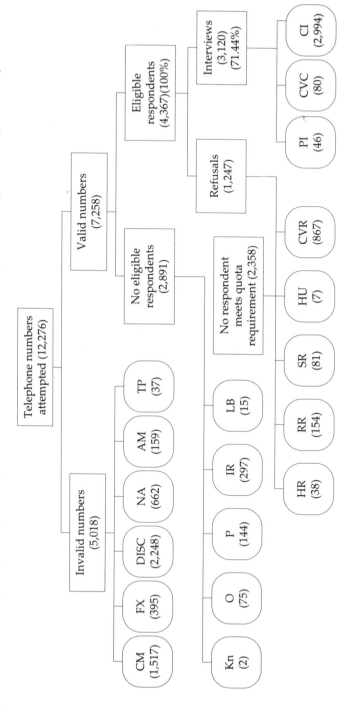

Appendix V

GLOSSARY OF TERMS USED
IN THE SAVI STUDY

Child Sexual Abuse

For the purposes of the SAVI study it was decided to ask about unwanted sexual experiences that occurred before age 17 as this is the legal age for consent to sexual relations under Irish law. Legally a "child" is defined as a person up to 18 years other than a married person.

No offence of Child Sexual Abuse exists under current Irish law although the Law Reform Commission's Report on Child Sexual Abuse (1990) recommended that such an offence be created. Prosecutions are brought under a variety of offences such as "unlawful carnal knowledge", buggery and sexual assault committed against a child or adolescent.

Contact Abuse (no penetration)

Refers to sexual assaults that involve the touching of the abused person's breasts and/or genitals or the forcing of the abused person to touch the perpetrator's breasts and/or genitals. Contact abuse (no penetration) in many cases corresponds to sexual assault in the law. A charge of aggravated sexual assault would be brought in cases where there is a high degree of violence or humiliation.

Gardaí (singular: Garda)

This (Irish language) term is used throughout the SAVI study to refer to the police force in the Republic of Ireland.

Incidence

Refers to the number of incidents that have occurred during a specific time period. In the context of SAVI it refers to the number of incidents of sexual harassment that have been perpetrated during the past year.

Incest

In the SAVI Study, incest includes contact and penetrative abuse by all intra-familial abusers — both blood relatives such as parents, grandparents, siblings and uncles, as well as non-blood relatives such as step-parents and in-laws — regardless of the age of the abuser.

The legal definition of incest in Ireland is very narrowly defined. For a man to be charged with incest, he must be aged 17 years or older and have had sexual intercourse with a woman who is to his knowledge his mother, sister, daughter or granddaughter. For a woman to be charged with incest, she must be aged 17 or older, and have consented to sexual intercourse with her father, grandfather, brother or son.

This definition was considered too narrow for the purposes of the SAVI study. It does not include, for example, rape under Section 4 (penetrative abuse other than vaginal), nor acts between two men (e.g., anal penetration), nor acts which occur between those under the age of 17 (e.g., a 16-year-old brother who abuses a 5 year old sister). The legal definition also limits incest to sexual acts between blood relatives, which would exclude other non-blood relatives or close family members. For this reason, we preferred to define incest as sexual abuse occurring within the familial network rather than define it on the basis of vaginal intercourse occurring between consanguine partners.

Non-contact Abuse

Refers to sexual assaults that do not involve the touching of the abused person's breasts and/or genitals. It also includes indecent exposure and, in the case of children, being exposed to pornographic material or being forced to strip in order to be photographed or filmed.

Penetrative Abuse

In the context of the SAVI study this refers to rape, rape under Section 4 and digital penetration.

Prevalence

Prevalence is the proportion of people who meet a criterion. In the context of the SAVI study, prevalence refers to the percentage of people who have had lifetime experiences of sexual abuse and violence.

Rape (as defined by law)

Unlawful sexual intercourse with a woman who, at the time of intercourse, does not consent to it, where the man knows she does not consent to it or is reckless as to whether she does or does not consent to it.

Rape (under Section 4)

Sexual assault that includes penetration (however slight) of the anus or mouth by the penis, or penetration (however slight) of the vagina by any object held or manipulated by another person. (Note: this does not cover digital penetration.)

Sexual Abuse

In the SAVI Study this term is used to describe sexual offences committed against those aged under 17 years.

Sexual Assault

In the SAVI Study this term is used to describe sexual offences committed against those aged 17 and older. It combines the legal categories of sexual assault and rape.

Sexual Assault and Aggravated Sexual Assault (as defined by law)

Aggravated sexual assault is a sexual attack (other than rape) that involves serious violence or causes grave injury, humiliation or degradation to the person assaulted. Sexual assault is a sexual attack with a less serious level of violence.

Sexual Harassment

The Employment Equality Act of 1998 defines sexual harassment as:

> ". . . any act of physical intimacy, any express request for sexual favours, any other act or conduct including spoken words, pictures or other material . . . if the act, request or conduct is unwelcome and could reasonably be regarded as sexually, or otherwise on the gender ground, offensive, humiliating or intimidating" (Section 23.3).

In the SAVI study questions regarding sexual harassment were not limited to the workplace but were asked about "events that you may or may not have had in your daily life".

Sexual Violence

In the SAVI Study the term sexual violence is used as an inclusive term to describe all sexual offences, be they committed against adults or children.

Stalking

In the SAVI study, stalking was defined as being followed in a way that was frightening, having someone wait for you "without your approval, writing or talking to you against your wishes, or implying threats".

Appendix VI

Irish Legal Definitions Associated with Sexual Abuse

Irish criminal law provides for a wide range of sexual offences. However, there are grey areas and a need for further clarification and reform. Discussion with key informants (two barristers who work in the area of sexual offences) led to the following redefining of the questions used in the SAVI study in terms of legal practice.

Adult [1]

- 1: A charge of attempted sexual assault may be made depending on level of severity.

- 2: Sexual assault.

- 3: Sexual assault in the vast majority of cases. If, for example, **verbal** intimidation were used a charge of sexual assault might **not** be brought.

- 4: Sexual assault.

A charge of **aggravated sexual assault** would be brought in cases where the victim was humiliated, hurt, tied up, etc.

- 5: Rape

- 6/7: Rape under Section 4 except "performed oral sex on you" = Sexual assault

---

[1] The numbers correspond to the item numbers in Table 4.4, pp. 65–66.

- 8: Digital penetration = Sexual assault; Penetration by an object = Rape under Section 4
- 9: Attempted rape.

Child (female) [2]

- 1: Not a sexual assault. A charge such as "possession of child pornography" might be brought.
- 2: Either a sexual assault or a charge relating to child pornography.
- 3: Either "indecent exposure" or a sexual assault.
- 4: If child feared being assaulted a charge of sexual assault might be brought; otherwise "indecent exposure".
- 5: Sexual assault
- 6: May be sexual assault if event happened because of fear or threat.
- 7: Sexual assault
- 8: Attempted rape.
- 9: Rape.
- 10: Rape under Section 4 or sexual assault (as 6).
- 11: Rape under Section 4.
- 12: Digital penetration = Sexual assault; Penetration by an object = Rape under Section 4.

Child (male) [2]
As above except:

- 8: Sexual assault (not rape).

---

[2] The numbers correspond to the item numbers in Table 4.3, p. 63.

WEIGHTED PREVALENCE RATES

Since the demographic profile of the SAVI sample differed somewhat from the general population, prevalence rates were recalculated using values weighted to take account of the differences. The weighted values made virtually no difference to patterns of estimates of the prevalence of various forms of sexual violence (see tables below). The disadvantage of calculating weighted estimates of population prevalence is that we could only apply the weightings to persons aged 20 and over because this is how the data is collated by the Central Statistics Office. Furthermore, analyses which examine relationships between variables do not need to be adjusted, which would lead to the use of two different sample sizes in the analysis, depending on whether population prevalences or interrelationships were being calculated.

The prevalences given in this appendix are therefore based on a sample of 2,956 persons because the 18- and 19-year-olds could not be included. Because the adjusted prevalences did not differ materially from the unadjusted, we have calculated unadjusted prevalences throughout this report, which means that all analyses are based on the same sample size.

Lifetime History of Sexual Abuse, Sample Values and Population-Prevalence-Adjusted Values for Participants Aged 20 and Over

Lifetime Category	Women	Population Adjusted	Men	Population Adjusted
None	57.7	59.5	70.6	71.0
Abuse NEC/NOS	9.9	9.1	7.2	7.3
Contact abuse	19.3	18.7	17.0	16.7
Attempted rape	2.9	2.7	2.0	1.9
Rape	10.2	10.0	3.2	3.1

The table shows the results of applying reweighting to the sample percentages in order to correct for over/undersampling of some age groups within each sex. While there are small changes to figures, the substantive values remain similar.

	Women	Population Adjusted	Men	Population Adjusted
Child Abuse				
None	68.9	70.7	75.8	76.3
Pornography	0.8	0.9	2.7	2.8
Indecent exposure	9.4	8.6	4.7	4.7
Contact SV	13.2	12.5	12.6	12.1
Attempted penetration	2.1	2.1	1.5	1.5
Penetration	5.7	5.3	2.7	2.7
Adult Violence				
None	74.7	75.3	87.4	87.3
Unspecified	5.1	4.6	2.9	3.0
Contact	12.9	12.7	8.3	8.4
Attempted rape	1.3	1.3	0.6	0.5
Rape	6.0	6.1	0.8	0.8

Examining the detailed prevalences, it is again clear that neither adult nor child abuse prevalence is substantively different when population weights are applied.

INDEX